Who Was Jacques Derrida?

Who Was Jacques?Derrida

An Intellectual Biography

DAVID MIKICS

Yale University Press   New Haven *&* London

Set in Minion Roman type by Integrated Publishing Solutions.

Printed in the United States of America.

Library of Congress Cataloging-in-Publication Data

Mikics, David, 1961–

    Who was Jacques Derrida? : an intellectual biography / David Mikics.

      p. cm.

Includes bibliographical references and index.

ISBN 978-0-300-11542-0 (hardcover : alk. paper)

1. Derrida, Jacques.   I. Title.

B2430.D484M48 2009

194—dc22

[B]   2009011984

A catalogue record for this book is available from the British Library.

This paper meets the requirements of ANSI/NISO Z39.48–1992 (Permanence of Paper).

10 9 8 7 6 5 4 3 2 1

For VM

Contents

Acknowledgments

John Kulka and Jennifer Banks, my editors at Yale University Press, accompanied me every step of the way. This book would not exist without their care and enthusiasm. The anonymous readers for Yale were also extraordinarily helpful, and Jack Borrebach provided expert copyediting. Harvey Yunis read and usefully commented on my discussion of Plato. I greatly appreciate the support of David Bromwich and John Hollander, as well as the patience of Harold Bloom, Michael Fox, and Tzvetan Todorov, who answered my questions about their personal experience of Derrida.

The Martha Gano Houstoun fund at the English Department of the University of Houston supported the writing of this book in essential ways. I am grateful to the Houstoun family and to the English Department's Houstoun Committee. Richard Armstrong and Rob Zaretsky, of the Honors College at the University of Houston, offered help and insight; the Honors College was a true intellectual home during my work on the book. In New York, the Frederick Lewis Allen Room of the New York Public Library provided a place to work and an inspiring sense that I was surrounded by many distinguished writers, past and present. I thank my father, Lewis J. Mikics;

also Wendy Scheir and Farnoosh Fathi. Jenn Lewin provided
cheer and intellectual guidance. And completing this book without the presence of Victoria Malkin now seems impossible.
My writing coincided with the American presidential
election campaign of 2008. When election day arrived, I had
just finished the book, with its reflections on the role of the intellectual in public life. On that November night in Brooklyn,
I felt that my country had remade its promise, and that intellectual commitment to our common existence had, perhaps
more than ever before, proven possible in America. The sudden awakening of responsibility and hope, larger than the
book I had written, still helped me to frame the experience of
writing it. The basic questions of human identity, political decision making, our curiosity about one another—questions
that Derrida often avoided in the service of a self-enclosed academic vocabulary—might, in the end, matter to us all.

Preface

At the age of eighteen, I became a follower of Jacques Derrida. The year was 1980. The school was New York University, later one of the American universities where Derrida taught regularly, along with Yale and the University of California at Irvine. My freshman writing instructor, serious-minded, bespectacled, and slightly milquetoast, had come to NYU from Johns Hopkins. Hopkins was the university where deconstruction, in the person of Derrida, first hit the shores of America, at the famous 1966 conference "The Languages of Criticism and the Sciences of Man." For honors freshman English, my instructor assigned us Plato's *Gorgias,* J. L. Austin's *How to Do Things with Words,* and finally the pièce de résistance: Derrida's essay "Signature Event Context," a critique of Austin.

Austin was a sly, fastidious Oxford don who had been a spy during World War II, and who wrote essays with titles like "How to Talk: Some Simple Ways" and "Three Ways of Spilling Ink." For me, the freshman, he proved a consistent and surprising delight: my first real taste of philosophy. I had dipped into Sartre in high school and had been excited by his way with intellectual melodrama. But Austin was something else again: sneaky in his insights, blithely funny where Sartre was excitable and soul-wringing. Sartre was about love and death, religious belief, murder and suicide. He made you feel like a member of the disillusioned, tough-minded elite: daring you to know the world's harsh truths, and still to act in lonely independence. Austin, unlike Sartre, talked about ordinary actions like promising, betting, and making excuses; about speech acts that "misfire" (an eccentric bishop's blessing of the penguins, or the bigamist's "I do"). I had no idea that philosophy could be so attentive to small things, could show them in a new light, one that made me think harder than I ever had before. Austin opened my eyes to how philosophy might be about life, as we meet it every day—trivial, significant, odd.

But Derrida, from my eighteen-year-old's perspective, blew Austin away. He accused Austin of trying to tether people to the statements they made and the actions they performed, so that situations would always be stable and reliable. For Derrida, such stability was an impossible fantasy. Our words are drifting, uncontrollable: once they leave our mouths, they take on a life of their own. Speech, Derrida asserted, is not so different from writing. Plato called the written word an orphan. You never know who will pick up and read a book, or what that reader will make of it. Writing wanders ceaselessly. The author has no control over his work's future interpretation. Derrida went further than Plato, arguing that not just writing, but speech, is a homeless drifter. Even in our conversations, Derrida insisted, we have no mastery over our meaning, however much we insist that we do.

I did not know it at the time, but Derrida was my introduction to skepticism, a long tradition in philosophy. When I chose Derrida over Austin, in spite of my fascination with Austin's stance and style, I was giving in to the skeptic's classic argument: that we cannot trust the evidence of our words and our senses, that nothing is reliable. Every belief system claims an anchor in the way things really are. But, the skeptic asks, how can we prove that the world is what we say it is? Someone else, always, is bound to disagree.

This book tells the story of Derrida's skepticism, which proved so influential in the American academy. But it also pays close attention to Derrida's even more influential departure from his rigorous method of doubting everything: the prophetic tone he assumed when he evoked the revolutionary properties of writing or, in later years, of justice. This tone was an attempt to reach outside the enclosure of skepticism, to proclaim the emergence of a world that would not be merely linguistic.

When he practiced skeptical doubt, Derrida turned away from the human psyche, whose rich complexity had occupied philosophers from Plato to Austin. His rejection of psychology will be an important theme of this book. When Derrida became dissatisfied with skepticism, he also realized that his own thought had become rarefied and unreal. He needed a new motif, something that would reconnect him with his era and with the reality around him. He found this new motif not by concerning himself with individuals, their motives and life histories, but by proclaiming an ethics (derived from the religious thinker Emmanuel Lévinas) that could rise above psychology and confront humanity in its most stark and urgent dimensions. Derrida became, like Lévinas, a voice for justice. Derrida relied on this transformation to exclude the dramas of the psyche that he had been determined to avoid from the beginning of his career. But a philosophy so stridently opposed to psychology merely damages its own persuasiveness; it refuses the most palpable sign of our existence, our inner life.

Derrida's denial of psychology also denies biography. But

his thought, in spite of itself, is deeply personal: the thinker's intellectual existence cannot be isolated from his emotional life. So this book presents an account of Derrida's life, as well as his thought—especially his intense attachment to his friend Paul de Man, source of Derrida's greatest misstep and professional trauma. Derrida's resistance to thinking about the personal life cannot prevent biography (de Man's as well as his own) from coming back to haunt him.

Thanks to Derrida, college teachers and their students deconstruct everything from meals to clothes to ideas. His impact has been large; and his books can be fascinating, as I hope to make clear in my account of his career. Derrida was instructive in his uncertainties, more so than in his lofty pronouncements. It is my sense that the general reader, not merely the adept in theory and philosophy, can benefit from following the course of his work.

The culture wars are over and, in the universities, the theory camp has won. In the larger culture, however, grave doubts persist about the worth of theoretical work in the humanities. Increasingly, there is a division between the academy and the public, which knows little and cares less about the university's reflections on books and ideas (often seen, whether fairly or not, as cultlike, obscurantist, and doctrinaire). If we are to find a way past this impasse, we must learn from the central polarizing figure of literary study in the past few decades: Jacques Derrida. In this book, I exercise the same vigilance that he so often recommended, this time with respect to his own words.

Abbreviations

WORKS BY JACQUES DERRIDA

Acts = *Acts of Religion*. Ed. Gil Anidjar. New York: Routledge, 2002.

Counterpath = *Counterpath: Traveling with Jacques Derrida*. With Catherine Malabou. Tr. David Wills. Stanford: Stanford University Press, 2004.

Dissemination = *Dissemination*. Tr. Barbara Johnson. Chicago: University of Chicago Press, 1981.

For What = *For What Tomorrow: A Dialogue*. With Elisabeth Roudinesco. Tr. Jeff Fort. Stanford: Stanford University Press, 2004.

Grammatology = *Of Grammatology*. Tr. Gayatri Chakravorty Spivak. Baltimore: Johns Hopkins University Press, 1976.

Introduction = *Edmund Husserl's "Origin of Geometry": An Introduction*. Brighton: Harvester Press, 1978.

Jacques Derrida = *Jacques Derrida*. With Geoffrey Bennington. Chicago: University of Chicago Press, 1999.

Margins = *Margins of Philosophy*. Tr. Alan Bass. Chicago: University of Chicago Press, 1982.

Negotiations = *Negotiations, Interventions, and Interviews, 1971–2001*. Ed. and tr. Elizabeth Rottenberg. Stanford: Stanford University Press, 2002.

Of Spirit = *Of Spirit, Heidegger, and the Question*. Tr. Geoffrey Bennington and Rachel Bowlby. Chicago: University of Chicago Press, 1989.

Paper Machine = *Paper Machine*. Tr. Rachel Bowlby. Stanford: Stanford University Press, 2005.

Philosophy = *Philosophy in a Time of Terror: Dialogues with Jürgen Haberman and Jacques Derrida*. With Giovanna Borradori. Chicago: University of Chicago Press, 2003.

Points = *Points . . . Interviews, 1974–1994*. Ed. Elisabeth Weber. Tr. Peggy Kamuf and others. Stanford: Stanford University Press, 1995.

Post = *The Post Card: From Socrates to Freud and Beyond*. Tr. Alan Bass. Chicago: University of Chicago Press, 1987.

Speech = *Speech and Phenomena, and Other Essays on Husserl's Theory of Signs*. Tr. David B. Allison. Evanston, IL: Northwestern University Press, 1973.

Veils = *Veils*. With Hélène Cixous. Tr. Geoffrey Bennington. Stanford: Stanford University Press, 2002.

Writing = *Writing and Difference*. Tr. Alan Bass. Chicago: University of Chicago Press, 1978.

WORKS BY OTHERS

Atlas = Martin Gilbert, *The Routledge Atlas of Jewish History*. Revised edition. New York: Routledge, 2003.

Beyond = Sigmund Freud, *Beyond the Pleasure Principle*. Tr. James Strachey. New York: Norton, 1990.

Blindness = Paul de Man, *Blindness and Insight: Essays in the Rhetoric of Contemporary Criticism*. 2nd revised edition. Minneapolis: University of Minnesota Press, 1983.

Course = Ferdinand de Saussure, *Course in General Linguistics*. Ed. Charles Bally and Albert Sechehaye, with Albert Riedlinger. Tr. Wade Baskin. New York: Philosophical Library, 1959. [The standard pagination common to all texts of Saussure's work is used here.]

De Gaulle = Michael Kettle, *De Gaulle and Algeria 1940–1960: From Mers El-Kebir to the Algiers Barricades*. London: Quartet Books, 1993.

Derrida = Kirby Dick and Amy Ziering Kofman, *Derrida: Screenplay and Essays on the Film*. Manchester: Manchester University Press, 2005.

Dhimmi = Bat Ye'or and David Maisel. *The Dhimmi: Jews and Christians Under Islam*. Revised edition. Teaneck, NJ: Fairleigh Dickinson University Press, 1985.

Dialogue = Diane P. Michelfelder and Richard E. Palmer, eds., *Dialogue and Deconstruction: The Gadamer-Derrida Encounter*. Albany: State University of New York Press, 1989.

Edmund Husserl = Maurice Natanson, *Edmund Husserl: Philosopher of Infinite Tasks.* Evanston, IL: Northwestern University Press, 1974.

Heidegger Controversy = Richard Wolin, ed., *The Heidegger Controversy: A Critical Reader.* New York: Columbia University Press, 1991.

How to Do = J. L. Austin, *How to Do Things with Words.* Ed. J. O. Urmson. Cambridge, MA: Harvard University Press, 1962.

Jews = Norman A. Stillman, *The Jews of Arab Lands: A History and Source Book.* Philadelphia: Jewish Publication Society, 1979.

JPS = *JPS Hebrew-English Tanakh.* Philadelphia: Jewish Publication Society, 1999.

Logical = Edmund Husserl, *Logical Investigations.* London: Routledge, 2001. Cited by investigation and section number.

Papers = John L. Austin, *Philosophical Papers.* 2nd edition. Ed. J. O. Urmson and G. J. Warnock. Oxford: Clarendon Press, 1970.

Passion = James Miller, *The Passion of Michel Foucault.* New York: Simon and Schuster, 1993.

Philosophical = Stanley Cavell, *Philosophical Passages: Wittgenstein, Emerson, Austin, Derrida.* New York: Blackwell, 1995.

Poetry = John Koethe, *Poetry at One Remove: Essays.* Ann Arbor: University of Michigan Press, 2000.

Reckless = Mark Lilla, *The Reckless Mind: Intellectuals in Politics.* New York: New York Review Books, 2001.

Responses = Werner Hamacher, Neil Hertz, and Thomas Keenan, eds., *Responses: On Paul de Man's Wartime Journalism.* Lincoln: University of Nebraska Press, 1989.

Rising = Pierre-André Taguieff, *Rising from the Muck: The New Anti-Semitism in Europe.* Tr. Patrick Camiller. Chicago: Ivan R. Dee, 2004.

Signs = David Lehman, *Signs of the Times: Deconstruction and the Fall of Paul de Man.* New York: Poseidon Press, 1991.

Strategies = J. Claude Evans, *Strategies of Deconstruction: Derrida and the Myth of the Voice.* Minneapolis: University of Minnesota Press, 1991.

Yale = *Yale French Studies* 69: "The Lesson of Paul de Man" (Special Issue). 1985.

Introduction

During his lifetime, Derrida elicited both intense celebration and intense scorn. Rather than judging him in the manner of his disapproving critics, or celebrating him like his followers, I aim to explain his career. Now that Derrida is gone, it is time for a more measured assessment of his worth. His thought was neither as world changing as his disciples claimed nor as dangerous (or absurd) as his critics suspected. It does, however, offer us a necessary lesson concerning the self-imposed limits of philosophy: the way that it tries to purify itself, and the hazards of such purity. Derrida's work, at once frustrating, diverting, and impressively self-sustaining even in its contradictions, contains a crucial message about what philosophy wants to exclude from its view—and what it finds itself forced to reckon with.

Derrida's work consisted of two interlocking parts: an argument about metaphysics and an argument about the self. First, Derrida redefined metaphysics (the search for an essence behind or above sensible appearances) as a wish for utter clarity: its aim was to make meaning fully available to consciousness. The conscious mind had to be the master of thought. In order to combat this metaphysical project (called, in Derrida's lexicon, logocentrism), Derrida promoted skeptical method. He associated skepticism with another key term, *différance*, which conveyed the unreliability inherent in meaning. The skeptic questions the dependability of our words and actions, so that, finally, the assumption of a consistent self becomes impossible. The world begins to seem a realm of illusion, where we have tricked ourselves into supposing that we are real.

Skepticism of this world-doubting kind had been a key thought of philosophers since Descartes, but Derrida turned it into a rule. The whole history of ideas seemed to him to be a debate, carried on between the lines of great philosophical texts, between the masterful coherence of metaphysics and its deconstructionist opponent, skepticism. Derrida proclaimed that there is nothing outside the text. He argued that we live in a fundamentally written and therefore phantom-like world, one that denies us the reality we seek.[1]

Derrida's choice of the metaphysics-skepticism problem as his governing thought meant, throughout his career, a determination to separate philosophy from psychological interest. He insisted that we are confluences of words and deeds, rather than souls with individual pathologies (or characters). The effort to purify philosophy by freeing it from the myths of the psyche began very early in Derrida's work. His first mature philosophical interest, which he developed in the 1950s and early 1960s as a young man studying at the École Normale Supérieure in Paris, was in the philosophy of Edmund Husserl. Husserl had developed the discipline of phenomenology: the study of how things appear to us and of how we receive, and make, meaning. In choosing Husserl as his guide, Derrida rejected the presiding spirit of French intellectual life, Jean-Paul Sartre, then the most prominent philosopher in the world. Sartre had taken Husserl's ideas in a psychological direction, portraying phenomenological themes in terms of human drama: for instance, scenes of voyeurism and seductive manipulation. The spirit of Husserl himself was completely alien to such psychologizing and therefore proved suitable for Derrida's project.

In his treatment of Plato and Freud, in particular, Derrida argued against the psychological. In his lengthy account of Plato's *Phaedrus,* he omitted any consideration of the dialogue's central tableau: the myth of the charioteer, which gives a picture of the divided psyche as Plato's Socrates conceives it. Plato adheres to a necessary myth of the self, one that cannot be demystified by any superior knowledge. By neglecting to mention this aspect of Plato, Derrida showed his intent to free philosophy from psychological concern.[2] Similarly, in his writings on Freud, Derrida saw as Freud's great discovery the fact that the unconscious is linguistic in nature and therefore an environment in which skepticism can swim freely. He rejected Freud's commitment to understanding the soul of the neurotic, as well as his interest in the dynamics of patient-therapist interaction. Derrida remained indifferent to the therapeutic or educative aspect of Freud, as he did to that of Plato. Instead, Derrida detected an exiguous individuality in fragments of language, in odd, undecipherable traces: the factors that conceal identity rather than reveal it. (Derrida's emphasis bears a relation to Jacques Lacan's notion of the Real, the absurd bit of reality that we anchor our identity to and that remains fundamentally unintelligible. But Derrida has a sentimental impulse to guard the cryptic aspect of our identity; Lacan scorns such concern for human vulnerability.)

As a result of the Paul de Man affair of the late 1980s, in which Derrida's friend de Man was revealed after his death to have been a pro-Nazi journalist during World War II, Derrida was forced to a crisis over the question of psychology. He insisted that de Man's accusers could not know his inner life, and therefore should not judge his involvement with fascism. In the very effort to place de Man's psyche off-limits to others, however, Derrida claimed it for himself. He described a noble struggle within de Man, who (as Derrida imagined it) secretly resisted the Nazism that he outwardly collaborated with. Derrida's anguished writings on de Man mark a turning point in his career because they demonstrate that the purification of philosophy from psychological interest cannot hold. Despite declarations that the self cannot be known, and therefore in a sense does not exist, we still yield to the inclination to imagine this unknowable self. Under the pressure of his attachment to de Man, Derrida was impelled to psychologize. The unwilling implication of Derrida's writings is that these two disciplines, philosophy and psychology, cannot be made separate. The desire for separation is a symptom, sometimes well worth studying (as when, working from the other side, Freud unconvincingly declares that he is not a philosopher). But the philosopher can never accomplish the separation any more than the psychologist can.

Psychology in the de Man affair stands for the presence of the real world, which tampered with the judiciously defined project of Derrida's thought and required him to imagine the inner life of another person. That such interventions occurred makes Derrida's long career a rich object of study. The other main instance of reality's interruption of thought was brought on by Derrida himself, when he assumed the stance of a prophet rather than just a careful analyst of intellectual history. Starting in the mid-sixties, Derrida cast his enterprise of deconstruction as a revelation, or a compelling message. This act was not merely a search for wider appeal and authority, but a recognition that there was something outside the perpetual recapitulations of the text. Derrida wanted a commanding truth, one that would change the way the world looks. Such a desire responded to the religious urgency of the Jewish philosopher Emmanuel Lévinas, with whom Derrida felt a close kinship. But Derrida also invoked a different prophetic tradition: Friedrich Nietzsche's vision of radically new horizons of thought.

I have emphasized that Derrida began his career in the early 1960s by exiling psychology from philosophy. He chose Husserl over Sartre as his inspiration and upheld a clarified version of metaphysics that he could combat by means of an equally refined skepticism. When this debate started to become self-enclosed, Derrida sought a way out of the cave of the metaphysics-skepticism quandary and into the light of a reality larger than skeptical method, with its narrow diagnostic concerns. Instead of restricting himself to showing how metaphysics overreaches, Derrida adopted, beginning in the mid-sixties, a prophetic attitude: he himself became an overreacher and hinted at the world-changing import of his pronouncements. The exact nature of the millenial promise remained deliberately vague; but, Derrida implied, the advent of the thought of writing, or différance, would utterly revolutionize the way we think, see, and live.

The world outside the cave, the scene of Derrida's prophetic message, took two contrary forms. The first was a liberated realm that Derrida associated with Nietzsche. Invoking Nietzsche's esteem for play and artistry, Derrida (in his lecture "Structure, Sign and Play") declared that irresponsibility and the lack of a determining center were required by the highest of human aspirations. Only through randomness, hypostatized as free invention, would we liberate ourselves. In a later lecture, "The Ends of Man," Derrida used Nietzsche to respond to the mood of student protestors, all the while leaving it unclear whether he was honoring, parodying, or subtly altering their rhetoric.

Rather confusingly, Derrida (in the same book of essays, *Writing and Difference,* in which he published "Structure, Sign and Play") countered his Nietzschean celebration of unfettered invention with an opposing vision: the world of Emmanuel Lévinas, who calls us to responsibility for our fellow humans. Derrida, following Lévinas, drew on the Hebrew scriptures, with their demand that we attend to the suffering of those we encounter rather than shielding ourselves behind the evasions of thought. This Judaic invocation was a far cry from Derrida's version of Nietzsche, for whom imagination, the playful expression of newness, promises to transform our perception.

Because of such contradictions, Derrida was seen by many as a mere dodger of coherence. But the interest of his work consists in his grappling with differing impulses, even when he could not reconcile them. By rebelling against the enclosed purity of the metaphysics-skepticism debate, Derrida opened himself to alien influences. These influences—chief among them, Lévinas and Nietzsche in his apocalyptic mood—led in opposing directions.

Writing itself, since it was the "becoming-absent . . . of the subject" (*Grammatology* 69), was too enmeshed in the metaphysics-skepticism conflict to have prophetic substance, despite Derrida's frequent hints in this direction in the sixties. He had to find, instead, a more fitting candidate for a prophetic opening to the outside of philosophy. It was, finally, Lévinas's ethics rather than Nietzsche's creative violence that filled this role. Significantly, Lévinas offered a superior form of the this-worldly emphasis that Derrida disdained in Claude Lévi-Strauss, Ferdinand de Saussure, J. L. Austin, and others. These thinkers' addiction to presence (as Derrida described it) was matched by the empirical fact of the face-to-face, the encounter with the other person, in Lévinas. The way out of the cave had to point toward a supervening reality. For Derrida at the end of his career, this reality was Lévinasian justice. One can speculate that Lévinas offered an acceptable path to Derrida not just because of the prestige associated with ethical judgment, but because Lévinas rejects psychology in favor of a more primal confrontation with the suffering person, whose motives and character do not matter.

There is another aspect of Derrida that demands discussion: his entanglement in what his fellow deconstructionist Paul de Man named, in a famous book, the "blindness and insight" model. For de Man, every text necessarily misreads itself, and therefore each author misunderstands the meaning of his own writing. Ironically, this pattern of misreading is just as true of the critic who sets to work uncovering an author's self-deceptions. So, de Man remarked, Derrida deliberately misreads Rousseau in order to attain the advantage over him: but Rousseau's text, which is richer and more knowing than Derrida will admit, has the last word, and exposes the critic as diminisher of his subject's complexities.

In this book I address Derrida's readings of several fascinating thinkers whose blindnesses become Derrida's insights. Derrida's readings of Rousseau, Plato, Husserl, and Austin were, as de Man predicted, misreadings. Derrida obscured their individuality and turned them into examples of a monolithic logocentrism. (By *logocentrism* Derrida meant the self-validating pride of a reason that can explain itself, securing on its own behalf a masterful logos, or account of the world.)

Derrida, the promoter of otherness and irreducible difference, transformed these texts into a reflection of his own preoccupations: the superiority of writing over speech, and the "violence" of human reason (that is, its attachment to the self-confirming character of thought). Plato, Austin, and Husserl became for him key examples of "Western metaphysics," the "phallogocentric" tradition that, he said, ought to be doubted, even overturned.

Derrida attacked the proud, naïve assertions of the conscious ego, which thinks that it has its expressions under its control, that it knows what it means and means what it says. Even more than psychoanalysis, deconstruction showed (in Freud's famous phrase) that the ego is not "master in its own house." Metaphysics was blindness, deconstruction the purveyor of insight.

Other philosophers have, of course, dissected the pretensions of the self-satisfied ego that claims to be the infallible master of its own meanings. Such an ego does many a comic turn in Austin's work, and Freud and Nietzsche diagnose it as well. But Derrida, in his skeptical mode, excludes the psychological dimension that these thinkers rely on. We are dominated, according to Derrida, by an invariable structure: the network of signifiers that speaks through us. Though we can comment knowingly on our own captivity, we find no escape from it. Skepticism provides the commentary, but commentary is not enough. We want freedom; and, as well, a more motivated view of necessity than the picture of a systematic imprisonment can offer.

Derrida here courted the same dangers as Michel Foucault, the other major French influence on theory in the humanities. Derrida, like Foucault, began with an insistence on the inescapable character of a system. For Derrida, the system was Western metaphysics; the institutions of modernity since the Enlightenment played a similar role in Foucault. In the sixties, both thinkers sought a radical alternative to the system, one that would give an outsider's perspective: for Derrida, the apocalyptic Nietzsche (and his echo in the announcements of avant-garde writers like Georges Bataille and Antonin Artaud); for Foucault, the madness that could be repressed, but not contained, by Western disciplinary practices. As an antidote, an "other" to the reign of the same, such exuberance opened onto a realm of free play (even if it was doomed free play, like the madness that Foucault celebrated).

But Nietzsche was not enough. The reintroduction of responsibility by way of a Lévinasian emphasis on extremes—so that I become a hostage to my fellow human, who is threatened with destruction—provided, for Derrida, a way to avoid the anarchic recklessness of Foucault. Obligation became more necessary than Nietzschean freedom. Lévinasian responsibility was, in the end, also a way for Derrida to escape from psychology, since in Lévinas the other person becomes a sheer presence, without history or personality.

But Lévinas and Derrida lose sight of our complexity. Even in extreme situations like the ones Lévinas describes, we are psychological beings, fantasizing and inventing our lives. There is, then, an alternative to Derrida's approach. The Romantic idea, which still animates so much of fiction and poetry, demands that we ally ourselves with the soul-making movements of thought and language—rather than unmasking these gestures as mere appearances, in the skeptical way of deconstruction.[3] Life depends on the contingent, the exultant and necessary building of a fiction. By exposing the world as merely contingent, and therefore insufficient, Derrida reduces our powers. Harold Bloom's notion of misreading, based as it is on the psyche of the author, remains more useful than the deconstructionist idea that misreading occurs within texts and that authorial personality is a mere illusion.

Derrida's knowing skepticism relieves us of responsibility for our words and deeds: he reduces us to mere parts of the signifying machine. By contrast, Freud and Austin, demystifiers of the self-confident ego, still give the self a central place in the world. They are philosophical detectives, intent on figuring out why we do what we do. They recognize the moments when we are forced to improvise, even to write our own script. Sometimes—often—systems fail, giving us the task of being original. Our condition, vexing and promising as it is, can only be understood by admitting the psychological dimension that Derrida tried so hard to exclude from his work.

Avoiding the psyche is a continual temptation of philosophy. Derrida gave in to this temptation, but then searched for a way out of the diminished version of philosophical thinking that resulted. In doing so he inadvertently, but crucially, pointed to the reasons why psychology and philosophy remain bound to each other.[4]

I

From Algeria to the
École Normale:
Sartre, Hegel, Husserl

Derrida's thought cannot be understood apart from his life. From the beginning, he was an intellectual outsider, a rebel. His efforts to redefine the discipline of philosophy took place against the rigid institutional system of the École Normale Supérieure. The young man from Algeria, a colonial backwater, confronted the powers that be in Paris, the vibrant center of advanced thought. Throughout his life, Derrida retained his early sense of being excluded from the sophisticated hierarchy that told students what and how to think. Even when deconstruction became a dominant institutional force in America, Derrida still felt that he was a marginal figure, persecuted by the press and its opinion makers. A close look at Derrida's biography explains much of his tendency to see deconstruction as an embattled, even quasi-revolutionary force: a dangerous truth that the men in charge cannot stomach.

After a brief account of Derrida's youth in Algeria, his family and his early reading, I describe in this chapter the major philosophical figures that Derrida encountered when he arrived in France in 1949, at the age of nineteen. The first is Jean-Paul Sartre, whom Derrida reacted against. Repelled by Sartre the psychologist, and the theatrical scenarios that were necessary to Sartre's version of philosophical inquiry, Derrida pursued a purer, more abstract form of thinking, Edmund Husserl's phenomenology. G. W. F. Hegel rivals Husserl as an epitome of metaphysics, but he includes history whereas Husserl does not: so Derrida's choice of Husserl over Hegel in his early work can also be seen as a purification of philosophy.

Both Sartre and Hegel (the latter long dead, the former very much alive in 1950s Paris) strongly influenced the fashionable Marxism of the École Normale Supérieure, where Derrida was first trained in philosophy. By breaking with these figures, and specifically with their engagement in politics and history, Derrida declared his intellectual independence.

Derrida's first work is an admiring account of Husserl's essay on the origins of geometry. But as Derrida develops his skepticism, his suspicion of metaphysical certainty, he turns against Husserl. He misreads Husserl as a one-sided exponent of logocentrism and a resister of différance. Such distortion is necessary in the blindness and insight model that Derrida follows: skepticism is always bound to metaphysics as its opponent and satirist, and as a result it exaggerates metaphysical vices. Conscious of the limits of this hyperbolic dialogue, Derrida begins, in the mid-sixties, to explore the possibility of an outside realm, an "other" to philosophy. He searches for this realm in the prophetic announcements of Nietzsche and the ethical imperatives of Emmanuel Lévinas. (These developments are explored in chapter 2.)

Jackie Derrida, later known as Jacques, was born on July 15, 1930, in El Biar, Algeria, near Algiers. Both his parents came from old Algerian Jewish families. His mother was Georgette Safar, whose family had lived in Algeria for at least three generations. In 1923 she married Aimé Derrida, a young traveling salesman. Their first son, René, was born in 1925. Paul Derrida followed in 1929 and died a little less than three months later. Then came Jackie in 1930. Jackie's younger sister, Janine, was born in 1934. A third brother, Norbert, was born in 1938 and died, like Paul, several months later. Derrida later said that the fact he was a middle child explained everything about him. He often quarreled with his elder brother, but never with his adored younger sister.

The Derridas' house was in the rue Saint-Augustin in El Biar, a fact that later attracted the attention of their son, the most famous North African thinker (along with Albert Camus) since Augustine. In 1934 the Derrida family moved to a larger house in El Biar that they called, with affectionate mockery, "the villa."

The ordinary, hardworking Derrida family lived in a mysterious and dangerous country, a place that would prove central to the identity of France because of its rebellion against colonial rule in the 1950s and 1960s. (Algeria was never, strictly speaking, a French colony, but rather a department of France— a fact that would be of crucial importance to the struggle over its future.) Algeria, for thousands of years fought over and conquered in turn by the Phoenicians, the Romans, the Vandals, the Byzantine Empire, the Arabs, and the Turks, had been invaded by France in 1830. The move was part of France's effort to establish firmer control over trade in the western Mediterranean. More important, it represented the attempt of Charles X, the Bourbon king, to distract attention from his failing rule.

Charles abdicated that same year, but the conquest of Algeria continued under his successor, the Orleanist Louis-Philippe.

At the time of the French incursion into Algiers, the pirates of the Barbary Coast were still routinely raiding helpless merchant ships. A host of Christian states paid the pirates yearly tribute money. The Algerian countryside was full of rebels. The French made slow progress battling these dangers; their control of the country was at first limited to a few small regions along the coast. Nomadic tribes of Berbers, fierce and proud, inhabited much of Algeria, along with Muslim Arabs. The Berbers were nominally Muslim, but far less pious than the Arabs, who often disdained them for their lack of devotion.

In the 1840s, a ruthless war under Louis-Philippe succeeded in subjugating Algeria to France. Louis-Philippe was exiled by the Revolution of 1848; his successor, Louis Napoleon (President of the Second Republic in 1848, and soon to be emperor) declared Algeria part of metropolitan France. The 1840s were a presage of the barbarism that overtook the country during the Algerian revolt of the mid-twentieth century, a conflict marked by terrible violence on both sides.

A flood of European settlers arrived with the French. Most of them were from the Mediterranean countries: Italy, Spain, Malta, Portugal. The colonists came to call themselves *pieds-noirs* (blackfeet), a name suggesting their impoverished, hardscrabble existence. *Pied-noir* originated around 1900 as a nickname for the native Algerian stokers on coal ships, who worked barefoot. The European immigrants to Algeria took over the name for themselves, just as they took over the country. Stubborn and proud, the pieds-noirs defined much of the character of colonial Algeria. By 1917 there were about 800,000 pieds-noirs; only one in five had direct French ancestry (*De*

Gaulle 12). The pieds-noirs, though vastly outnumbered by the Arab population, had the upper hand economically and socially.

Jews like Aimé Derrida and Georgette Safar belonged to a group set apart from both the Arabs and the pieds-noirs. The Jews had been natives of Algeria since Phoenician times, in the first millennium before the common era. This original group of Jews, brought to North Africa as traders allied to the Phoenician-Carthaginian empire, was augmented later on by Jewish refugees fleeing Roman repression and those expelled from Spain in 1492. When the French arrived in 1830, the Jewish community of Algeria numbered some 25,000 and was quite destitute. Many of the desperate Jews embraced the French as trading partners, seeing in them a long-needed route to prosperity.

The condition of the Jews of Algeria before the French conquest was indeed dire. William Shaler, the American consul general in Algiers, reported in 1825 that the Jews "are in Algiers a most oppressed people; they are not permitted to resist any personal violence of whatever nature, from a Mussulman; they are compelled to wear clothing of a black or dark colour; they cannot ride on horseback, or wear arms of any sort, not even a cane . . . they are pelted in the streets even by children, and in short, the whole course of their existence here, is a state of the most abject oppression and contumely" (*Dhimmi* 300–301).

During the hundred and thirty years in which Algeria was a colony of France, the French improved the lives of the Jews, whom they relied on in business dealings. But France also subjected them to its control; in this case as in all others, the French government held sway over religious institutions (*Jews* 16). In 1845, the government of Louis-Philippe established a central rabbinate in Algiers, and two others in Oran and Constantine. The chief rabbi in each of the three towns was imported from France, to insure French influence over the Jewish denizens of its colony.

The Crémieux decree of 1870 made the "indigenous Jews" of Algeria French citizens. Now literate and introduced into the modern world, the Jews were, technically at least, Frenchmen. Their improved status led to persecution. The pogrom of May 1897 began with the sacking of the synagogue in Mostaganem, near Oran. Rioters demanded the repeal of the Crémieux decree and charged the Jews, in classic anti-Semitic fashion, with being capitalist parasites who exploited the population. In fact, the majority of Algerian Jews were still living in poverty in 1897.

The dangerous situation of Jews in North Africa continued into the twentieth century. Albert Memmi, a Jewish author born in Tunis, wrote in 1974 that his grandfather, living under Muslim rule, was regularly beaten in the street by Arab boys in a ritual known as the *chtáká*.[1] After Algeria won its independence from France in 1962, Jews were deprived of all legal rights by the Algerian Supreme Court and were forced out of their professions. The Jewish population of Algeria, which stood at 140,000 in 1948, sank to a mere 500 by 1974 (*Atlas* 94). Eventually, there was not one Jew left in Algeria. It is no surprise that Derrida's parents were among the Algerian Jews who fled the new regime in the early 1960s.

Anti-Semitism in Algeria had a long history and was particularly intense in the 1930s, the first decade of Derrida's life. From the time of the Nazis' rise to power in Germany, the threat of pogroms loomed, supported as well by a tradition of anti-Semitism in France. Derrida was three years old in 1933, the year of Hitler's seizure of power; he and his family could hear French mobs in Algiers celebrating the Nazi victory. In August 1934, Arabs murdered twenty-five Jews in Constantine, in eastern Algeria. In 1936, a Jewish soldier was killed in Algiers for tearing down an anti-Semitic poster (*Atlas* 94).

Not a single German soldier set foot in Algeria during World War II. Even in the absence of the Nazis, though, the Vichy regime's persecution of the Jews was extreme. Jews were stripped of their citizenship and expelled from the professions and from schools. In Algeria as in France proper, Vichy imposed a strict *numerus clausus:* only two percent of doctors and lawyers could be Jewish, and all Jewish teachers were dismissed (except for teachers in Jewish schools; *Jews* 126). In 1942, on the first day of the school year, the twelve-year-old Derrida was made to leave his school, the Lycée de Ben Aknoun, without being told why: an event he often recalled in later life as a kind of primal scene, the submission to an authority that had no need to explain itself. Until the spring of 1943 young Jackie attended the Lycée Emile-Maupas, comprised of expelled Jewish students and teachers. The exclusively Jewish environment made Jackie uncomfortable. He had spent his childhood largely with gentile schoolmates. Suddenly, he was thrown together with a people he was not accustomed to thinking of as his own. His own bar mitzvah was approaching, but he resisted the rituals of Judaism, dragging himself unwillingly through rote memorization of the prayers he would need to recite before the bimah.

In a November 2002 interview with Kristine McKenna of the *LA Weekly,* Derrida remembered that he went regularly to synagogue as a child in Algiers, and that "there were aspects of Judaism I loved—the music for instance." But by the time of his teenage years young Jackie Derrida was, as he later remarked, "shocked by the meaningless way my family observed religious rituals—I found it thoughtless, just blind repetitions. . . . The privilege of holding, carrying and reading the Torah was auctioned off in the synagogue, and I found that terrible" (*Derrida* 118).

Derrida's bar mitzvah was in 1943. He achieved intellectual maturity, though, not through his obedience to Jewish ritual but by reading German philosophy. In 1943, he recalled, "I read Nietzsche for the first time, and though of course I couldn't understand him completely, he made a big impression on me. The diary I kept then was filled with quotations from Nietzsche and Rousseau, who was my other god at the time. Nietzsche objected violently to Rousseau, but I loved them both and wondered, how can I reconcile them both in me?" (118).

By this point, Allied troops had already landed in North Africa (on November 8, 1942). The massive incursion of American and British soldiers led to Jackie Derrida's first encounters with foreigners: his "discovery of America," as he later put it (*Counterpath* 27). The next year, Jackie returned to his previous school, once again studying alongside gentile pieds-noirs in an Algeria liberated from Vichy control. The threat of Nazism was ebbing; Jackie played soccer until dark with his teenage friends.

In 1943 Charles de Gaulle, as leader of the free French, promised emancipation to the Arab population of Algeria. The pieds-noirs protested de Gaulle's offer, increasing political tensions. Before long Algeria was hit by the wave of Arab nationalism that accompanied the end of the Second World War. In the 1945 Sétif massacre, Algerian Muslims hacked to death over a hundred Europeans, castrating the men and ripping open the bellies of the women. The French response was merciless: they murdered thousands of Muslims. The Arab rebel-

lion had been brutally quieted, at least until the cataclysm of
1955–62, the Algerian war.[2]

The revolt of native Algerian Arabs against French rule
was inevitable, given their oppressed status. A French government report of January 1955 revealed that the average gross in-
come of a European settler in Algeria was twenty-eight times
that of a Muslim; that among two thousand government em-
ployees, only eight were Muslim; and that only fifteen percent
of Muslims attended school.[3] When the rebellion finally arrived, it came with unbridled rage on the part of the colonized
masses.

For about a year, beginning in 1954, there were murmurs
of revolt among the Arabs. In October 1954, terrorists attacked
the French police and military. Then, in August 1955, responding to the cry "slaughter the French" that was issued from
Nasser's Egypt, the Algerians rose. As muezzins gave the signal
from their minarets, pied-noir men, women, and children
were mutilated, their throats cut, their bodies thrown in the
streets.

The Algerian war took its horrifying path, with atrocities
on both sides. The French army's widespread use of torture
against Arabs still haunts France today. In 1961, Maurice
Papon, the Vichy collaborator who had become the Paris pre-
fect of police, ordered the Paris massacre: two hundred Algerian protestors were shot and their bodies cast into the Seine.[4]
But the tide had already turned against French occupation.
The following year the French finally gave in, and Algeria attained its independence. In the summer of 1962, three quarters
of the pieds-noirs departed for France.

Jackie Derrida left Algeria as a nineteen-year-old in 1949,
years before the war of independence. But the earlier rebellion
of 1945 shook him and his family. In neighboring Libya, over a

hundred Jews were killed by Arab mobs in November 1945 (*Atlas* 93). Years later, he recalled, "Even for a child who was unable to analyze things, it was clear that it would all end in fire and blood. No one could escape that violence and that fear" (*Points* 120).

Derrida was growing up in an environment full of violent upheaval. He responded by throwing himself into books: Swift's *Gulliver's Travels,* Rousseau's *Reveries of a Solitary Walker,* Chateaubriand's *René,* and the novels of André Gide (*Counterpath* 27). (He also kept a silkworm collection, a peculiar, delicate hobby that rewarded the young Derrida with a burst of color when the cocoons were stained blood-red and the moths emerged [*Veils* 87–91].) In an interview, Derrida remembered how he first "got into" literature and philosophy. "Very early I read Gide, Nietzsche, Valéry, in ninth or tenth grade." He especially loved Gide's *Les nourritures terrestres* (*Earthly Nourishment*): "I would have learned this book by heart if I could have. No doubt, like every adolescent, I admired its fervor, the lyricism of its declarations of war on religion and families. . . . For me it was a manifesto or Bible: at once religious and neo-Nietzschean, sensualist, immoralist, and especially very Algerian" (*Points* 341–42). Gide's book is headlong, rhapsodic; it breathes an air of youthful ardor, a desire to experience all of life in its fullness, virtues as well as vices. Suffused with the atmosphere of North Africa, the setting of *Les nourritures terrestres,* Gide's characters praise the earth: "Amorous beauty of the earth, the touch of your surface is marvelous. O landscape where my desire sinks deep! Open country where my pursuit strolls; path of papyrus that covers the water; reeds bent over the river . . . I watched the spring unfold."[5] This was heady stuff for a sheltered, bookish teenager like Derrida.

Derrida's intellectual interests marked a departure from family tradition. For generations, the Derridas had been small businessmen; Jackie's parents read few books. For almost forty years Jackie's father Aimé, like his father before him, was a salesman for the Tachets, a French Catholic family who dealt in wines and spirits. Aimé, suffering under his "cruel and paternal chief," M. Tachet, seemed to spend his whole life traveling, though he always returned home to El Biar to stay the night with his wife and children (*Counterpath* 32).

Derrida remembered his industrious father going over his account books while sitting at the dining room table before dawn, about to depart for a long day of journeying to Algerian towns, perhaps Kabylie or nearby Vialar. With cash spread out on the table, young Jackie would help his father balance the books. When the books didn't come out right, "it was a catastrophe, all was not well with the world" (31–32). After he had learned to drive at eighteen, Jackie would sometimes accompany Aimé on his trips (32).

Derrida's father "would leave the house by car at five o'clock in the morning and return late in the evening. . . . He would come back exhausted, stooped over, a heavy briefcase in his hand, full of money and orders for goods. . . . My first political experiences linked the unjust suffering of two unfortunates: the 'Arab,' and my father, the 'traveler'" (32).

Years later, Derrida summed up his sense that, as a child in Algeria, he was an outsider to French literature and culture. The Frenchman of Paris was the arbiter of proper style. "He was the model of distinction, what one should say and how one should say it" (*Points* 204). Yet, at the same time, Derrida noted, the pieds-noirs thought of Frenchmen from the continent as naïve and credulous (205).

Jackie's parents had no idea what the École Normale

Supérieure was. But their teenage son, the brilliantly curious bookworm, already had his sights set on this immensely prestigious inner sanctum of French intellectual life. In the course of the twentieth century, the École produced Jean-Paul Sartre, Simone de Beauvoir, Raymond Aron, Maurice Merleau-Ponty, Claude Lévi-Strauss, and Michel Foucault, along with other distinguished French intellectuals. Jackie was to become one of this impressive company.

He prepared for the École Normale entrance exam by studying philosophy at the Lycée Gauthier in Algiers and then, for three years, at the Lycée Louis-le-Grand in Paris. Rigorous, day-and-night study preparation was demanded of all who aspired to admission to the École Normale. The school admitted only a minuscule portion of the teenage students who applied: several dozen each year, out of many thousands of candidates.

Derrida failed the entrance exam to the École in 1950. He redoubled his efforts, and after a new course of demanding study, he finally passed, entering the École Normale in 1952. A few years earlier, in 1947, Derrida had failed the baccalaureate exam required for graduation from a French lycée. These were not to be the last failures in Derrida's academic career. In 1955 he failed his *agrégation,* the École Normale's exit exam. (He passed the exam the following year, guaranteeing him a state job for life under the French system.) Throughout his career, and despite his enormous success, Derrida felt himself to be something of an outsider, a misfit prone to running afoul of the ruling powers of academic and intellectual life. Like his fellow Algerian Camus, he saw himself permanently in opposition. In later years, he bridled at any suggestion that he had founded an institution called deconstruction: even at the high point of his success, he preferred to cast himself as a rebel against our usual ways of reading, rather than the founder of a new, academically favored method.

Derrida first saw France in 1949, as he arrived at the bustling port of Marseilles, full then as now with lively, and partly illicit, street life. It was the first time he had ever been away from his home in El Biar, apart from day trips with his family to Algerian towns. By the time he reached Paris, homesickness hit him with unremitting force.

The nineteen-year-old Derrida tried to adjust to life in Paris. He "was sick all the time . . . on the edge of a nervous breakdown," as he later recalled (*Points* 342). The competitive examinations for entry to higher levels of schooling, so characteristic of the French system, were "monstrous torture" to him. If he failed, he would be forced to return to Algeria, a place that he now found "unbearable" (*Points* 343). Derrida's initial homesickness had faded, giving way to absorption in his daunting schoolwork.

During these early years in France, Derrida was frequently exhausted and sleepless, afflicted by the stress that accompanies youthful ambition within a rigid, hierarchical system. He began to take sleeping pills and amphetamines, which exacerbated his despondent, frantic moods. (Sartre was also a heavy user of amphetamines, then widely available over the counter and popular among overworked students.)

Jackie Derrida was now enrolled in the unique French institution known as the *hypokhâgne,* a boarding school that prepares teenage students intending to compete for admission to the École Normale Supérieure. The boarding house where Jackie lived was crowded and depressing. Things weren't much better after he started at the ENS. He stayed for a year near the Place Maubert in the heart of the Latin Quarter, in a tiny maid's room without running water (*Counterpath* 291).

The École Normale, concentrated in the rue d'Ulm, occupies the narrow streets of the Latin Quarter. Its looming, cramped buildings can have an oppressive air. These stone fortresses, constituting "a kind of monastery for boy geniuses" (as James Miller describes the École Normale in his biography of Foucault), make up the chilly, elite pinnacle of French academic tradition (*Passion* 45). To this day, they are animated by their students' ceaseless rounds of intense study, and by haughty, bristling debates among students and faculty, often culminating in the rapier-swift demolishing of an opponent's position.

Derrida's studies were nearly all-consuming; he had little time for leisure activities. But he did take several ski trips in the French Alps, and he visited Normandy and the Loire. On one of the ski trips, in 1953, he met Marguerite Aucouturier, the sister of a fellow student at the ENS. The handsome Jackie was tawny-skinned, his hair still black. (In childhood photographs, he appears much darker than the rest of his family.) Marguerite, from Czechoslovakia, was a blonde beauty of dazzling intelligence, interested in psychoanalysis (she would later become a psychotherapist). She and Jackie felt an instant rapport, both intellectual and emotional. The two began a love affair, which quickly became an item of gossip in the small, elite world of the ENS.

In 1956 Derrida made his first trip, by boat, to the United States. He was to study at Harvard for a year under a rather thin pretext, as he himself admitted: that he needed to consult microfilms of Edmund Husserl's manuscripts in the Harvard library. A year later, in June 1957, he returned to France on the same ship that brought him to America, *La Liberté* (*Counterpath* 25). While at Harvard, Derrida worked on his translation of and introduction to Husserl's "Origin of Geometry," which was to appear as a book six years later.

Derrida was impressed by the openness and seriousness of American academic life, as he first experienced it in Cambridge. At cocktail parties, people expressed real curiosity about his research; genuine intellectual exchanges appeared more possible than in France. His later popularity in the United States seemed to be presaged, even before any of the books that were to earn him such fame in the American academy.

The major event of Derrida's year in America was undoubtedly his wedding to Marguerite Aucouturier, which took place in Boston in June 1957. The marriage would last for nearly fifty years, until Jacques Derrida's death. The couple had two sons, Pierre and Jean; a third son, Daniel, was born out of wedlock to Derrida by Sylviane Agaçinski, a philosopher who later became the wife of French prime minister Lionel Jospin. (In the final interview before his death, Derrida expressed his disdain for marital fidelity. Still stirring up trouble in his last days, he complained that monogamy was "imposed upon Jews by Europeans," and that it is "neither Jewish nor, as is well known, Muslim.")[6]

As a teenager in Algeria, Derrida had devoured Sartre's *Nausea* and had seen his play *No Exit* (*Negotiations* 264, 277). After his arrival in France, he read Sartre's *What Is Literature?* and *Situations,* two books that introduced him to many of the writers he would care about most, including Francis Ponge, Maurice Blanchot, and Georges Bataille (*Points* 345). He was later to find fault with Sartre, and to choose Husserl instead as his major intellectual influence. But Derrida still had to reckon with Sartre, the dominant intellectual figure of postwar France, and he measured himself against Sartre at the start of his career. Derrida followed Sartre's idea that we wish to, but cannot, achieve a seamless, confident identity; but in contrast to Sartre, he denied value to this striving for authenticity.

Sartre, born in 1905, was the very model of the engagé intellectual, devoted to political causes from Algeria to Vietnam.

(In 1960, Sartre was one of the key authors of the Manifesto of the 121, a petition denouncing the French actions in Algeria, and encouraging French soldiers to disobey orders in order to destroy the war effort.) Sartre proved the axiom that the French judge their philosophers by the political party they vote for. In Sartre's era, the Communist Party held sway among the intellectuals. Stalinist rhetoric pervaded the classrooms and hallways of the rue d'Ulm, often spilling out onto the cobblestoned streets of the Latin Quarter.

Sartre had himself been a student at the École Normale in the 1920s. While studying at the École, Sartre also exercised himself as a novelist and, of all things, a boxer. His short, ugly, tenacious physique, the frog-like face with its walleye and ever-present cigarette, were familiar to all at the ENS. Strange to say, these physical peculiarities gave him an odd, powerful appeal to women, and he became a champion seducer.

At the École, Sartre met Simone de Beauvoir, his match as thinker and life partner, and later a central feminist intellectual. Until Sartre's death, he and de Beauvoir (called by Sartre *le castor*, "the beaver," for her assiduous nature) pursued an open relationship in which they shared details of their romantic encounters, often with the same young women.

In 1932, Raymond Aron, who was later to become the most important political philosopher of postwar France, told Sartre about Edmund Husserl's challenging approach to philosophy, his new science of phenomenology. Sartre, immensely excited, immediately read Emmanuel Lévinas's pioneering study of Husserl. For Sartre, phenomenology became the royal road to understanding human consciousness.

Phenomenology suited Sartre's already estranged view of humanity. People were, to Sartre, foreign presences, lost in a world of objects that remained indifferent to them. Husserl appealed to Sartre because he thought of the object world as a cause of philosophical wonder and disorientation. But Husserl was too calmly reflective for Sartre's taste. So Sartre gave Husserl's ideas his own twist, emphasizing psychology and political action over the detailed, abstruse studies of perception that Husserl preferred to pursue.

In October 1945 Sartre delivered a momentous lecture, "Existentialism Is a Humanism," to a packed house in a Right Bank theatre in Paris. In his talk, Sartre declared that "man is condemned to be free." Faced with the heroic, epochal choice between authenticity and inauthenticity, how could we not commit ourselves to authentic existence, and thereby to self-realization?

The straightforward bravado of "Existentialism Is a Humanism" catapulted Sartre to immense fame. In 1945, after the German occupation during which so many of the French felt they had acted in bad faith, or in quiet alliance with the evil of the times, the Sartrean endorsement of authentic choice came like an unexpected blessing. And, even better, it came from a man who presented himself as a hero of the resistance. (Soon afterwards Sartre's lecture drew a scowl from one of his main inspirations, Heidegger, in his "Letter on Humanism": Sartre, Heidegger wrote, "stays with metaphysics in oblivion of the truth of being" [*Passion* 47]. Derrida, in the midst of the tumult of the sixties, would look back to the debate between Sartre and Heidegger in his essay "The Ends of Man.")

As important as Sartre's ideas and his books was his career as the archetypal politically engaged intellectual. In this respect he inadvertently delivered a warning to Derrida concerning the perils of taking sides in the Cold War. Sartre's relation to Communism was vexed and uncertain at times, but for the most part he loyally defended the Soviet Union. Sartre's decision, typical of Stalinist intellectuals, was to conceal his knowledge that the Soviet Union was a police state "pour ne pas décourager Billancourt" (so as not to discourage Billancourt, the Paris suburb full of Renault workers).

In the question and answer session at New York's Film Forum following the premiere of the film *Derrida* in October 2002, Derrida was asked about Sartre by a member of the audience. His response was notably cagey. Derrida said, "I read him intensely when I was young, and then I departed from him. I realized he was not a strong philosopher.... It's still a question for me how this man, who is not a very powerful philosopher, not a very good writer, either; who made so many mistakes in politics—who made mistakes all the time—nevertheless, is still such an admired figure in France.... But no, I don't owe him anything in philosophy" (*Derrida* 110). In another interview, Derrida went much further and called Sartre's example "nefarious and catastrophic" (*Points* 122).

The voluble leftist Sartre was a warning sign for Derrida in the 1950s. Derrida, by contrast, never praised an authoritarian regime.[7] Instead of the revolutionary violence that Sartre approved, Derrida spoke of the strictly metaphorical "violence" done by philosophical concepts.

Derrida rejected Sartre the political prophet. But Sartre's philosophy remains a powerful ancestor of Derrida's. Like Sartre, Derrida sees the human impulse toward undivided consciousness, and therefore integral selfhood, as a basic part of us. In reality, Derrida and Sartre agree, such wholeness is a fond delusion. Derrida decentered the subject, but Sartre had already deprived the subject of security, of stable identity. Iris Murdoch notes that for Sartre "the urge toward 'self-coincidence' ... is the key to our being."[8] This drive toward unified, substantial identity can never succeed; we remain empty strivers yearning for fullness. In Sartre's terms, we are each the for-itself that wants to be in-itself. Yet Sartre insists on what Derrida denies: that we can at least achieve the authenticity of the striver, as we focus our aim on a human goal.[9]

Sartre and Derrida share a diagnosis of the human condition as the pursuit of certainty and stability in an unreliable, inconstant world. But Derrida was always more attracted to Sartre's influence, Husserl, because Husserl avoids the psychological approach that Sartre relies on.[10] Husserl's more rarified perspective appealed to Derrida because Husserl, in his quest for a truly impersonal theory, avoids the entanglement with ideas of heroic authenticity and political commitment so characteristic of Sartre.

Derrida wants a role for the philosopher freed from Sartrean melodrama: he wishes philosophy to achieve a sufficient detachment from the turmoil of its time, and from human pathology in general. Husserl, who in this respect is an important guide for Derrida, argues against the entwining of psychology and philosophy that is so apparent in Plato, Nietzsche, and Freud. As I discuss in the next chapter, Derrida would recognize the pressures of his era in the late sixties and respond to them by adopting, at times, a voice of prophetic exhortation reminiscent of the youth movement. But until then, he took his stand as a critic of metaphysics rather than a Sartre-like analyst of twentieth-century humanity.

Sartre, then, is less important for Derrida than the phenomenologist Husserl and the nineteenth-century idealist Hegel. As Dermot Moran suggests, Husserl and Hegel are the definitive philosophers for Derrida. (Martin Heidegger comes a close third.)[11] In his early career, Derrida chooses Husserl over Hegel because Husserl allows him to retain a distance from history. Rather than deciding on the relation between thought and its historical epoch, as Hegel does, Derrida remains concerned with the transhistorical assertions of metaphysics and its critical counterpart, skepticism.

Hegel in his *Phenomenology of Mind* (1807) posits a realm of absolute knowledge attainable at the end of history. (The latter-day Hegelian Francis Fukuyama asserted in 1992 that the end of history had arrived, although Fukuyama later retracted this apparently premature conclusion.) The philosopher who has gone through the entire history of thought—none other than Hegel himself—can arrive at the promise of absolute knowledge, and perhaps even at absolute knowledge itself.

There is no right or wrong position in philosophy, in the Hegelian approach. Instead of trying to determine the merits of particular philosophical views, Hegel recounts these views in their historical succession, with great ingenuity and dramatic flair (and in prose so virtuosic and self-reflexive it can seem stunningly opaque at times). Plato yields to Descartes, who gives way to Hume, who is overturned by Kant . . . and then all is fulfilled in Hegel himself. Or so Hegel tells us. Philosophy for Hegel, then, is simply the whole history of the ideas developed by philosophers through the ages. If we recount this story with care and devotion, we will be narrating as well the career of the Spirit (in German, *Geist*): the universal mind to which only philosophers are fully attuned.

Hegel was a central presence in twentieth-century French thought. Alexandre Kojève, a Russian exile in Paris and a glamorous ladies' man (and lately accused of being one of Stalin's spies), introduced a number of French writers and thinkers to Hegel in the 1930s, through his well-attended weekly seminar on the *Phenomenology*. Among them were Raymond Aron, Georges Bataille, André Breton, Maurice Merleau-Ponty, and Jacques Lacan: a truly star-studded cast (*Reckless* 122). Bataille and Breton were already presences in French intellectual life; the others would become famous later on.

Kojève was fond of referring to Hegel eagerly penning the final lines of his *Phenomenology* as Napoleon's guns sounded victory at the battle of Jena, the town where Hegel lived and taught. Napoleon was the world spirit writ large, monumental and unavoidable proof of history itself. With Napoleon spearheading Enlightenment, overthrowing princes and ready to impose the power of reason on Europe in the form of tolerant local regimes, political and philosophical history confirmed each other. Hegelian thought and world-historical events moved in perfect synch.

For Hegel metaphysics is a total project, reaching with soaring ambition and grand intricacy toward its culmination in Napoleonic Europe. *Consummatum est:* the story of Western thought was complete—now that it had been understood by Hegel himself. (Great thinkers are not usually modest, but Hegel probably takes the cake when it comes to self-confidence.)

Derrida, always insistent on the importance of Hegel, remains doubtful about Hegel's emphasis on the totalizing power of reason, its vaunted ability to complete itself. He shares with Hegel the idea that philosophy is really the history of philosophy. But he interprets the thought of the past by emphasizing its ambiguities and contradictions rather than its slowly increasing grasp of the truth, as Hegel does.

For Derrida, Hegel is an arch-logocentrist. Derrida's most fundamental concept is probably logocentrism. The term can be defined as the prizing of a reasonable account, one provided by lucid thought—and the elevation of such lucidity into self-sustaining empowerment. In Greek, *logos* means word, reason, account, or story. It is opposed to *mythos:* also story, but in the sense of a possibly ungrounded rumor or tale. In effect, Derrida turns the logos into a mythos, albeit a powerful, all-pervasive one.

According to Derrida the dominance of reason, of the logos, is linked to the archetypally masculine will to control society (*phallogocentrism* is one of Derrida's many coinages). Logocentrism also emphasizes the notion that thoughts can be accurately conveyed by speech, and that the task of writing is to serve speech by representing it faithfully. The logocentrist believes that both words and thought, if they are clear and sensible, offer a transparent view of reality.

A logocentrist believes that thought, and therefore the world, is self-verifying, capable of establishing and securing itself. The logocentrist contends that we may be confused at times, muddled or fantastic in our thinking, but that these moments are aberrations. We really define and justify ourselves by our conscious, sensible thoughts, the ones we can articulate clearly to ourselves. Arguments should be lucid and logical: in this way they are most persuasive, and most true. Rhetorical tricks and sly efforts to hoodwink an audience get in the way of truth. Things make sense to the degree that they reflect, or are rooted in, reality.

These beliefs form the credo of the commonsensical logocentrist. We cannot avoid going through some part of life as this simple character. But Derrida argues that logocentrism can be proven false. Meaning, he asserts, is generated by différance; not, as we commonly think, by the connection between language or thought and the "real world." (For Derrida, there is no such place.)

First revealed to the world in the essay "Différance" (1968), Derrida's invented word incorporates two meanings implied by the French verb *différer*: "to differ" and "to defer," or postpone. Derrida, in his wide-ranging essay, finds the idea of différance in the works of the linguist Ferdinand de Saussure, as well as those of Freud, Nietzsche, Heidegger, Bataille, and Lévinas. For Derrida, following Saussure, there stands behind any written or spoken utterance a matrix of differences that enables meaning to exist. In Saussure, the difference between phonemes creates meaning; significance does not reside in any particular phoneme. This idea of the "betweenness" of meaning applies to language as a whole, and appears most audibly in puns. (A pun works only because it plays with the difference between two words.)

This spatial aspect of différance exists in the gap between one word and another, whether the gap is in the dictionary or in the competence of the person who speaks or writes. But différance also has a temporal aspect: it defers, in addition to differing. Only a series of uses of a word, built up over time, can create linguistic meaning. Each of the occasions of use will be related, but these occasions will also differ from one another. Here Derrida departs from Saussure, who emphasized the synchronic, or present-tense, character of language, dramatized in the act of conversation. (As we shall see in chapter 2, Derrida offers a fierce critique of Saussure in *Of Grammatology*.)

For Derrida, différance implies that there is no firm distinction between speaking and writing, though these two aspects of linguistic expression often seem opposed to each other. We assume that speech takes place on a single, present occasion, and that the speaker is in control of what is said, whereas writing sometimes comes to us from an indefinite source and raises questions about whether its author's intentions are reliable, or even discernable. Derrida argues that both the written and the spoken word signify only by means of difference. What we take to be the substantial presence of a speaker understanding a thought and communicating it as a message to listeners is actually just as elusive and uncertain as a scrap of writing, full of obscure expressions, by an unknown author.

Yet Derrida does not advocate an abandonment of reason. He is not a Dadaist revolutionary babbling nonsensical verses or an absurdist performance artist rampaging on a stage. Instead, as a philosophical skeptic, he devotes exhaustive efforts to analyzing the very writings that are the most logocentric in their inclinations. When read carefully, these works, by Hegel, Heidegger, and others, also cast intense doubt on logocentric prejudices. Oppositions like truth versus lie or presence versus absence are inevitable: we cannot think, talk, or live without depending on them to structure our world. So the trick is to rely on these oppositions, as we must, while also keeping in mind that they are subjected to intense questioning even in the words of their advocates, the great philosophers (who, often, want to find a more genuine truth, or a more absolute form of presence: Plato's episteme, Heidegger's Dasein).

Derrida's idea is to adopt a shrewd, two-faced consciousness, at once logocentric and skeptically antilogocentric. Derrida's attention to the power of changing contexts to shift meaning provides a crucial key to his work. He is, perhaps above all, the philosopher of contingency, insisting that anything can turn out to be something else if it is reinterpreted or seen from a different perspective. For him, there are no absolutes: no protection from the instability of changing circumstances and, therefore, no protection from new meanings. This underlining of contingency is the form of his skepticism.

This skepticism requires that Derrida derive from the fact of contingency the much more dubious notion (basic to much current theory) that anything contingent is unworthy of our belief. (As I explain in chapter 2, Derrida's embracing of Nietzsche in the late sixties turns such skepticism inside out: suggesting the apocalyptic promise of contingency, which appears in the form of the utterly unpredictable and unanchored statement. Such an emphasis requires him to deny the specific weight of the contingent, its place in a context, as his opposition to Austin demonstrates.) The poet and philosopher John Koethe points out that doubting the contingent is one means that theorists rely on to partition themselves off from the rest of us. Koethe emphasizes that poets, in particular, value the contingent and consider it worthy of our trust. For the poet, who sees meaning in the fleeting and the elusive, mutability is no argument against importance. Not for nothing does Wallace Stevens include "It Must Change" as one of the desired aspects of his supreme fiction (in "Notes Toward a Supreme Fiction"). Koethe remarks that "locating the source of our notions of language, thought, and the mind in contingent human practices does not automatically render them illusory" (*Poetry* 46).

Skeptics like Derrida claim that if a thing is not absolute—if it is contingent, its meaning changing over time—then it has proven unreliable. The skeptic reaches toward an impossible standard of evidence, and as a result breaks faith with the familiar world, the one we all live in. Just because we know that some societies have approved of murder does not mean that we cannot consider murder wrong. The mere fact of social diversity does not prove moral relativism.

When Derrida began to assert the centrality of ethics in his thought, in the last decade of his career, his assertions about justice could not be coherently combined with relativism (the natural child of his skeptical approach). For years,

Derrida had explored the skeptical response to metaphysical statements about the certainty of meaning. How could ethical imperatives exist in a world where all meanings were uncertain? Derrida was forced, however covertly, to admit a role for moral revelation: for the idea that certain values, once disclosed to humanity, cannot easily be retracted (for example, the commandment to care for one's neighbor, or the prohibition against murder).

Edmund Husserl provides the original stimulus for Derrida's skepticism. Husserl is the perfect target for Derrida: a diehard logocentrist who quests after clarity. Husserl wants to prove his thinking, render it certain. Derrida, in opposition to this metaphysical ideal, becomes the champion of the undecidable. He argues the indeterminacy of meaning, and seizes on the contingent, the random, the fragmented—everything that Husserl abhors. Yet Husserl is a necessary starting place for Derrida because he tries (and fails) to bridge the gap between the contingent and the absolute. As Derrida occupies himself with Husserl's "Origin of Geometry," what fascinates him is Husserl's attempt to understand the historical genesis of Western thought. Husserl grapples with the ideas of objectivity and abstraction that are basic to Western scientific and philosophical consciousness. Where do these ideas come from? Husserl's answer is: a particular time and place, ancient Greece. But the conjunction of universality and particularity remains an insoluble problem for him. (In Hegel, by contrast, universal ideas are incarnated without difficulty in particular historical moments.) Derrida takes from Husserl the notion of an inescapable, but permanently puzzling, relation between universal truth and the occasion when it arises.

As his career develops, Derrida the skeptic drifts far away

from this Husserlian problem and toward a simplified sense that metaphysical claims are always undermined by the contingency of the occasions when they appear. Because ancient Greece is not naturally, but only accidentally, the birthplace of geometry, geometrical truth is not stable in the way Husserl wants it to be; because mental life cannot verify itself continuously, but instead loses track of its activities, our experiences of distraction or forgetfulness damage the validity of consciousness. For these reasons, Derrida argues, scientific truth or conscious thought cannot be certain in the way Husserl desires.

Derrida began his intellectual journey by following Husserl in restricting metaphysics to abstract statements about perception, action, and signification and excluding both Sartrean psychology and the ethical commands familiar from religious tradition. In the mid-sixties, with Derrida's writings on Emmanuel Lévinas and Edmond Jabès, religion entered his work. An aspect of existence appeared that could not be easily subsumed under the metaphysics-skepticism pairing that governed Derrida's treatment of Husserl—the Lévinasian encounter with the other, a fellow human in need. (This interest in Lévinas came to the fore during Derrida's ethical turn in the 1990s.)

Husserl, a German Jew who had converted to Christianity, was fastidious and abstract in his manner and in his voluminous writing. (In addition to Husserl's published oeuvre, there exist about twenty thousand pages of his phenomenological "research," recorded in his peculiar shorthand.) In his photographs, he stands stiffly intent, a proud sage with a massive beard. As professor of philosophy for many years at the University of Freiburg, Husserl was the teacher of the celebrated Martin Heidegger, along with Hannah Arendt, Herbert Marcuse, and other important figures. Heidegger, crucially influenced by Husserl, dedicated to him the first edition of his magnum opus *Being and Time* (1927). (He retracted the dedication after the Nazis came to power, when Husserl, as a Jew, was removed from his teaching position.)

Phenomenology derives its name from the Greek verb *phainomein*, "to appear." The phenomenologist studies appearances: how we perceive the world, and how our acts of perception provide the basis for our understanding of life. Husserl intended phenomenology as a way of making philosophy return to its authentic vocation: the close consideration of how human knowledge is possible, and of how we live our lives as thinking and perceiving beings.

Husserl saw a grave danger for philosophy in scientific naturalism, which is as current now as it was in Husserl's era. Naturalism (in the sense of the word that Husserl relies on) tries to explain human experience, including mental events, in terms of natural processes. (Cognitive science, now a serious influence in many disciplines, is a leading form of naturalism.) As Husserl saw it, naturalism had not established a truly scientific basis for itself; it was rooted in experimental results, rather than reason, and therefore could not develop a coherent picture of the mind.

Husserl vowed to base his philosophy neither in the language of natural science favored by naturalism, nor in what he saw as the mythic hypotheses of psychology—nor, finally, in the ready observations of common sense, so often proved faulty by philosophers from Socrates on. Instead, he searched for a realm that could be the basis for both science and everyday experience: two ways of understanding that usually seem to be divided from each other. Although Husserl's thought may at first glance seem abstract and unbending, it is in fact a metaphysics that accepts, and tries to explain, contingency.

Husserl was devoted to the importance of human reason, increasingly so as Europe sank into the morass of totalitarian ideology in the 1930s. He attended to Max Weber's warning concerning the dangers of separating reason from value. Husserl, following Weber, cautioned against basing life either on reason detached from values, the route of technological advancement, or on values devoid of reason, the path of European nationalism (*Edmund Husserl* 180).

In Husserl's view, philosophy was needed to clarify science. What do we really mean by basic terms like *thing, event, consciousness?* How do we attend to an object's wholeness while still being able to understand the object's separate features? The answers cannot be found by scientific experiment, but rather must be sought through phenomenology, the study of how things definitively appear to us. For Husserl, our shared world is the real arena of study (*Edmund Husserl* 111). And, Husserl adds, it is this world's typical character that allows it to be shared. Typification underlies the common possibility of experience. For this reason, Husserl attends to the sameness, the givenness or continuity, of experience. But he also notices what interrupts such continuity: when self-consciousness, wonder, or doubt arise suddenly and unexpectedly, throwing us out of our usual complacency. Suddenly things look strange, unaccountable. Only philosophical reflection can tell us about such matters: insight cannot be found through research into the structure of the brain or familiar platitudes about what life is like.

Husserl is also intent on understanding what he calls the foundational character of science. There is something about a scientific discovery (for example, the revelation of Euclidean geometry) that enables us to rely on it; the discipline created by the discovery may be modified as time goes on, but always on the basis of its original premises. The permanence of a discipline like geometry consists in the way it offers possibility for new knowledge, for development, but still remains the same discipline.

As the catastrophe of Nazism encircled the Europe of the 1930s, Husserl yearned after a rational continuity in the life of nations that would be analogous to the lucid power of scientific knowledge. He hoped for a revival of philosophical reason in its noblest forms. This reawakening of reason, linked by Husserl to the idea of Europe as the home of science, was, as he saw it, the only way out of the growing insanity of nationalist ideology. Husserl wrote in a diary entry in 1906, "I have been through enough torments from lack of clarity and from doubt that wavers back and forth. . . . Only one need absorbs me: I must win clarity, else I cannot live; I cannot bear life unless I can believe that I shall achieve it."[12]

For all Husserl's influence on Derrida, it is hard to imagine a passage more inimical to the deconstructionist point of view than Husserl's diary entry, with its wholehearted, and rather desperate, declaration of faith in clear truth. Derrida argues against Husserl's fervent wish for a clarity that we can trust. He spurns the quest for certainty that has animated philosophy since its beginnings in ancient Greece. Instead, he favors constant ambiguity. Derrida wants to frustrate certainty; he chooses to celebrate diversions and digressions. Husserl, by contrast, wants with all his being to get to the core: the unknown but knowable basis of all our experience. In this sense, Husserl provides a perfect foil for Derrida, since he represents philosophy's attachment to the ideal of certain truth. Derrida sees the phenomenologist's hunger for such truth as fearful and defensive: a flight from différance.

Husserl does, in fact, have his defensive side. A number of

dangerous, important elements are overlooked in his attempt to establish the truth. Consider the aspects of life addressed in Antonin Artaud, or Nietzsche, or Lévinas: terror, anxiety, guilt. Philosophy starts from such emotions, too, not just from the calm wonder and thoughtful abstraction that Husserl preferred to dwell on.

In spite of his temperamental differences, Derrida was profoundly drawn to Husserl. He saw Husserl not merely as a benighted opponent, but as a thinker who investigated the connection between history and philosophy with unprecedented originality. For Derrida, again, Husserl represented an antidote to Sartrean theatricality. He stood for a more studied approach to the question of how thought and history intersect, in opposition to the heated Sartrean emphasis on engagement.

Derrida, while still at the École Normale, wrote his dissertation on Husserl (although the dissertation remained undefended until 1980, when the fifty-year-old Derrida finally received his doctorate of letters). A distillation of that dissertation was given in Derrida's first lecture at an academic conference, after he came back from his work on Husserl during his Harvard year. The talk, "'Genesis and Structure' and Phenomenology," was delivered by the twenty-nine-year-old Derrida in 1959 at a conference in Cérisy-la-Salle, a picturesque town in Normandy. (Since 1980, Cérisy has hosted a series of academic meetings devoted to discussion of Derrida's work.) "Genesis and Structure," first published in 1964 and then reprinted in *Writing and Difference* (1967), is by any measure a remarkable work. It is especially ambitious and challenging for a scholar still in his twenties.

In "Genesis and Structure," Derrida aptly sums up the peculiar strength of Husserl's inquiry. Husserl, Derrida writes, returns to the things themselves, as philosophy should. He remains "self-effacing before the originality and primordiality of meanings" (*Writing* 155). We all perceive, we all think: Husserl attends to these basic facts. He is faithful to experience and opposed to any tendency on the part of philosophy to impose its will on the world. (In this respect, Husserl differs starkly from Hegel.)

Derrida goes on to argue that Husserl's ideal fidelity to phenomena takes two divergent forms. On the one hand, Husserl aims for a descriptive clarity concerning the structure of experience (how perception or imagination work, for example). On the other, he tries to uncover origin rather than structure: the historical roots of the way we see and know the world. Notably, Husserl attempts this understanding of the genesis of our experience in "The Origin of Geometry" (1936), which Derrida studied so intensively in the late fifties and the beginning of the sixties.

Husserl refuses to believe that numbers or geometrical shapes simply "fell from heaven." Instead, they were invented, or discovered, by particular people, who then transmitted their discovery to others. Here, though, Husserl runs into what Derrida calls the difficulty of "accounting for a structure of ideal meaning on the basis of a factual genesis" (*Writing* 158). Derrida suggests that genesis and structure—that is, the birth of geometry and its systematic nature—cannot be coherently related, despite Husserl's wishes. Yet these two aspects are, nonetheless, conjoined in some way.

Ideal geometrical shapes somehow came out of pre-geometrical experience. But how? It could not be the case that evidence for geometry accumulated in someone's mind, leading to an inevitable conclusion that such ideal forms must exist. Instead, this was a true intellectual revolution: a world-historical stroke of imaginative transformation, whose author and motive remain unknown to us.

The fascinating question that Husserl encounters in a work like the "Origin of Geometry" is, as he puts it, "the problem of the foundation of objectivity" (*Writing* 159). Actual people, who lived at a certain point in history, developed the notion of objective truth. They founded objectivity in the form of the pure propositions of mathematics, which were not a matter of opinion, and not, therefore, subject to historical conditions. In spite of their universal nature, though, geometry and higher mathematics remain rooted, according to Husserl, within a certain civilization, that of Europe (and the cultures influenced by Europe). Husserl yields to the temptation to associate the truth of geometry with the place of its genesis in ancient Greece, the source of European civilization. For Husserl, Europe is the culture that invented the scientific consciousness, and therefore it remains the home of truth.

Husserl thus emphasizes the fact that a basic way of perceiving the world, as a collection of precisely defined geometrical shapes, had a historical origin, in ancient Greece. He adds, though, that once geometry is discovered, it *becomes* universal. Similarly, one might argue, there may be cultures whose members lack a sense of fear, or shame, or fairness. But, if they existed, we would think of them as incomplete, waiting to acquire a fuller sense of humanness. They would be like the archaic people before geometry who, unable to see quantifiable shapes, were waiting to acquire a fuller sense of what things look like. So a discovery becomes a norm.

Derrida points out that Husserl cannot at the same time both describe a structure and explain its genesis. A permanent gap remains between the ideal meaning encoded in geometry and the fact that geometry was invented in a particular place and time. It is hard to believe that geometry is an essentially European science, given its universal applicability. Husserl's belief in the West as the native realm of philosophical thought, the historical source of the objectivity necessary to science and mathematics, comes under fire in Derrida's "Genesis and Structure." But Derrida remains ambivalent on this question, as he acknowledges the necessity, the true importance, of Husserl's project. He suggests that Husserl's inclination to associate structure and genesis, to link scientific truth with the culture that discovered it, might well illuminate the character of our knowledge. Derrida refuses to unmask Husserl as a mere ethnocentric European. Instead, he implies, rather uneasily, that thought is unavoidably allied to its cultural surroundings. Europe remains, then, the home of objectivity, much as we might squirm at the ethnic favoritism such an idea conveys. Derrida implies that Husserl, instead of just exhibiting the symptoms of our inevitable tendency to connect genesis with structure, genuinely helps us to understand this connection. And yet Derrida does not go further, though we want him to; he does not explain what the understanding is, exactly.

The nature of Husserl's discovery, and of Derrida's attitude toward it, remains unclear in the early "Genesis and Structure." We can surmise, though, that Derrida is sympathetic to Husserl's effort. We will see in the next chapter how Derrida faults Foucault for being an unrepentant historicist. Husserl, by contrast, remains valuable to Derrida because he combines a sense of historical origins with a universalizing emphasis—even if Husserl (like Derrida) is unable to fully explicate the combination.

In 1962, Derrida continued his work on Husserl with an introduction to the "Origin of Geometry." Husserl's essay on geometry is twenty-three pages long; Derrida's introduction occupies over a hundred pages. Derrida was finding in Husserl what the other philosophers of the École Normale looked for in Marxist politics: an epochal intersection between knowledge and everyday life. Geometry, for Derrida as for Husserl, offers an example of ideas that change the world, that change experience itself. Every day, we see and feel the strict forms that were not there before geometry first appeared. In this way, the geometrical becomes firm evidence for itself.

Beginning with Plato's *Meno*, geometrical truth has been identified with (as Husserl puts it) what is "objectively there for 'everyone'" (*Introduction* 65). It is of crucial importance for Husserl that this ideal objectivity has a history. No final state of geometrical knowledge will ever be reached: instead, we are treated to an infinite progress of understanding. Husserl associates this infinite progress with European culture, the home of the exact sciences. But the source of the idealizing ability that stands behind exact science, and that therefore supports phenomenology, remains obscure. As Derrida puts it, "the Logos cannot appear as such, can never be given in a philosophy of seeing" like Husserl's (141). There is no "phenomenology of the Idea" (138).

Derrida, then, implies that Husserl's philosophy is anchored in something that remains external to it, and that cannot be subjected to phenomenological investigation. What is missing, and must remain missing, is a story about how the difference between mere facts and ideal objects first arose. On the one hand, as Husserl phrases it, "the human surrounding world is the same today and always" (*Introduction* 180). Phenomenological investigation, like geometrical truth, can take place anywhere, at any time. On the other hand, the "Origin of Geometry" suggests that objective truth is less at home in civilization than it once was, given the rampant irrationalism of early twentieth-century politics. Husserl dwells on the difference between the work of reason involved in mathematics, which requires the activity of making things self-evident and objectively true, and the ready-made opinions and prejudices of "the whole modern age" (169). Husserl calls upon science as the cure for the easy, half-plausible doctrines of contemporary politics.

Husserl, then, enlists mathematical objectivity as a potentially saving counter to the myths and lies of the 1930s, Auden's "low dishonest decade." He fervently hopes that a new attention to the kind of lucidity and standards of evidence that mathematical science requires will reform the public realm. As geometry once leapt out of a merely factual context, giving experience a new dimension, so it may once again change our understanding of the world around us.

In the "Origin of Geometry," as in his Vienna lecture (1935) and his *Crisis of the European Sciences* (1936), Husserl implicitly relies on Plato's sense that there is a vast difference between the world of the ideas (which mathematics helps us perceive, according to Plato) and our everyday shifting universe of opinion, emotion, and unreliable narrative. But he also draws from Plato the notion that attention to the ideas can purify the everyday, enabling us to see it truly, as if for the first time. The ideas bring us out of the cave into the accurate light of reality.

As in "Genesis and Structure," Derrida in his introduction to Husserl emphasizes Husserl's sense that geometry had a beginning. Geometrical objects did not exist prior to the discovery of the discipline. Yet the particulars of history cannot explain this beginning. If we knew the names and biographies of those who invented geometry, we would learn little about what the founding of geometry was like, or what it meant. Instead, these merely factual circumstances would miss the point. (In this sense geometry is fundamentally unlike psychoanalysis, on which a study of Freud's personality sheds much light.)

The introduction contains a startling digression on, of all figures, James Joyce. In the midst of his knotty reflection on Husserl's idea of meaning, Derrida suddenly juxtaposes Husserl's attitude toward meaning with Joyce's. Joyce, he writes, "take[s] responsibility for all equivocation." The Irish writer sees "the greatest potential for buried, accumulated, and interwoven intentions within each linguistic atom, each vocable, each word, each simple proposition, in all worldly cultures and their most ingenious forms (mythology, religion, science, arts, literature, politics, philosophy, and so forth)." Joyce, Derrida concludes, sets as his aim "to travel through and explore the vastest possible historical distance that is now at all possible" (*Introduction* 102). Husserl, by contrast, attempts "to reach back and grasp again at its pure source a historicity or traditionality that no de facto historical totality will yield of itself. This historicity or traditionality is always already presupposed by every Odyssean repetition of Joyce's type" (103). Joyce may know history, but Husserl, more profoundly, wants to understand where history comes from.

The invoking of Joyce was an omen. Derrida was already, in the mid-sixties, on his way to becoming the most literature obsessed of philosophers. But far from turning philosophy into a kind of literature, Derrida in his pairing of Joyce and Husserl implies that Joyce's wild, word-spinning freedom depends upon a "historicity or traditionality" that Husserl can grasp as Joyce cannot, because Husserl goes to the source, meaning's origin. In this way, Derrida remains loyal to Husserl and to philosophy. He suggests that philosophy has an understanding of origins, and an explanatory prestige, that literature cannot match. Joyce's reliance on many-faceted ambiguous meaning remains secondary to Husserl's effort at solid transparency. Logocentrism, with its home in philosophy, remains the alpha and omega; literature, the vast wandering space in between.

For the Derrida of the introduction to Husserl's *Geometry*, the logocentric was not yet doubtful. But it was about to come under his far-reaching suspicion. Never again would philosophy be able to assert its superiority over the oblique and playful twisting of meaning that is literature's habit. And Derrida himself was poised to become a Joycean corrupter of words.

For the five years before the introduction appeared in 1962, Derrida had moved between America, Europe, and North Africa, often restless and uncertain of the future. For more than two years, beginning in 1957, he served France in the Algerian war, teaching at a school for soldiers' children at Koléa, near Algiers. In 1959 and 1960, afflicted with a serious depression, he taught at a lycée in Le Mans with his friend from the École, the future literary theorist Gérard Genette.

In 1960 began a happier time, the decade of Derrida's greatest achievements. Back in Paris and teaching at the Sorbonne, he took a trip to Prague with Marguerite in a "tiny Citroen deux cheveux" (*Counterpath* 291). He returned to Algeria in 1962, the year of the Husserl *Introduction*, to help his parents relocate to Nice (he had tried, without success, to convince them to remain in Algeria after the revolution). In 1963 a first son, Pierre, was born to Jacques and Marguerite Derrida; the second, Jean, would follow in 1967. In between, in 1965, the Derridas took a memorable trip to Venice and spent a month on the Lido. Derrida was settling into his role as a rising intellectual presence, cemented in part by his triumphant appearance in 1966 at the Johns Hopkins Sciences of Man symposium (an event I will return to in the next chapter).

The year 1967 was Jacques Derrida's annus mirabilis. He published three major books, including his two most famous works, *Of Grammatology* and *Writing and Difference.* The third book, *Speech and Phenomena,* is less well known, but Derrida confessed in the early seventies that it was his favorite of the three.

In *Speech and Phenomena,* Derrida continues the investigation of Husserl begun in "Genesis and Structure" and his introduction to the "Origin of Geometry." He does more than just furnish a commentary on Husserl's thought, however. With *Speech and Phenomena* Derrida definitively turns against Husserl, a philosopher whom he clearly admired in his earlier writings. A full eight years after Derrida gave his "Genesis and Structure" lecture, and five years after the equally sympathetic *Geometry* introduction, Derrida conceives a stark opposition between himself and Husserl.

Speech and Phenomena presents a sustained critique of *Logical Investigations* (1900), one of Husserl's first important works, in which he proposes a brilliant, groundbreaking treatment of how meaning occurs. Husserl's innovative discussion in his first logical investigation begins with a distinction between indication and expression. In all communications between one person and another, Husserl writes, speech is bound up with indication. Husserl's examples of indication are canals on Mars (which, if they existed, would indicate the presence of living beings on the planet) and fossils (which indicate the past existence of vanished animals). Similarly, a shouted denunciation is an indication that someone is angry. Our tone of voice, our choice of words and gestures, indicates our meaning.

Expression, in contrast, normally (but not always) relies

on indication as its vehicle. Indications can be expressions if they have been selected by someone in order to convey a meaning. (The canals and the fossils are indications but not expressions, since they are not products of intention.) We can tell something about the mood of those we listen to because they express themselves, and because their expressions are also visible or audible indications. As Husserl remarks, "we 'see' their anger, their pain etc." (*Logical* 1.7 [190]). Not all human gestures are expressions. Involuntary facial tics may also communicate something to a hearer: that the speaker is nervous, for example. Such tics are indications, pieces of visible evidence. But they would not be expressions, since they have not been chosen by someone as a means to say something.

Indication and expression are therefore, for Husserl, the two basic aspects of meaning. It is important for Husserl that these two aspects remain separable. I have already mentioned cases in which indication exists without expression: the canals of Mars, or facial tics. But for Husserl, expression can also occur apart from indication, a point that will rouse Derrida to fierce disagreement. When we have an interior monologue with ourselves, argues Husserl, we engage in expression, but not indication.

In a decisive passage, Husserl considers the case of "solitary mental life" as an example of pure expression that needs no indication:

> Shall one say that in solitude one speaks to oneself, and thus employs words as signs, i.e. as indications, of one's own inner experiences? I cannot think such a view acceptable. . . .
>
> One of course speaks, in a certain sense, even in soliloquy, and it is certainly possible to think of

oneself as speaking, and even as speaking to oneself, as, e.g., when someone says to himself: "You
have gone wrong, you can't go on like that." But in
the genuine sense of communication, there is no
speech in such cases, nor does one tell oneself anything: one merely conceives of oneself as speaking
and communicating. In a monologue words can
perform no function of indicating the existence of
mental acts, since such indication would be there
quite purposeless. For the acts in question are
themselves experienced by us at that very moment.
(*Logical* 1.8 [190–91])

Husserl's argument seems convincing, if difficult. I can
perform acts of indication in silent, inward soliloquy. But I cannot actually indicate anything, since there is no other person
who has adopted a discerning relation to me, trying to figure
out what I mean. The performance is therefore a pretended action (though in certain cases a useful form of self-therapy: "You
can't go on like that"). I can discover something about myself
in solitary reflection, but the discovery remains independent
of any later mental playacting. If I decide to dramatize my
thought, say in order to drum up my courage or reinforce my
desires, the communication remains merely imagined, and
therefore secondary to the original thought (*Strategies* 115).

Husserl's point is comparable to Ludwig Wittgenstein's
argument against our tendency to picture our mental lives as a
drama of articulated, quasi-verbal thoughts. Wittgenstein, like
Husserl, makes the case that we cannot possibly experience
our lives and our thinking in the way we suppose we do. For
example, we do not follow a rule by saying to ourselves, "I've
got to take the next step now," any more than we walk by de-

ciding to put one foot in front of the other. When we dwell on our decision to take a particular step and tell ourselves that we follow rules not automatically but thoughtfully, we deliberately remove ourselves from what rule-following is actually like. Such articulation makes a theatrical gesture where, usually, none is required. As Husserl argues, expression occurs prior to any "speaking to oneself."

In Husserl's interpretation, when I use emphatic declarations in solitary mental life—"you have gone wrong"—I indulge in an imaginary performance, since the thought I am dramatizing cannot possibly be obscure to me. But when I interact with other people, the performance is real, since I am at times unclear to them, and they to me. (Freud, of course, argues that the central region of mental life, the unconscious, remains profoundly inaccessible to the self. But Husserl remains loyal to consciousness, seeing it as the basis of all thinking.) In the case of solitary thinking, then, meaning resides in the expression, before anything else. In social life, however, meaning depends on indication as well as expression: on what other people make of what we say and do. When we try to figure someone out on the basis of limited evidence, we rely on indication. But the fact that we can still mean something without engaging in indication shows that there is a contrasting expressive side to language. For Husserl, again, expression does not require verbal signs. When I am asked to tell someone what I am thinking, the frequent sense of strain, of having to translate a thought forcibly into verbal form, shows that I express myself in solitude in a more intimate way than can easily be captured in words.

Derrida argues that all expression, including conscious, solitary meditation, is a form of indication: that thinking requires signs, whether verbal or gestural. In his argument, indication takes over the realm of expression. For Husserl, by contrast, indication and expression may occur together, or they may not; they do not contaminate each other. When Derrida, against Husserl, argues that expression is really indication, he contends that the material of indication—words and gestures performed in time—insinuates itself into, and permanently colors, the thing indicated, the expression.

Derrida charges that Husserl wants a self for which meaning is utterly present, constantly available (*Strategies* 108). But despite Derrida's claim, Husserl does not adhere to such a simple view of the self and its meanings. For him, communicable meaning is not, in fact, easily available: a gap remains between inward expression and social indication. Husserl suggests that we are intimately related to our own thoughts, and that it is therefore absurd to picture the self explicitly formulating its every mental impulse. According to Husserl, I am deeply mistaken if I think that I must constantly take silent mental notes in order to think or perceive. (Such note taking, occurring on an unconscious level, constitutes, in rough terms, Derrida's picture of the mind.)

For Derrida, Husserl's belief in a thinking that precedes articulation marks him as a metaphysician par excellence. Husserl asserts that an idea can be possessed by a private, interior self, and therefore that the self remains prior to language. The self would then be prior, as well, to culture, history, tradition: a notion that current theory finds, perhaps more than anything else, anathema. Derrida is not a believer in culture in the currently fashionable sense; but he does insist that the self is secondary to, even reducible to, the series of signs generated in time: that is, language. (The idea of a cryptic, hidden self develops slowly in Derrida's work, and is related to the importance of linguistic signs, since Derrida tends to identify the secret self with opaque, fragmentary bits of language.)

Derrida, ascribing the metaphysical notion of the self to Husserl, also charges him with a dangerous adherence to the temporal present tense. Time, and what he claims to be Husserl's misunderstanding of it, will prove to be a crucial subject for Derrida, as he offers his critique of Husserl's effort to separate expression from indication in the *Logical Investigations.* Now Derrida decisively turns toward a skeptical critique of metaphysics, in the form of an attack on Husserl. The project requires a distortion of Husserl's view: a transformation of him into a strident, defensive logocentrist.

Derrida paints Husserl as a thinker addicted to presentness as the necessary form of the availability of meaning. In *Speech and Phenomena,* Derrida states that for Husserl "self-presence must be produced in the undivided unity of a temporal present so as to have nothing to reveal to itself by the agency of signs" (*Speech* 60). This claim is inaccurate. As the philosopher Natalie Alexander points out, Husserl is concerned not with a punctual, self-sustaining present moment, but rather with a "temporally extended whole," in which a now-phase is shadowed by what has just been and what is about to come. Husserl does not claim that the now is a sufficient, self-sustaining foundation. Instead, the now is dependent on, and intertwined with, its past and its future.[13] For Husserl every moment has a forward and backward horizon: it implies past and future moments. This temporal span is required by our need for context. Every time we see something, we are *seeing as:* seeing the thing as part of a larger whole. This means that each perception must be prepared for by a sense of how or why it occurs and what it might lead to. Husserl's attention to the context of the moment shows that he is not the simplistic adherent of self-presence that Derrida claims he is.

Husserl, though not a believer in the "pure present," still remains far removed from Derrida's idea that moments are indicative signs—that there is no present, only representation. We represent (that is, indicate) time to ourselves, Derrida writes, in order to live our temporally extended lives. Time means the reading of signs. In a reading that owes much to the early sections of Hegel's *Phenomenology*, Derrida argues that the "now," the ostensibly present moment, is in fact insubstantial, a nothing, because it is negated by the past and the future, just as the self is a nothing because it will someday be dead. Whenever I say "now," whenever I notice the current instant, I furnish a mere representation. I can never make my way into the present.

Here, for the first time, Derrida establishes a central role for death, the sine qua non of his philosophy. Derrida remarks that "my nonperception, my nonintuition, my *hic* and *nunc* absence are said by that very thing that I say, by *that* which I say and *because* I say it" (*Speech* 93). It is not just that my statements can still function even after my death (if they are written down, or if people remember them). Rather, death is required for my words to mean anything at all. As Derrida puts it, with a somewhat chilling touch: "The relationship with *my death* (my disappearance in general) thus lurks in this determination of being as presence, ideality, the absolute possibility of repetition. The possibility of the sign is this relationship with death. . . . The appearing of the *I* to itself in the *I am* is thus originally a relation with its own possible disappearance. Therefore, *I am* originally means *I am mortal*" (54).

Derrida's credo is not "I think, therefore I am," but rather, "I die, therefore I am (not)." Death creeps into our very selfhood. He even describes indication as "the process of death at work in signs" (*Speech* 40). For Derrida everything is a sign, which for him means that everything is founded on repetition (on what he calls iterability) and on the false promise of permanence. This promise must fail because death is "inscribed" in the sign itself.

Derrida, again, is assuming that all significance depends on indication. But Husserl asserts that things may have meaning without being indications. My expressions are never *completely* readable by others. I am still expressing, even when close friends cannot tell whether I am grimacing or grinning—when they can't read me. Odd as it is, my expression embodies my meaning whether or not this meaning is available to someone observing me. It is (so Husserl would argue) not *originally* a sign, but an expressive motion.

In Husserl, then, the most telling case of meaning is one in which I express something, even if no one sees or reads me. For Derrida in *Speech and Phenomena,* by contrast, all meaning implies the absence of the one who means, who expresses. This is deeply counterintuitive. In the typical skeptic's fashion, Derrida wants to give the lie to our common sense of ourselves. My expressive gestures feel like part of my living present. Rather than being produced or "written" by me, my gestures, one might almost say, *are* me. But for Derrida a truer witness of meaning would be not my internal feeling for my body's gestures as expression, but rather a video recording of my body's motions. All that feels most inward is in fact, he insists, merely outward. In this way, Derrida converts expression into indication. Derridean meaning resides in signs that function in the absence of both sender (writer or speaker) and referent: "The total absence of the subject and object of a statement—the death of the writer and/or the disappearance of the objects he was able to describe—does not prevent a text from 'meaning' something. On the contrary, this possibility gives birth to meaning as such, gives it out to be heard and read" (*Speech* 93).

"The living present springs forth out of its nonidentity with itself," Derrida concludes (85). Even when I do something as simple and present-tense as waving my hand or jumping happily in the air, I should be aware that this present has been invaded by a non-presence: the fact of my own future disappearance, my death.

The grim determination with which Derrida sets out to sour the "living present," to make it wilt and subside into a matrix of nonidentity, testifies to his will to alienate us from our experience. In this, he takes part in a tradition. Characteristically, philosophy pulls rank on our native feeling, our desired sense of ourselves. This can be a salutary effect, comparable to the Christian moralist's desire to remind us in the face of our self-congratulation that we are but dust and ashes, or the psychoanalyst's critique of the comforts of fantasy. But like the moralist's dismal rigor or the analyst's reductive truth telling, the philosopher's commitment to alienation may drift too far from ordinary life. In a certain mood, I may feel that the prospect of death really is inscribed in each of my statements and gestures. But the mood cannot be a permanent one: the memento mori remains a partial view.

The Derridean philosopher David Wood writes of *Speech and Phenomena* that "Husserl scholars have not reacted too favorably to it."[14] This is a considerable understatement. Husserl scholars have found it difficult to take Derrida's book seriously; they see in it an attempt to get the better of Husserl by misrepresenting his texts. This is especially the case with Derrida's insistence on the theme of voice and speech. He claims that "there is an unfailing complicity between idealization and speech" in Husserl (*Speech* 75); but Husserl simply does not emphasize speech, or connect it to idealizing. Derrida asserts that Husserl names "the voice that keeps silence" (70) as the basis for meaning. This is Derrida's image, and Derrida's idea— not Husserl's.

One might be reminded of a comment by Paul de Man, who charged that Derrida in his *Grammatology* "deliberately misreads Rousseau for the sake of his own exposition and rhetoric" (*Blindness* 139). Derrida performs the same kind of misreading of Husserl in *Speech and Phenomena*. The Husserl scholar Claude Evans even suggested, with tongue in cheek, that *Speech and Phenomena* might be a satire, given the bizarre picture of Husserl it delivers to its readers (*Strategies* 172).

Evans, as he knew, went too far. Derrida is surely serious in his treatment of Husserl. But just as surely he reduces Husserl to a much lesser thinker than he is. In Derrida's hands, Husserl becomes a rather simplistic exponent of "being as presence," determined to exile everything contingent and worldly. The strange combination of contingent origin (Greece) and absolute truth (geometry) that intrigued Derrida when he commented on Husserl's "Origin of Geometry" has been eliminated. Now, five years later, Derrida charges that Husserl wants to expel all contingency.

Derrida's Husserl wishes to escape death and flee into the fantasyland of transcendental thought, free of space and time. According to Derrida, Husserl promises that "I can empty all empirical content, imagine an absolute overthrow of the content of every possible experience, a radical transformation of the world. I have a strange and unique certitude that this universal form of presence, since it concerns no determined being, will not be affected by it" (*Speech* 54). In effect, Derrida turns Husserl into a representative of one-sided Neoplatonic idealism, determined to float free of actual experience. But the starting point of Husserlian phenomenology is exactly the opposite of what Derrida claims. Husserl returns to the things themselves: how we perceive, imagine, think, and feel the world. He wants to see what happens when we have an insight or realize a truth.

In answer to the charge that Derrida betrays Husserl, Derrida's defenders might reply that this move is typical for a philosopher: turning on his own ancestry, engaging in a Bloomian misreading that enhances his own strength and decreases his precursor's. Heidegger misread Nietzsche, Hegel misread Kant, Nietzsche misread Plato . . .

This defense of Derrida has some validity. Heidegger, one of Derrida's crucial ancestors and his rhetorical model in many ways, shared Derrida's pious insistence that he was reading earlier philosophers with rigor and responsibility: missing nothing, with the sole aim of being true to the text. Yet Heidegger, just like Derrida, produced distorted, though brilliantly interesting, versions of Kant, Plato, and Nietzsche. He saw in these earlier philosophers only what he wanted to see.

Derrida on Husserl emulates Heidegger in this enterprise of revision—and, at times, falsification—of earlier philosophers. But he goes further by suggesting, however fleetingly, his antipathy to one of the basic motifs of philosophy, the search for truth. Countering Husserl's prizing of clarity and insight, Derrida in *Speech and Phenomena* tries to show that the insightful is a subset of the non-insightful, never able to escape a tangled web of glitches, nonsense, and semantic misfiring (*Strategies* 53). The problem is that Derrida is then left unable to explain how understanding, meaning, and truth actually occur.

Speech and Phenomena differs decisively from Derrida's

earlier work on Husserl. No longer would he make the bold literary experimentalism of writers like Joyce and Mallarmé yield priority to the staid Husserlian attitude to meaning, as he did in his introduction to the "Origin of Geometry." Derrida in his later work celebrates literary explosions of meaning, at times preferring them to the firmer, if narrower, ground of philosophy.

The antilogocentrism of experimental writing is important to Derrida because it unmasks meaning as unstable, unreliable in its contingency. Such a vision of literature prevents it from bearing much weight, whether cultural, historical, or emotional. Instead, the object lesson of the avant-garde becomes a negative one, asserting the dominion of mere randomness (though Derrida transforms this randomness into a cataclysmic Nietzschean message in his 1966 essay "Structure, Sign and Play," which I discuss in the next chapter).

The confrontation between an inventive, potentially explosive approach to meaning and a careful, methodical one marks Derrida's struggle with Husserl's work. The contest was a close one, but the wild, centrifugal text (the kind that Derrida was about to produce) was bound to win out over the more confined and predictable one (Husserl's oeuvre). Beyond mere skeptical assertion, Derrida now reaches toward the radical and the innovative, the world-changing. This prophetic attitude appears in many of Derrida's texts from the late sixties (often in conjunction with the name of Nietzsche, as in "Structure, Sign and Play" and "The Ends of Man").

Speech and Phenomena, like its companion volumes *Writing and Difference* and *Of Grammatology*—both of them more unbuttoned and extravagant in style than Derrida's relatively restrained study of Husserl—was published at a time when France, like America, was breathing the atmosphere of a politicized avant-garde. Writers and thinkers reckoned with the sometimes chaotic discontent of the times and instilled an ardent energy into their work. As shown in the next chapter, Derrida's writing shared in such energy. However rarefied his thought may seem, it was not immune from the turbulent currents of the sixties.

II

Writing and Difference and *Of Grammatology*

In this chapter I devote extensive attention to two books that Derrida published in 1967, *Writing and Difference* and *Of Grammatology*. In both works, Derrida insists on the skeptical position he had established in his studies of Husserl. Yet, more important, he also moves beyond the battle between metaphysics and deconstructive skepticism. The real story of *Writing and Difference* and *Of Grammatology*, especially the former, is Derrida's desire for a new, even revolutionary, truth. This truth cannot be found through the mere act of debunking metaphysical assertions. Derrida seeks something more, an empirically present reality: the encounter with the face of the other in Lévinas; the traumatic origin of history in Freud; Nietzsche's embrace of a coming, palpably transformed world. There are other kinds of empiricism that Derrida rejects: in Lévi-Strauss, Foucault, Husserl. And his continuing opposition to the psychological reduces the explanatory force of his stance in the late sixties. But the fundamental fact is that he recognizes the shortcomings of a merely negative, demystifying skepticism.

Derrida needs an outside of philosophy, a glimpse of the real world. The need becomes stronger in the face of the revolt of 1968. With their privileging of life over mere books, the student revolutionaries present a threat to Derrida's text-centered approach. Derrida meets this challenge by evoking a Nietzschean apocalypse in which the free play of meaning abolishes all previous forms of metaphysical security and proves our old assumptions illusory. Derrida's heralding of the Nietzschean future is one instance of the prophetic style he frequently indulged in the late sixties. But such broad proclamations carry little explanatory power; they demonstrate only Derrida's desire to share in the mood of his era. A liberated reality cannot, after all, be so easily attained; the traumatic and constraining realities described by Lévinas and Freud will prove more significant for Derrida's future development.

The major theme of *Writing and Difference* and *Of Grammatology*, then, is the question of empiricism and its possible relation to an outside of philosophy. Derrida scorns the empirical commitment of Foucault to discover the history of madness, as well as the empirical anthropological research of Claude Lévi-Strauss. Madness will not be a key term for Derrida, because it implies the psychological perspective that he warns against. Saussure's emphasis on empiricism, his grounding in the evidence of conversational practice, is seen by Derrida as an aspect of the same devotion to presence that characterizes Husserlian phenomenology (charged with an overestimation of voice, as we saw in chapter 1).

But the empirical begins to take on a different, more positive light in *Writing and Difference*, a collection of essays mostly composed of pieces that appeared in the avant-garde

theoretical journals *Tel Quel* and *Critique* between 1963 and
1966. The commitment of Emmanuel Lévinas to the face-to-
face encounter with another person is Derrida's prime instance
of an empiricism that genuinely challenges philosophy. Similarly, Freud's idea of traumatic origins exposes a determined,
unavoidable fact that stands behind our experience. Derrida's
persistent references to the Hebrew Bible in his treatment of
Freud, as well as his commentary on the Jewish writer Edmond
Jabès, indicates that Jewish tradition, for Derrida, implies an
encounter with the historical real—and an escape from the
sterile dialogue between metaphysics and its opponent, deconstructive différance.

In the light of such strong empiricism as Freud's and
Lévinas's, Derridean writing (theorized most extensively in
the *Grammatology*) is revealed as an insubstantial force, not
affirmative enough to carry us into any genuinely new territory. Writing remains bound up with claim and counterclaim,
presence and absence; it shows how death insinuates itself into
life, hollowing out expression. Derrida needs to surmount the
parasitic character of such statements, the way that deconstruction thrives on the mere exposure of paradox. And so he
turns, at different moments, to the laughter of the overman
(Nietzsche) and the suffering of the neighbor (Lévinas), as well
as to the Freudian notion of trauma. (Trauma proves to be
more challenging to Derrida than the Freudian unconscious,
although the unconscious elicits far more pages from him.)
Freud, of course, raises the specter of psychology, but Derrida
takes care to avoid it. Derrida's interpretation of trauma in
Freud remains distant from any consideration of personality
or individual development. He takes from Freud only what he
wants: themes that can be detached from any connection with
therapeutic practice or the mysteries of human interaction.

Derrida's most significant encounters in the sixties, then, are with Freud, Nietzsche, and Lévinas. With all three figures, Derrida finds a path beyond the argument over metaphysical assertion and skepticism that occupies him in the case of Husserl. He juxtaposes to Freud and Lévinas the words of the Hebrew Bible, emphasizing the Jewish commitments of these two thinkers. Nietzsche is an equally prophetic figure, but in a different direction, pointing toward play and freedom rather than obligation to the past—and therefore appropriate to the student revolt of May 1968, which Derrida considers in his lecture "The Ends of Man." Finally, the history of his time is the empirical phenomenon that confronts Derrida most immediately at the end of the sixties. His response, a wary one, nevertheless testifies to his desire to link deconstruction to the historical moment.

In March 1963, Derrida, just thirty-two years old, delivered a lecture on Michel Foucault at the Collège Philosophique in Paris. Derrida's talk, later reprinted as a chapter in *Writing and Difference,* is not so much a commentary on as a cross-examination of Foucault, Derrida's former teacher at the École Normale Supérieure. Foucault was himself present in the audience at the Collège. As one reads through Derrida's lecture, one can almost feel his subject's growing nervousness. Derrida puts Foucault on the spot in a ceremonial, thoroughgoing way. Here Derrida, wrestling with his precursor Foucault, sizes up Foucault's way of writing intellectual history—and finds it wanting. He argues that Foucault misrecognizes madness, seeing it as an empirically evident, historical phenomenon. For Derrida, madness actually resembles geometry in Husserl: an ideal entity detached from history, and paired permanently with philosophical reason. But madness is not Derrida's key term in the sixties, since it implies the psychological element that he tries to exile from philosophy. Instead, he chooses writing, celebrated in *Of Grammatology.*

By 1963, Derrida and Foucault already had a long personal history. In the early fifties, Derrida had been a student in Foucault's course on psychology at the École. Their most significant encounter came in 1955, after Derrida gave a paper he had written on Husserl to his supervisor, Louis Althusser. Derrida wanted the paper to count for his degree. Althusser confessed that he was unable to evaluate Derrida's work on Husserl ("It's too difficult, too obscure," he remarked). So he gave the paper to Foucault, who commented, "Well, it's either an F or an A+" (*Negotiations* 148). Foucault, like Althusser, resisted any public acknowledgment of Husserl's importance. Derrida, the budding Husserl scholar, was not to forget, or forgive, his teacher Foucault's blind spot.

Two years before Derrida's lecture, in 1961, Foucault had published his landmark *History of Madness in the Age of Reason.* (In English the book is more commonly known as *Madness and Civilization,* the title of Richard Howard's abridged translation.) Foucault argued that insanity, which had been an accepted, if frightening, power in the ancient world, was stigmatized during the Enlightenment, when it became the "other" of reason. Madmen were confined to asylums, whereas in the Middle Ages and earlier they had run free in the streets: reviled and feared, but also sources of a fierce oracular wisdom.

Derrida begins his essay, entitled "Cogito and the History of Madness," by circling warily around his prey, his old teacher Foucault. "Having had the good fortune to study under Michel Foucault, I retain the consciousness of an admiring and grateful disciple," he remarks uneasily (*Writing* 31). Derrida then describes himself as a disciple with an "unhappy consciousness." When he starts to write against his "master" Foucault, he notes, he "finds himself already challenged by the master's voice within him" (31). Despite this elaborate preliminary footwork, Derrida proves bold enough. His chapter on Foucault clearly rejects the "master."

In his relentless critique, Derrida makes the case that Foucault engages in crude, ineffective historicizing. In fact, Derrida asserts, the position of madness is similar in the ancient, medieval, and modern worlds, not different as Foucault claims. Derrida argues that nothing changed in respect to madness with the Cartesian revolution in philosophy. Socrates and Descartes share a wish to exile insanity, "the other of reason," from philosophical thought: from the logos (40).

Derrida stakes out his terrain, announcing that he will be a thinker of Western metaphysics as a whole, not a student of epochs like Foucault. Foucault called the global revolutions that occur every few centuries changes of episteme (epistemes being, in the Foucauldian vocabulary, regimes of information and knowledge that govern how one thinks and acts). For Derrida, all of European intellectual history is one long episteme.

Derrida, then, opposes Foucault's historicizing bent. He makes another point against Foucault as well. Foucault, Derrida charges, acts as if he knows what madness means, as if it could be defined by reason (incarnated by Foucault himself, the synoptic thinker). Yet his polemical aim is to liberate madness from the domination of reason. This is a basic contradiction, one that Foucault seems unaware of, writes Derrida.

Derrida takes issue with Foucault's assertion that there is something outside reason called madness. In fact, Derrida claims, madness is internal to reason, present within it from the beginning. Foucault, he argues, should admit that madness is the age-old underside to reason: an antagonistic aspect that reason relies on to define itself, but that also challenges reason's coherence. Taking as his guide the example of Descartes, who raised the possibility of the philosopher's madness in his *Meditations,* Derrida suggests that every thinker, even (or, rather, especially) at his most stringent and lucid, fears insanity. "I philosophize only in *terror,* but in the *confessed* terror of going mad" (62).

Foucault's biographer James Miller hypothesizes that Derrida's remark was a chilling and vindictive one, since Foucault's fear of insanity and his repeated suicide attempts were well known at the École Normale Supérieure (*Passion* 120). (The death-obsessed Foucault would later advocate "suicide-festivals" and "suicide-orgies" designed to accelerate the "limitless pleasure" of dying. Foucault seems to have thrown himself into a dangerous orgiastic whirlwind during his final, AIDS-afflicted years, when his visits to San Francisco bathhouses became frenetic and compulsive [*Passion* 55].)

Derrida now gives his final verdict on Foucault. The latter, he asserts, fails to see that "reason has been divided against itself since the dawn of its Greek origin" (*Writing* 40). Foucault, says Derrida, translates the eternal and immutable question of the logos and its other, the force that erodes reason from within, into convenient historicizing, with the result that he dodges the question's profundity. Derrida's attack on Foucault faults his empiricist attachment to presence: to the idea that madness is a historical phenomenon. In this respect, Foucault resembles Husserl, with his supposed championing of the voice that hears itself speak. He becomes an example of attachment to the merely evident rather than the properly paradigmatic. In the course of the sixties Derrida also accuses Lévi-Strauss, Saussure, and Rousseau of committing this fault.

But Derrida's most telling choice in the sixties is his approval of an empiricism of a different kind, which he endorses in prophetic style: the traumatic encounters described in Freud and Lévinas.

Derrida ends "Cogito and the History of Madness" with a tepid compliment to his former professor: "What Michel Foucault teaches us to think is that there are crises of reason in strange complicity with what the world calls crises of madness" (*Writing* 63). This concluding gesture of approbation does not disguise the largely unfriendly character of Derrida's appraisal of Foucault.

Derrida was rewarded by the École Normale for his rebellious inclinations, demonstrated by his bold assault on Foucault. He was proving himself an innovator, willing to spark controversy. And he chose the right person to attack: Foucault's relation to the École was fairly marginal. Althusser, who ruled the intellectual roost at the École, was never criticized by Derrida, despite the latter's disapproval of Althusser's theories and his politics.

In October 1964, Derrida, now thirty-four years old, was appointed as a *maître-assistant,* or instructor, at the École, where he had already been teaching for the past year. He was recommended to his new post by Althusser and by Jean Hyppolite, the great Hegel scholar who had instructed many of Derrida's generation. Derrida was to stay at the École Normale for the next twenty years, making it his base of operations and his intellectual home (*Negotiations* 150).

The École Normale of the sixties was, in effect, governed by Althusser, a devout Marxist. Althusser had a tragic end. In 1980, afflicted by dementia, he strangled his wife—and then wrote a memoir, *The Future Lasts Forever,* in which he confessed that he was an intellectual fraud and that he had actually read very little of Marx's work. Already in the sixties Althusser was suffering from severe manic depression, and he often failed to show up for his classes at the ENS.

Althusser was a fervent Communist Party member, unbending in his loyalty to Moscow. The literary theorist Gérard Genette, who shared his friend Derrida's political misgivings, recalls going to see Althusser in 1956. Genette was troubled by the Soviets' brutal suppression of the Hungarian revolt. Althusser, baffled by Genette's criticism, remarked, "But if what you're saying is true, the Party would be in the wrong!" A defect in Communism was as unthinkable for Althusser as a flaw in God would be for a Christian believer. Struck by Althusser's instinctive support of tyranny, Genette immediately left the Communist Party. The exchange between Genette and Althusser had a marked effect on Derrida who, while personally fond of Althusser, became increasingly skeptical of his political allegiances (164).

Derrida was not a member of the Communist Party, unlike most of his colleagues at the École. When he was a student there, Derrida later noted, the Party "dominated in a very tyrannical manner" (151). There was an atmosphere of "*intellectual,* if not personal, *terrorism*": a relentless "theoretical intimidation" on the part of the Marxists (152). Discussion of phenomenology, even the mere mention of Husserl or Heidegger, was considered reactionary, the mark of a counterrevolutionary. As a student and then an instructor at the École, Derrida felt isolated and unhappy, a victim of political persecution (153–56). For the rest of his life, he was to remain a liberal rather than a radical in politics.

Against this background of conformist thinking, Derrida readied his declaration of independence. In the summer of 1965 Derrida wrote the two essays that were to become the core of his best-known work, *Of Grammatology*. He later recalled his visit to Venice that summer with his wife, Marguerite. Derrida remarked to her as they rode the vaporetto that he had discovered something very big (*Derrida* 111). This summer was his breakthrough, the real beginning of his championing of writing as the hidden presence in Western metaphysics. In a miracle of invention, Derrida had come upon the basic idea of deconstruction. *Of Grammatology*, the book that spread the deconstructionist word, would not appear for another two years, but Derrida was already set to assume his evangelical duties.

The title page of the *Grammatology* was featured in one of Jean-Luc Godard's movies, flitting by in the course of *Le Gai Savoir* (1967). A brief moment in a rapid-fire montage sequence was sufficient to give Derrida the hip, revolutionary imprimatur of Godard, the avant-garde hero of the counterculture. Indeed, Derrida at the time of *Grammatology* was increasingly associating himself with the cutting-edge aesthetic experimentation of *Tel Quel*, the intellectual journal that published, in the winter of 1967, his brilliant, lengthy essay "Plato's Pharmacy" (discussed in chapter 3).

In keeping with Derrida's association with *Tel Quel*, *Of Grammatology* leans heavily on the rhetoric of avant-garde polemic. In the opening pages of his book, Derrida sees himself as the midwife of a monstrous, apocalyptic birth, worldwide in its dimensions and earthshaking in significance: "The science of writing—*grammatology*—shows signs of liberation all over the world, as a result of decisive efforts. . . . The future can only be anticipated in the form of an absolute danger. It is that which breaks absolutely with constituted normality and can only be proclaimed, *presented*, as a sort of monstrosity" (*Grammatology* 5).

In his *Grammatology* Derrida forecasts "the death of the civilization of the book." This impending demise "manifests itself particularly through a convulsive proliferation of libraries" (8). He aims to "designate the crevice through which the yet unnameable glimmer beyond the closure can be glimpsed" (14). With a resounding blast, then, Derrida's *Grammatology* announces, in the title of an early chapter, "The End of the Book and the Beginning of Writing."

What is this rough beast that carries the strange new name, grammatology? Before all else, grammatology (from the Greek *grammê*, "letter") exalts writing. More specifically, it proclaims the liberation of writing from speech. The speaking voice, Derrida claims, has been the central value for all Western thought. And this age-old championing of voice oppresses us. Speech is naturally attractive, writing naturally threatening, in the eyes of Western metaphysics. "*The history of* (the only) *metaphysics* . . . from the pre-Socratics to Heidegger," he writes, is "the debasement of writing, and its repression outside 'full' speech" (3). For over two thousand years, writing has been in exile. Derrida invites it back into the philosophical fold.

Speech—so it seems—offers the assurance of an available, fully graspable meaning. When you say something to yourself, you must know exactly what you mean. And this certainty is philosophy's ideal: notably in Descartes' cogito. As Descartes sees it, I prove my existence by saying something to myself. I think, and therefore—so I tell myself—I am. Not just for Descartes, but for all the rest of philosophy, writes Derrida, "the voice . . . has a relationship of essential and immediate proximity with the mind" (11). And this closeness of voice and mind leads to an idea of "the absolute proximity of voice and being, of voice and the meaning of being, of voice and the ideality of meaning" (12).

All the philosophers agree, Derrida asserts: they constantly favor speech over writing. Descartes imagines the cogito as spoken, not written. Socrates elevates philosophical conversation, with its ability to respond to the objections of an interlocutor, over writing that says the same thing forever, to whatever reader happens upon it. (This concept forms the thesis of the *Phaedrus*, which Derrida attempts to puncture in "Plato's Pharmacy.") Heidegger pictures himself listening to the voice of Being, rather than reading its signs. All three philosophers, according to Derrida, are trapped by a wrongheaded metaphysical attitude: for them, speech has an authenticity that writing could never attain. Speech seems available to empirical proof in a way that writing does not, according to Derrida. Voice tempts us to the idea of presence: we can hear it, we can feel it happening. So once again, empiricism becomes a danger to philosophy, as in the case of Foucault's insistence on the experience of madness when he should have stayed on the plane of ideas. The experience of speaking, like the fact of madness, seems immediate and therefore convincing. But Derrida suggests that the drifting, ungraspable phenomenon of writing is a better guide, even in its elusiveness. (As I have indicated, Derrida eventually proves unable to uphold this preference for the nonevident; he needs a breakthrough into reality.)

For Derrida, writing is naturally devious. It surprises us, disconcerts us, he argues, in a way that speech cannot (at least not in its straightforward, ideal version). When I say "I think, I am," I congratulate myself on my powers of thought—and demonstrate these powers in the most immediate, present-tense way possible. This dream of an instant, direct line from thinking to immediate expression is, for the deconstructionist, metaphysics' major fault. As metaphysician, I claim that meaning is at my disposal, that I am its master. But, according to deconstruction, this claim cannot be sustained. In the *Grammatology* as in his study of Husserl, Derrida repeatedly attacks our inclination, as he sees it, to assume a reassuring identification of meaning with the present moment: an assumption he attributes to the speaking subject (who comes off as something of a metaphysical bully).

In Derrida's world, as he charts it in the *Grammatology,* writing proves superior to speech. Writing plainly lacks the harmony between the spoken word and the present tense implied by the naïve metaphysics of voice. Because we can't ask a dead or inaccessible author what he meant (and even if we could, we'd probably receive an evasive answer), writing floats away from its biographical source. This is even the case with our own writing. I might stumble across a grocery list, or a diary entry, that I have forgotten I ever wrote. Writing comes back to haunt us in a way that speech, with its attachment to the present, does not. A disheveled stack of lecture notes from college, or a file of old emails, gives perpetual surprises, pleasant or unpleasant, to the author who reads them years later.

But, one may object to Derrida, surely speaking is not purely, or always, a present-tense activity. We replay our conversations on a tape recorder, slip an audiobook in the car CD player, listen again on our iPods to a downloaded lecture. Speech might feel archaic; it might, just like writing, be a relic, a sign of the past. And a conversation with a friend, or an intimate enemy, can be just as dizzying and intricate as any postmodern novel.

Derrida in the *Grammatology* surmounts these obvious

objections by redefining the word *writing* to include speaking as well. He suggests that speech is a kind of writing. "Language is first, in a sense I shall gradually reveal, writing" (37). But since writing was a relatively late invention in human history, and infants learn to speak before they learn to write, how can writing come first, before speech?

Derrida recognizes the objection and considers it obvious. And he has a (nonobvious) answer. Speech, although we imagine that it comes before written language, is actually secondary to writing. When we replay a conversation, whether in our heads or on an iPod, we are treating speech as if it were writing. We are even—so Derrida presses the argument— *showing that speaking is a subset of writing.* It is blatantly ethnocentric (a word Derrida wields with a certain abandon in *Of Grammatology*) to say that some societies are illiterate. "Actually, the peoples said to be 'without writing' lack only a certain type of writing" (83). Derrida shows himself unwilling to acknowledge that there are differences between societies that possess writing and those that do not. As anthropologists have long recognized, the transmission of memory, of the history of the tribe, takes place differently in an oral culture and a literate one. Where there is no writing, and therefore no fixed records to be consulted, history tends to become the property of rumor and legend.

Rather than such anthropological distinctions, Derrida concerns himself with our common plight as humans who (as in Sartre's philosophy) are condemned to self-division. He argues that there is always an alienation from "self-presence," however directly we express ourselves. No matter how immediately, spontaneously, or sincerely we speak, we are still not transparent to ourselves (as Freud showed with his study of unconscious motivations and slips of the tongue). The pure voice that hears itself speak may be the wished-for model, but in fact our talk is full of mistakes, wrong directions, and half-hearted indications. The person who listens to me probably has a better grasp of my meaning than I myself do, just as the reader of a book may be able to summarize its significance more accurately than its author could.

Derrida makes a valid if familiar point when, following Freud's lead, he declares that we are not privileged knowers of our own meaning. His bigger charge, that metaphysics is inhabited by an assumption that one can know exactly what one is saying and doing at every moment, remains profoundly dubious. If the philosophical tradition really assumed this, it would be trumpeting an indefensible, and rather simple-minded, credo.

There is a further problem with the way Derrida sees the contrast between voice and writing in Western culture. Derrida's *Grammatology* depends on the hypothesis of a widespread, age-old prejudice against writing and in favor of speech. Writing is repressed, he claims; we prefer the living voice. But if we look beyond the pathos of Derrida's poor orphan writing, crushed by speech, a persuasive counterargument—an answer to the *Grammatology*—emerges. Intellectuals like Derrida have been champions of the book, and profoundly opposed to the ephemeral and conversational, for centuries. Authority resides on the shelves of libraries, and in the pages of journals: so the institutions of science, law, theology, and, yes, philosophy have always told us. Laws are written down, not relayed through conversation. Even professors of sociology and anthropology, who find their material in the lively chatter of social life, have usually resisted incorporating everyday conversation in their books. There is something about the quick give and take of talking, the way its rhythms evade the academic cadence, that tends to put off the mandarins. In this debate, Derrida is on the side of the mandarins, intent on proving that all is writing.

Derrida claims that, since we associate—wrongly—speech with life, we run in fear from the written word as from death itself. We desperately wish to disguise writing as speech. Taking on the role of counsel for the prosecution, Derrida in the *Grammatology* momentarily pretends to be a partisan of voice. Here is how he sums up what he sees as the usual case against writing: "What writing itself, in its nonphonetic moment, betrays, is life. It menaces at once the breath, the spirit, and history as the spirit's relationship with itself. It is their end, their finitude, their paralysis. Cutting breath short, sterilizing or immobilizing spiritual creation in the repetition of the letter, in the commentary or the exegesis, confined in a narrow space, reserved for a minority, it is the principle of death and of difference in the becoming of being" (25).

In a shaky generalization, Derrida goes on to assert that nonphonetic writing (for instance, Chinese characters and Egyptian hieroglyphics) is particularly suspect in the eyes of European tradition. In fact, both China and Egypt have long been regarded in the West as age-old sources of wisdom, their forms of script esteemed as more profound than the ones we know. Freud used hieroglyphics as a figure for the complex depths of the unconscious; Ezra Pound revered the Chinese ideogram. But Derrida argues that we are anxious to subordinate writing to speech, and that we are made particularly uneasy by forms of writing, like Chinese characters, that do not seem linked to the human voice. "A war was declared" on nonlinear writing systems like Chinese, he announces (85).

Is writing really seen by philosophers as (in Derrida's phrase) "the principle of death and of difference in the becoming of being"? If Derrida were right about this, one would expect generations of thinkers following Socrates, adhering to conversation and avoiding script. Socrates suggested that true thought can be transmitted only viva voce, through the face-to-face initiation of disciples. But the tradition he started deviates from his prizing of speech. Instead, philosophers characteristically produce vast tomes (or, nowadays, brief articles) that remain mostly alien to colloquial, spoken language. Nietzsche and J. L. Austin, among others, complained about this lack of connection to living speech in the philosophical tradition. These two—along with Wittgenstein, Emerson, and others—returned the human voice to philosophy, which had long avoided everyday conversational interaction. Derrida, by prizing writing over conversation, asserts a traditional philosophical privilege.

Pursuing the defense of writing against speech, *Of Grammatology* continues with an attack on Ferdinand de Saussure, the maverick French linguist who revolutionized his field with his series of lectures published as the *Course in General Linguistics* (1916). Saussure pioneered the area of study that later became known as semiotics: the study of signs. In the *Course,* he formulated a hugely influential distinction between the two halves of the sign: the signifier and the signified. For Saussure, a word (that is, a verbal sign) consists of two aspects, related to each other like, in his well-known image, the two sides of a sheet of paper: the signifier (the sound of the word) and the signified (the concept or idea implied by the sound). A picture is also a sign; in this case the signifier is visual rather than sonic, but it is still paired with a concept.

Saussure championed a system-centered view of language, based on the idea that meaning is generated by a network of differences. This is true on the level of the signifier, so that the sound "cat" is different from "cot" or "cut" and must be audibly distinct from both in order to mean what it does. More interesting, it is also true on the level of the signified. The concept "cat" only has meaning because it is different from the concept "lion," and different as well from the concept "dog." These differences, argued Saussure, can be understood as oppositions. A cat is "a domestic, rather than a wild, feline" (not a lion or a tiger); it is "the other main domestic animal, the one that does not bark or, generally, fetch" (not a dog). Signs are not individual units, picked out and matched to particular objects. Instead, they signify as halves of an opposition, members of a system. Signs signify structurally.

According to Saussure, a signifying system shapes the world. Reality is not a heap of referents, objects that exist prior to being named or described. The things that surround us, from cats and dogs and chairs and cars to ideas, nations, and families, are organized by signs. These signs help the things come into being. This much, the idea that signifying constructs the world, Derrida praises in Saussure. But he has other problems with Saussure's project. Derrida complains that Saussure shares the age-old logocentric prejudice against writing and in favor of speech. "Plato said basically the same thing" as Saussure, Derrida remarks, rather grumpily. For Saussure, Derrida judges, writing is "a garment of perversion and debauchery" (35).

As often, Derrida's brilliant rhetorical fervor runs away with itself here. Saussure did not say that writing is debauched and perverted, merely that conversational usage, not books, should be the prime resource for linguistic research. Saussure effectively combated philology's preference for staid scholarly investigation. Instead, he championed fieldwork as a necessary excursion into the messy arena of human talk and interaction.

In the nineteenth century, philologists built fortresses of dusty, antique books, immuring themselves in the library. Saussure protested this Casaubonesque ignorance of, and disdain for, the study of living conversation. (Similarly, in sociology, Erving Goffman and others provided an alternative to a dull, statistic-ridden discipline by arming themselves with a notebook and snooping around barrooms, hair salons, and gas stations.) Such empirical testing is, for Derrida, a dangerous temptation: by lending metaphysical assertion the status of palpable reality, it seduces us away from the suspicion we should foster toward metaphysics.

Derrida, in his discussion of Saussure, claims that the ancient philosophical and religious distinction between the soul and the body is "borrowed" from the contrast between speech and writing, which he insists is primary (35). Derrida wants to associate empirical realism, based on the fact of the body, with voice. This point seems rather dubious; in any case, it would be difficult to demonstrate. Derrida provides no evidence for his idea that the speech-writing difference precedes everything else. In addition, he asserts that the sign and religion appear at the same time in world history: "The sign and divinity have the same place and time of birth" (35). One longs for some explanation of such far-reaching insistence (and for possible evidence taken from studies of the origin of religion), but it is not forthcoming. Derrida offers no details about the close relation between the sign and godhead. At such moments, he assumes a high, unsubstantiating preacher's tone, borrowed from avant-garde polemic.

Derrida objects in no uncertain terms to Saussure's distinction between the signifier and the signified. Saussure allows that the signifier is a product of difference: one sound or written mark has meaning only because it differs from another. Derrida approves, and in fact regards as crucial, Saussure's emphasis on the differential character of the signifier. But then, he writes, Saussure goes wrong. He charges that Saussure aims to preserve and protect the signified. In Saussure, Derrida writes, "the signified is a meaning thinkable in principle within the full presence of an intuitive consciousness" (73). In fact, Saussure says nothing like this. As in the cases of Husserl and of Rousseau, who is considered next in the *Grammatology*, Derrida stigmatizes one of his influences by attributing to him the "metaphysical" and untenable idea that meaning is fully available to a self-conscious speaker—an idea that Saussure would never have endorsed.

Derrida argues, against Saussure, that the signified is "*always already in the position of the signifier*" (73). The letters on a page, the words in the air between us: these are signifiers and therefore fragile, apt to be misheard or misread. Their signifieds, the concepts the words are attached to, are, according to Derrida, just as precarious. Does the vulnerability to misunderstanding, on the part either of a word or a concept, render it *essentially* unstable, as Derrida claims? Philosophers, and ordinary people as well, have used the word *justice* for thousands of years now. Justice may be subject to misprision, but it remains recognizable. Even though no universally satisfying definition of it has been achieved, the idea of justice retains a powerful hold on us. We still have a stake in it—and so does Derrida, in his work of the 1990s. (In the 1990s, as I recount in chapter 5, Derrida makes justice the center of his own work, in somewhat implausible combination with his customary skepticism about identity and meaning.)

Saussure himself says that "in language there are only differences" (68). If only, Derrida adds, Saussure had realized that the signified too, not just the signifier, is afflicted by différance, he would have enabled us to go beyond phenomenology: to destroy the privilege granted by phenomenology to the world that consciousness perceives. Phenomenology thinks of the world in terms of experience. But in fact, Derrida insists, the world is *writing*. And "writing is other than the subject" (68): it means "the becoming-absent and the becoming-unconscious of the subject" (69).

The supposed attachment of Saussure to the voice, a necessary part of Derrida's argument against him, must also be addressed here. Despite Derrida's claim, Saussure did not fetishize speech. He did, however, regard it as central to the study of language. He argued that changes in the way a word has been pronounced over time occur regardless of its written form. Spelling does not influence speech: oral communication has its own tradition, one that remains separate from writing. Saussure's emphasis on speech is not metaphysical, as Derrida claims, but rather the product of a particular interest, the study of pronunciation: a field in which, as Saussure judged, oral communication outweighs writing in importance.

Saussure comments on the fact that human language has, from its very origins, been wedded to speech; he adds that it is not by accident that humans rely on the vocal organs for language. Instead, he writes, "the choice was more or less imposed by nature" (*Course* 26). At first glance, this sentence might seem to support Derrida's case that Saussure treats language as naturally bound to the voice. But in fact it shows that Derrida is mistaken. As Claude Evans notes, Saussure merely suggests that the voice was "more or less" the most fitting, or promising, site for language (*Strategies* 159). Derrida turns this empirical judgment into a metaphysical necessity, as if Saussure thought that language's essence is to be spoken.

For Saussure the connection between language and speech and the priority of speech to writing are historical facts, not essential truths. American Sign Language is presumably less capable than speech of a range of intonations. Saussure would have considered this a practical, not a metaphysical, disadvantage. The voice is simply better equipped than the hands to produce a variety of expressive nuances. Derrida reads Saussure's remark about speech as a statement of metaphysical need, rather than what it is, a merely pragmatic judgment.

If Derrida were correct, one would expect Saussure to embrace phonetic writing and reject nonphonetic systems like Chinese, which are more distant from the human voice. Instead, Saussure recognizes that Chinese does not represent spoken words—and he applauds this fact. Saussure writes that in Chinese, writing "does not have the annoying consequences that it has in a phonetic system, for the substitution is absolute; the same graphic symbol can stand for words from different Chinese dialects" (*Course* 48). Saussure protests against the confusion created for linguistic research by phonetic writing's often inaccurate or misleading effort to represent speech. He does not see writing itself as the enemy.

In the same section of his *Grammatology* that deals with Saussure, Derrida introduces C. S. Pierce, the eccentric nineteenth-century Harvard professor who was one of the founders of pragmatism. Pierce pioneered the study of signs: in a way, he was the first semiotician. According to Derrida, Pierce shows us that "from the moment there is meaning there are nothing but signs. *We think only in signs*" (*Grammatology* 50). Experience is an unwieldy, even a mistaken concept (60–61). Instead, we should train ourselves to think in terms of— and here Derrida pronounces a daring new word—the trace.

At times, Derrida writes about the trace in near-mystical terms. The trace "*does not exist*"; but it is the basis for all existence (62). And again, in rapt italics: "*The trace is in fact the absolute origin of sense in general. Which amounts to saying once again that there is no absolute origin of sense in general. The trace is the difference* which opens appearance and signification" (65). The trace is difference, deferral-différance: the gap between one word and another, or one moment and another, that makes meaning.

Derrida now brings out the big guns. The trace has been discovered by the ultimate legitimating authority: science. "And finally, in all scientific fields, notably in biology, this notion [of the trace] seems currently to be dominant and irreducible," he announces, without providing evidence (70). Is everything *really* just writing: the whole world the work of the trace, as Derrida asserts? What about visual pleasures, or the body's quick embraces? These too, Derrida insists, are forms of writing (or "writing"): based on absence rather than, as we naïvely thought, presence.

For all Derrida's fervent denunciations of logocentrism and his apocalyptic thundering in the *Grammatology,* he also suggests that there is no radical change possible and no real place for individual self-assertion. If we trumpet our own originality, we merely turn ourselves into benighted examples of logocentric prejudice. Instead, we should adopt the practice of commenting subversively on previous thinkers, while also admitting that their thought is the inevitable basis of our own. We can only disturb the universe; genuine newness is ruled out from the start. The metaphysics-skepticism paradigm has already determined our thinking.

Here is an example of the Derridean way of diminishing originality in the *Grammatology.* In this passage, Derrida, with some shuffling, explains his use of the word *trace:*

> Why of the *trace?* What has led us to the choice of this word? I have begun to answer this question. But this question is such, and such the nature of my

answer, that the place of the one and of the other must constantly be in movement. If words and concepts receive meaning only in sequences of differences, one can justify one's language, and one's choice of terms, only within a topic (an orientation in space) and an historical strategy. The justification can therefore never be absolute and definitive. It corresponds to a condition of forces and translates a historical calculation. Thus, over and above those that I have already defined, a certain number of givens belonging to the discourse of our time have progressively imposed this choice upon me. The word *trace* must refer to itself to [*sic*] a certain number of contemporary discourses whose force I intend to take into account. Not that I accept them totally. But the word *trace* establishes the clearest connections with them and thus permits me to dispense with certain developments which have already demonstrated their effectiveness in those fields. (70)

Derrida claims that "a certain number of givens belonging to the discourse of our time have progressively imposed the choice" of the word *trace* on him. Listening to Derrida, we hear the expression of history itself, along with his own nervous and habitual qualifications. (One thinks, perhaps uncharitably, of William Kerrigan's remark that reading Derrida can be like watching a man study his facial tics in a mirror.) He is nothing more, he would have us believe, than a conduit, and a rather tentative one, for current "discourses." (He is careful to note that he does not "accept [these discourses] totally.") It is discourse, not the self, that speaks.

This is not the whole story, though. Surprisingly, Derrida

at key moments in the *Grammatology* reveals that he wishes to give the self a role in his theory, even though it does not hold sway over meaning as the logocentrists claim it does. The self, in Derrida's account, is "testamentary." By uttering words that will signify equally well after I am dead and gone, I recognize a "relationship with [my] own death." We are not mere passive bystanders overshadowed by the work of the trace, but instead gloomy surveyors of our own mortality. "Spacing as writing," Derrida remarks, "is the becoming-absent and the becoming-unconscious of the subject. By the movement of its drift/ derivation [*dérive*] the emancipation of the sign constitutes in return the desire of presence. That becoming—or that drift/ derivation—does not befall the subject which would choose it or would passively let itself be drawn along by it. As the subject's relationship with its own death, this becoming is the constitution of subjectivity. On all levels of life's organization, that is to say, of *the economy of death*. All graphemes are of a testamentary essence. And the original absence of the subject of writing is also the absence of the thing or the referent" (69). Here Derrida echoes Heidegger's *Being and Time*. In Heidegger, anxiety for its own death defines the self: this is its "constitution of subjectivity." (Heidegger, though, did not make the connection between death and writing, as Derrida does.) Derrida, in the passage above, is careful to note that the subject does not "choose" its own becoming; neither, however, does it simply drift "passively" with the reigning discourse. Instead, it is called upon to recognize itself as a mortal being.

This passage heralds Derrida's emphasis, decades later, on the self that is subject to the great questions (above all, death and the life-giving obligations we bear to others: the key themes, respectively, of Heidegger and Lévinas). Already in the *Grammatology*, Derrida's focus on the impersonal force of writing, which scatters the self, is modified by a Heideggerian description of selfhood as "the subject's relationship with its own death." Even this early, he is unable to remain a pure skeptic, a total denier of human identity.

Derrida begins the central section of *Grammatology* with a brief discussion of the pioneering French anthropologist Claude Lévi-Strauss, specifically Lévi-Strauss's brilliant book *Tristes Tropiques* (*The Sad Tropics,* 1955). Lévi-Strauss in *Tristes Tropiques* elegantly delivers a combination of autobiography, travel book, and reflection on anthropology as a discipline. For a large part of the book, he focuses on the time he spent among the Nambikwara, an Amazon Indian tribe. It is this section of Lévi-Strauss's account that provokes Derrida's ire. Lévi-Strauss, Derrida charges, is a follower of Rousseau's idealistic primitivism. He displays all the faults of the "Age of Rousseau": "The critique of ethnocentrism, a theme so dear to the author of *Tristes Tropiques,* has most often the sole function of constituting the other as a model of original and natural goodness, of accusing and humiliating oneself. . . . Rousseau would have taught the modern anthropologist this humility of one who knows he is 'unacceptable,' this remorse that produces anthropology" (114). As in the case of Foucault, with his esteem for a madness that he describes as the stark opposite of oppressive Enlightenment reason, Lévi-Strauss (so Derrida charges) sees in his Amazonian tribe a perfect, primitive alternative to all that is corrupt in Western civilization.

Lévi-Strauss, Derrida points out, idolizes the Nambikwara because they are peaceful and because they do not possess writing. Lévi-Strauss, much to Derrida's distaste, sees a fatal connection between these two things: violence and the ability to write. Evil first appears among the Nambikwara, Lévi-Strauss believes, "with the intrusion of writing come from *without* (*exothen,* as the *Phaedrus* says)—the Nambik-wara, who do not know how to write, are good, we are told." (This is Derrida's rendition of Lévi-Strauss's point.) Parody-ing Lévi-Strauss's argument, Derrida adds, "The Jesuits, the Protestant missionaries, the American anthropologists ... who believed they perceived violence or hatred among the Nambikwara are not only mistaken, they have probably pro-jected their own wickedness upon them" (116).

Derrida is especially perturbed by the idyllic picture that Lévi-Strauss draws of the Nambikwara sleeping on the bare earth at night, lying two by two beside their dwindling fires. The philosopher quotes with disdain the anthropologist's fond description of the Nambikwara. Lévi-Strauss writes, "Their embraces are those of couples possessed by a longing for a lost oneness; their caresses are in no wise disturbed by the foot-fall of a stranger. In one and all may be glimpsed a great sweet-ness of nature, a profound nonchalance, an animal satisfaction as ingenuous as it is charming, and, beneath all this, something that can be recognized as one of the most moving and authen-tic manifestations of human tenderness" (117). Derrida takes great offense at the authentic fellow-feeling Lévi-Strauss claims to see in his primitive tribe. "Never," Derrida fumes, "would a rigorous philosopher of consciousness have been so quickly persuaded of the fundamental goodness and virginal inno-cence of the Nambikwara merely on the strength of an empir-ical account" (117).

Lévi-Strauss does seem over-insistent on the innocence of the Nambikwara: he projects his desire for a "lost oneness" onto them. Still, Derrida's critique is peculiar. Instead of criti-cizing Lévi-Strauss for projection, he attacks his reliance on an "empirical account." No matter how "rigorous" we are, we fre-quently make judgments about the character of other people.

On what basis can anyone make such judgments other than empirical observation? If Derrida has a different hunch about the Nambikwara—if he sees them, for example, as malevolent and solitary—it would have to be substantiated by what could only be called an empirical account (whether from his own experience, if he were to journey to the Amazon, or from other travelers' reports). Derrida seems to want to change the rules of the human game, replacing the kind of experientially based suppositions we usually make with the strict results of philosophical analysis. But he fails to suggest how this might happen: what a more rigorous or philosophical approach to judging others and their societies might look like.

What especially rankles Derrida, one might guess, is that Lévi-Strauss links his praise of the Nambikwara to a critique of the academic philosophy that he had immersed himself in at the École Normale Supérieure before becoming an anthropologist. In *Tristes Tropiques,* Lévi-Strauss scorns the metaphysics he studied as a young man, seeing it as vacuous and ineffectual. When he plots his escape from French academic life and into the wilds of Brazil, he is on a search for a superior, more deeply felt way of life. Thankfully, he is able to escape what he calls the "claustrophobic, Turkish-bath atmosphere" of philosophical reflection for the "open air" of anthropology and the truly social disciplines of Marxism and psychoanalysis, which (Lévi-Strauss asserts) confront actual experience as philosophy does not. Having found his vocation as anthropologist and bold investigator of the wild life in the tropics, Lévi-Strauss derides what he deems the sterile intellectual contortions of Husserl and Sartre.[1] Lévi-Strauss's slurs on phenomenology and existentialism were not forgotten by Derrida, who takes his revenge on behalf of the philosophers in *Of Grammatology.*

In his heated objection to Lévi-Strauss's praise of the Nambikwara, Derrida may also be giving vent to a resentment of Lévi-Strauss's considerable novelistic talent, his fluent ability to write an "empirical account." *Tristes Tropiques* is marked by virtuosic passages of description, notably in the section "Crowds," derived from Lévi-Strauss's experience in Calcutta. Here Lévi-Strauss does reveal himself as a disciple of Rousseau; he prefers the countryside to the urban uproar. But he retains a perverse appreciation of city decadence. When he evokes the packed street life of India, he shows considerable mimetic flair: "Every time I emerged from my hotel in Calcutta, which was besieged by cows and had vultures perched on its windowsills, I became the central figure in a ballet . . . a shoeblack flung himself at my feet; a small boy rushed up to me, whining 'One anna, papa, one anna!'; a cripple displayed his stumps, having bared himself to give a better view; a pander—'British girls, very nice . . .'; a clarinet-seller . . ."[2] As a stylist, he does everything that Derrida does not: he writes economical, memorable sentences anchored in factual details. Such realism as Lévi-Strauss's presents a disciplinary threat to Derrida. He wishes to ward off the possibility that the anthropologists, nurtured by mere empirical observation, might rival the philosophers.

Along with his objection to Lévi-Strauss's empirical tactics, Derrida criticizes his remarks about writing. Derrida admits that Lévi-Strauss's connection between writing and social hierarchy (and, therefore, violence against the lower orders) is historically warranted. The first large urban civilizations—Babylon, Egypt—used writing as an elite mechanism for social control. The secrets of the realm remained in the hands of the few who had knowledge of script.

Derrida, then, concedes Lévi-Strauss's point that the

written word works to ensure social stratification. He disagrees, however, with what he sees as Lévi-Strauss's narrow, conventional definition of writing, a definition most of us share. Derrida wants to assert that writing is everywhere, in some unexpected form. The Nambikwara, he points out, draw family trees in the sand: isn't that a form of writing? Most readers would say that it is not: that writing consists of expressive sentences inscribed in script form (rather than, say, diagrams or sketches). But Derrida is undeterred. The zigzags that the Nambikwara etch on their calabashes are, for him, another form of writing. So too is body language: the flesh writes in Derrida as well.

Derrida's point, again, is that our lives are dependent on the trace, that crucial concept. While the trace may become more explicit when writing (in the conventional sense) arrives, in fact it has always been there. Moments in our experience are best pictured as scribbles in a notepad that are then amended or covered over by other scribbles as we get older. Medieval scribes, short of vellum, would sometimes rub out the traces of a text and write another on top of it, making what was called a palimpsest (a favorite image of Derrida's). Life, he suggests, is a multilayered collection of traces, a palimpsest rather than a continuous, linear plotline. (Derrida's influential essay on Freud from *Writing and Difference,* which I discuss later on in this chapter, describes the unconscious as a palimpsest.)

Derrida's attack on Lévi-Strauss in *Grammatology* prepares him for his duel with Lévi-Strauss's great ancestor, Rousseau. Rousseau denounces the "non-self-presence" (17) of the man artificially isolated from nature, swaddled in the corrupting habits of European industrial society. He wants "self-presence in the senses, in the sensible cogito" (17): a return to the nature we can feel within ourselves, if only we attend to it properly. For Rousseau, Derrida asserts, writing is "a tragic fatality come to prey upon natural innocence" (168), the native strength enshrined in living speech. Natural presence—which for Rousseau takes the form of maternal love, as well as the speech that comes before writing—"*ought to be* self-sufficient" (145).[3]

In his commentary on Rousseau, Derrida describes how a "dangerous supplement" insinuates itself into the values of presence and natural being. This serpent in Eden, the supplement, is, in the realm of sexuality, masturbation, with its attachment to artificially generated fantasy images (masturbation receives significant attention in Rousseau's *Confessions*). In the realm of communication, the supplement is writing, which erodes speech by substituting itself for it.

Derrida suggests that we need to reverse the terms of valuation: the supplement proves essential, rather than corrupting. Once we have realized that even pure nature itself is a substitute, that it is constituted retroactively as a nostalgic vision—the Eden we never had—then we are liberated, at least to a degree, from such fantasies of innocence. "One can no longer see disease in substitution when one sees that the substitute is substituted for a substitute" (314). Liberation (of this rather thin, shadowy sort) would consist in recognizing writing for the original, pervasive factor it is, rather than as a falling-off from speech. Derrida's treatment of Rousseau suggests, however partially, a realm of freedom at the far end of metaphysics: the end of fantasies of voice, and the acknowledgment of writing.

But writing is still too insubstantial for Derrida's purposes. It is a creature of skepticism, of absence, rather than a true, revolutionary otherness. Derrida turns instead to Nietzsche and (in a different vein) to Lévinas for the overcoming of philosophical tradition he seeks. Both Nietzsche and Lévinas, instead of merely criticizing philosophical convention, turn toward new continents.

In 1966, at the age of thirty-six and with his massive *Grammatology* finished and ready for the press, Derrida undertook his first trip to America since his Harvard fellowship ten years earlier. He made the journey in order to speak at a conference at Johns Hopkins, one with a grand subject: the Languages of Criticism and the Sciences of Man. The conference had been organized by Richard Macksey, a polymath literature professor who was already cultivating an interest in the innovations stemming from France; and by René Girard and Eugenio Donato, two distinguished European scholars teaching at Hopkins.

Macksey, Girard, and Donato invited a stellar group of French intellectuals to Baltimore. Roland Barthes stood out as the most prominent of them: the apostle of the "pleasure of the text" and the "death of the author," and the great aesthete among French theorists. The reclusive Barthes, who lived with his elderly mother, was an inert conversationalist, but his writing sparkled. Along with Lévi-Strauss, he was probably the best stylist among the structuralists. Among the others who came to Johns Hopkins were Jean Hyppolite, an influential interpreter of Hegel; the baffling psychoanalyst Jacques Lacan, who had already attracted a small group of devoted disciples; Jean-Pierre Vernant, a scholar who was applying the new theoretical methods to the study of ancient Greece; and the renowned phenomenologist Lucien Goldmann. Also in attendance in Baltimore was a Belgian scholar of literature then teaching at Cornell named Paul de Man. Derrida and de Man were to meet for the first time at the Hopkins conference. Chatting about Rousseau at breakfast, they inaugurated a friendship that would last nearly twenty years, until de Man's untimely death in 1983.

Derrida arrived in New York in October 1966 and spent several days there before going on to Baltimore. He shared a room at the Hotel Martinique in midtown Manhattan with Tzvetan Todorov, also invited to lecture at the Hopkins conference. Todorov, a Bulgarian, had fled his country's repressive regime to live in Paris. Todorov was at the time one of the structuralists, but his true interest was political thought. He explained later that, since his parents were still alive and in Bulgaria, he had to avoid writing about politics, which would have exposed them to potential punishment by the Bulgarian Communist government.[4] After his parents' deaths, Todorov shifted to books on the European political tradition, the Nazi death camps, and other subjects—and he became a strong critic of structuralism and poststructuralism, in the name of a revived humanism. In a ringing riposte to Derrida's attempt to combine deconstruction with ethics, Todorov remarked, "It is not possible, without inconsistency, to defend human rights with one hand and deconstruct the idea of humanity with the other" (*Signs* 81).[5]

Derrida was given the honor of being the final speaker at the Hopkins conference, and he took full advantage of the opportunity. His talk, "Structure, Sign and Play in the Discourse of the Human Sciences" (later published in *Writing and Difference*), is one of his most dazzling performances. It is compact (an unusual feat for Derrida) and synoptic, enlisting Freud, Nietzsche, Rousseau, and other major figures to make his point. And Derrida's point in "Structure, Sign and Play" is nothing less than the demolition of structuralism, represented by the person of Claude Lévi-Strauss, Derrida's great precursor. As David Lehman observes, Derrida announced structuralism's death at the very event, the Sciences of Man symposium, that was supposed to celebrate its arrival in America (*Signs* 97).

Derrida argues that structuralism, like all of Western philosophy, aims to enshrine "Being as presence in all senses of this word" (*Writing* 279). For structuralism, Being takes the form of a center that anchors and determines all: "The concept of centered structure is in fact the concept of a play based on a fundamental ground, a play constituted on the basis of a fundamental immobility and a reassuring certitude, which itself is beyond the reach of play" (279).

In his speech at the Baltimore conference, Derrida plans to shake this center, to render it permanently uncertain. He also wants, in the process, to kill the father. The father in this case is Lévi-Strauss, the renowned anthropologist from the generation preceding Derrida's and the most influential structuralist of them all.

Derrida begins his critique of Lévi-Strauss in "Structure, Sign and Play" by focusing on Lévi-Strauss's treatment of the distinction between nature and culture, a staple of philosophical thought since the ancient Greeks. There is one thing, according to Lévi-Strauss, that troubles the nature-culture division, since it is hard to assign to either category: the incest taboo. The prohibition of incest seems to be shared by all human societies. It is, as Lévi-Strauss puts it, "a rule [and therefore cultural], but a rule which, alone among all the social rules, possesses at the same time a universal character" (cited in *Writing* 283). Instead of taking the baffling and paradoxical character of the incest taboo, halfway between nature and culture, as a telling fact about the nature-culture opposition, Lévi-Strauss simply accepts the fact that the taboo is universal. Derrida takes him to task severely on this account, though

Derrida himself hardly possesses an explanation of the law against incest. He suggests that this law escapes "traditional concepts" and is "probably ... the condition of [these concepts'] possibility" (*Writing* 283). That "probably" is a telltale indication of Derrida's uncertainty. According to Derrida, the incest taboo lies at the root of all knowledge, but its function remains unclear.

Derrida presents Lévi-Strauss in "Structure, Sign and Play" much as he does in *Of Grammatology*. Lévi-Strauss looks to him like a mistaken, if inventive, empiricist, a believer in those outmoded entities, facts and evidence. Immersed in fieldwork, the famed anthropologist doesn't care about ideas as much as he should. Lévi-Strauss, Derrida charges, retains "old concepts ... while here and there denouncing their limits, treating them as tools which can still be used" (284). Lévi-Strauss, in this respect a typical anthropologist, falls back on empiricism: on the facts of tribal behavior and belief, as if these facts were prior to the concepts he uses to explain them. "Empiricism is the matrix of all faults menacing a discourse which continues, as with Lévi-Strauss in particular, to consider itself scientific," announces Derrida (288). The "discourse" Derrida speaks of here is structuralism, whose proponents might be surprised to find it tarred as empiricist. He continues: "On the one hand, structuralism justifiably claims to be the critique of empiricism. But at the same time there is not a single book or study by Lévi-Strauss which is not proposed as an empirical essay which can always be completed or invalidated by new information" (288).

The contrast is stark between Derrida's attack on Lévi-Strauss's empiricism, for him a grave intellectual fault, and his respect for Emmanuel Lévinas's empirical emphasis, which in Derrida's estimation constitutes a permanent challenge to philosophy. Lévi-Strauss makes no claim to the ethical higher ground that Lévinas occupies, so Derrida rejects his empiricism. Derrida goes too far when he implies that anthropology could, or should, be nonempirical (as he has implied already in the *Grammatology*'s comments on Lévi-Strauss's *Tristes Tropiques*). But Derrida does point effectively to a central ambiguity in Lévi-Strauss's work: its combination of empiricism with a reliance on mythic structures.

Lévi-Strauss trusts in myth. His books are themselves examples of mythic thinking. Rather than stepping outside myth to provide a logos, a reasoned explanation for mythic narratives, he plays the mythmaker. Since both Lévi-Strauss and the tribes he studies engage in myth, he is forced to resort to his advanced capacity for observation, the advantage of the empirical scientist, in order to assert a difference between himself and these tribes. Like Freud, Lévi-Strauss defers to the primal, mythic power of certain stories. At the same time, both these thinkers base their arguments on close, empirical analyses of particular cases (Lévi-Strauss's primitive societies, Freud's neurotic patients). Pace Derrida, this approach may imply less a contradiction than an enabling feature of modernity, which harbors vestiges from the mythic past even in the midst of its cutting-edge science. Committed to the nuances of empirical analysis, we at the same time remain awed by the mysterious powers that stand behind all our behavior. W. H. Auden called them the Lords of Limit: remote, illiterate villagers know these deities as well as we.

The most powerful aspect of "Structure, Sign and Play" is its invocation of Nietzsche, Freud, and Heidegger, a triumvirate that Derrida enlists on his side against Lévi-Strauss's structuralism. (The absence of Marx is significant, and should be understood as a blow directed against Derrida's precursors: Sartre and company, the Communist intellectuals of the rue d'Ulm.) In a climactic passage, Derrida champions "the Nietzschean critique of metaphysics, the critique of the concepts of Being and truth, for which were substituted the concepts of play, interpretation, and sign (sign without present truth); the Freudian critique of self-presence, that is, the critique of consciousness, of the subject, of self-identity and of self-proximity or of self-possession; and, more radically, the Heideggerian destruction of metaphysics, of onto-theology, of the determination of Being as presence" (280).

By 1966, Lacan had already conjoined Heidegger and Freud in this manner; and Heidegger had elevated Nietzsche to preeminent status, as the crucial philosopher of the modern age (though capable of being corrected by Heidegger himself). But Derrida adds something characteristic of his own approach as he announces what was already becoming a familiar litany of cutting-edge thinkers. He insists that all three of these figures, Nietzsche, Freud, and Heidegger, depend on the concepts that they undermine. We may try to dismantle the edifice of metaphysics, but metaphysics itself remains standing. We can shake the self-congratulatory pride of reason, but not ruin it.

Derrida's emphasis in "Structure, Sign and Play" must be viewed in light of the sixties, when calls for revolution and the overturning of established order abounded. Derrida, citing great thinkers, insists on an alternative to hidebound ideas of reason, self-certainty, and logic. What he offers is the free play of language, unmoored from the center, the logos. But this alternative, unlike the revolutionists' agenda, relies on the familiar concepts, even as it bristles against them. The logos from which one has been liberated is still there, persisting as long as Western thought itself remains.

Unlike Lévi-Strauss, whom Derrida derides for his reliance on empirical facts, Derrida bases himself on philosophical tradition alone. Western metaphysics is his subject as
primitive society is Lévi-Strauss's. Because metaphysics unravels in Derrida's hands, it reveals itself as a mere mythos.
The metaphysician's proud self-certainty has been ruined. Yet
this mythos proves necessary; no radically other way of doing
things is available.

Or so it may seem, given Derrida's emphasis in *Grammatology* and elsewhere on the necessary intertwining of the logos
and its deconstructive antagonist. But it turns out there is a
route past deconstruction's imprisoning paradox. Derrida in
"Structure, Sign and Play" cites Nietzsche as a near-messianic
figure who is able to point beyond metaphysics altogether,
playing the role of apocalyptic liberator. This is a persistent
ambiguity in Derrida's work: he is attracted to the idea of a
realm liberated from metaphysics but cannot decide whether
or not such a place might be attained.

Elsewhere, it is Lévinas (or, in one essay, Artaud) who di-
rects us beyond metaphysics (and, therefore, beyond Derrida's
own skepticism, which is bound up with metaphysics). Whenever Derrida assumes a prophetic rhetoric, he is wishing for
an alternative to his usual pessimistic insistence that we are
all prisoners of discourse: unable to rely on the sheer, challenging presence of something that demands to be called reality. That reality takes different forms in Derrida's work—
Artaud's madness, Lévinas's face-to-face, Nietzsche's vision
of the future—but it plays the same role, promising a step beyond the weary, playful engagement with paradoxes of metaphysics that deconstruction trades in. The prophetic reality is,
in this sense, a successful form of the empiricism that Derrida
criticized in Lévi-Strauss, Rousseau, Saussure, and Husserl,

with their attachment to presence. Finally, in the 1990s, Lévinas wins out as Derrida's favored representative of this reality, the alternative to mere metaphysics.

In the late 1960s, Nietzsche seemed more suited to the revolutionary atmosphere than Lévinas. Musing on Nietzsche's messianism, Derrida is enthusiastic, hopeful. He chants with apocalyptic élan at the end of "Structure, Sign and Play" of something "as yet unnamable which is proclaiming itself and which can do so, as is necessary whenever a birth is in the offing, only under the species of the nonspecies, in the formless, mute, infant, and terrifying form of monstrosity" (293). Throughout the sixties, Derrida remained, for the most part, distant from politics. At the same time, he practiced (as in the sentence above) an annunciatory rhetoric similar to the one adopted by the student rebels.

If not siding with the peasant masses, the working class, or the angry students, what then was the Derridean specter doing as it stalked the academic corridors of Johns Hopkins in 1966? The following year, in *Grammatology*, this rough, threatening creature was unveiled as nothing other than *writing*: a fairly tame beast after all, in comparison to the truly Dionysian monsters entertained by so many as the sixties drew to their furious close. Dionysian radicalism led to a self-frustration that Derrida studiously avoided, by remaining on the level of the written text.

Derrida's sublime, catastrophic language in "Structure, Sign and Play" appears overdone, even skirting self-parody at times. But he has a serious, and significant, agenda: the replacement of politics with theory. He intends to challenge the growing liberationist dreams of the sixties and the New Left along with more traditional Communist messianism, putting his own candidate for world-changing upheaval in the ring. This candidate has various names in his work: writing, différance, and, in "Structure, Sign and Play," Nietzschean affirmation. Derrida poses Nietzsche against "the saddened, *negative*, nostalgic, guilty" Rousseau. Nietzsche, Derrida insists, gives us a joyous, active innocence in place of what he sees as Rousseau's wan, sentimental ideal. (Though rarely cited in the sixties, Rousseau was one of the main influences on the "back to the garden" aspect of hippie culture.) Derrida writes, "The Nietzschean *affirmation* . . . is the joyous affirmation of the play of the world and of the innocence of becoming, the affirmation of a world of signs without fault, without truth, and without origin which is offered to an active interpretation. *The affirmation then determines the noncenter otherwise than as loss of the center*" (292).

For Derrida's Nietzsche, then, there never has been any center. Everything is mythos, nothing logos. Nietzsche, "no longer turned toward the origin, affirms play and tries to pass beyond man and humanism." He refuses to dream, as Lévi-Strauss and Rousseau do, of "full presence, the reassuring foundation, the origin and the end of play" (292). Nietzsche becomes for Derrida the one figure in Western philosophy who wants definitively to overcome its premises, to "pass beyond man and humanism." In this way, skepticism is turned inside out, transformed into the source of affirmative, creative force. Because the logos is dead, we find ourselves stranded in "a world of signs without fault, without truth, and without origin." And in Derrida's fervent reading, this new world bears a utopian promise. Nietzsche offers us the "innocence of becoming": freewheeling, endless play without center.

Derrida borrows his powerful liberationist Nietzsche from two earlier French thinkers, Georges Bataille and Pierre Klossowski, who had written about Nietzsche during the 1930s.

But the real Nietzsche is far more complex than the one that Derrida, following Bataille and Klossowski, depicts. He is not the brave, festive inhabitant of a cosmos without truth. Instead, Nietzsche has a political program for the future: one that involves not abolishing the category of the true, but formulating a new truth and a new order of society.[6] As with Plato, the Nietzschean revolution will be activated by the philosopher-lawgiver: Nietzsche's *Übermensch,* or overman. (I will return to this subject when I consider Derrida's *Spurs,* his major statement on Nietzsche, in chapter 3.)

In 1966, the same year as the Johns Hopkins conference, Derrida delivered an exciting lecture on Freud at the Institut de Psychanalyse in Paris. His talk, called "Freud and the Scene of Writing," was published later in the year in *Tel Quel,* and then reprinted in *Writing and Difference.* Derrida's Freud exhibits a partiality similar to that of his Nietzsche. Both, in the Derridean view, discover an inherently powerful, self-sustaining region of signifying: the Freudian unconscious and Nietzschean aesthetic play. In both cases, Derrida de-emphasizes these thinkers' concerns with educating the psyche (in Freud, through therapy; in Nietzsche, through philosophical inquiry). He also discards their interest in how the social order is formed and governed: crucial for both the pessimist Freud and the world-remaking Nietzsche. In Freud as in Nietzsche, Derrida recognizes a prophetic element. The traumatic encounter with reality basic to Freud's theory will attain a signal importance for Derrida, as a way out of the self-enclosed philosophical tradition that Derrida has spent his energies dissecting.

It was in many ways appropriate that Derrida, still early in his career, tackle Freud, assessing his potential for philosophy. In the sixties and seventies, psychoanalysis flourished in

France. Sartre paid homage to Freud in *The Family Idiot* (1971), a psychoanalytic treatment of Flaubert. In 1967, Jean Laplanche and J.-B. Pontalis published their influential overview of psychoanalytic vocabulary, *The Language of Psychoanalysis*. Earlier, Octave Mannoni had applied Freudian ideas to the history of European colonization in *Prospero and Caliban* (1950).

Most important for Freud's legacy in France, Jacques Lacan, a prominent figure on the Parisian intellectual scene, had since the early fifties been busy injecting psychoanalysis with heavy doses of Heidegger and Hegel (the latter in Kojève's influential version). Like Derrida, Lacan had rebelled against the influence of Sartre, scorning Sartre's enthusiasm for Communism and his sense of human existence as a heroic struggle. Lacan opted for a grim, even cynical, sense of social life: a perspective informed by Freud's doubt about the nineteenth century's utopian hopes to transform society.

For all its partiality and obscurantism, Lacan's reading of Freud was a thorough and deeply personal vision. Derrida in 1966 had less of a sense of Freud's strength as a critic of modernity and as a vastly original spirit dedicated to redefining our sense of our lives. His lecture on "Freud and the Scene of Writing" is devoted almost exclusively to Freud's image of the unconscious, which Derrida aligns with his own concept of writing.

In his essay, Derrida shows little regard for Freud's main goal. Freud was dedicated to the cure: he wanted to enable individuals to recognize themselves and reimagine their lives, so that they could pass from immobilizing sickness to health. This process requires an argument within the self. Chiefly, what Freud demands is a challenge to the superego: a shattering of the false images of self imposed by the unreal powers of social law, powers internalized by the neurotic by means of drastic self-punishments. Even as he unmasks reason's tyranny over our psyche in the shape of the lordly superego, Freud still honors the god of reason, practising what a recent critic, Richard Armstrong, calls an "improvised Jewish Hellenism."[7] Freud sees the work of reason in a patient's effort to come to self-understanding. Derrida lacks sympathy for this therapeutic project and prefers to dwell on Freud's theory-making in isolation from his practice.

"Freud and the Scene of Writing" begins by distinguishing between psychoanalysis and deconstruction. Both Derrida and Freud use the word *repression*. But deconstruction is broader than and prior to psychoanalysis, Derrida tells us. "Logocentric repression is not comprehensible on the basis of the Freudian concept of repression," but the reverse is true, since deconstruction allows us to put psychoanalysis in its true place (*Writing* 197). Much as Marxists insist that without the categories of historical materialism nothing can be properly understood, so Derrida asserts that not Freud but rather a deconstructive knowledge of how logocentrism represses writing will explain the root of our maladies. Only deconstruction can demonstrate how "individual repression became possible within the horizon of a culture and a historical structure of belonging" (197). Not surprisingly, Derrida fails to deliver on his promise to account for the origin and historical context of psychic repression.

Derrida announces his agenda in "Freud and the Scene of Writing": to "locate in Freud's text several points of reference, and to isolate, on the threshold of a systematic examination, those elements of psychoanalysis which can only uneasily be contained within logocentric closure" (198). Freud, then, remains logocentric, even as he strives to pass beyond the standard metaphysical platitudes. He had a Pisgah sight of the Derridean promised land but was unable to arrive there.

Derrida begins his discussion on the very borderline of the Freudian corpus, the *Project for a Scientific Psychology*. The *Project*, left in fragmentary form and never published by Freud himself, was written in 1895, an important year for its author. In the 1890s Freud, along with his colleague Josef Breuer, uncovered the dramatic facts about hysteria: the ways in which hysterics "suffer from reminiscences." In May 1895 Freud and Breuer published their groundbreaking *Studies on Hysteria*, a collection of case studies marked by Freud's brilliant detective work and unrivaled storytelling abilities.

Studies on Hysteria is breathless, suspenseful in its narrative drive. With the exhilaration of discovery, Freud and Breuer come upon the thought of the "talking cure," as it was named by the "founding patient" of psychoanalysis, Bertha Pappenheim (called "Anna O." in *Studies on Hysteria*). Instead of subjecting patients to crude, random treatments—dousing them with water or forcing them to exercise were two popular options espoused by Freud's predecessors—Freud talked to them. Freudian analysis was a reciprocal process, a bringing of repressed thoughts to patients' attention with the help of the patients themselves. Their inner disquiet and outward restlessness spurred inquiry: a humane dialogue that Freud, the new Socrates, encouraged. This process marked the great revolution in the treatment of neurosis: the birth of therapy as we know it. With the talking cure, Freud, like Socrates (and like Saussure), asserted the power of conversation over ossified methods of research that rely solely on writing.

A few months after the publication of *Studies on Hysteria*, Freud took off in a new direction. In September 1895, he was on the train home from Berlin to Vienna, galvanized by one of his periodic "congresses" with his eccentric friend Wilhelm Fliess. During the long journey, Freud began drafting a "psychology for neurologists": his *Project for a Scientific Psychology*. The *Project* contains no narrative details concerning hysterical patients and no feats of deduction like those Freud gives us in the *Studies on Hysteria*. Here Freud employs his neurological knowledge by developing a model of the mind. (Freud began his career studying the gonads of eels; his background in hard science led to a neurological study of aphasia before his development of psychoanalysis.)

Freud focuses on the difference between the internal and external cases of stimulation: between being struck by a thought or desire and being struck by something in the world outside (light, heat, sound, and so on). Internal cases of stimulus depend on memory, whereas external cases depend on perception. By its nature, perception remains ephemeral and ever changing. Memory, by contrast, persists, both troubling and sustaining us. What the Song of Songs says about love and jealousy, Freud might have remarked about memory: it is as strong as death, and cruel as the grave.

Derrida is mainly interested in Freud's effort to define memory in terms of its reliance on differing quantities of energy, or energy that occurs at different intervals. Freud tries to explain what happens in the mind by understanding how quantity (the amount or frequency of excitation) becomes quality (a mental image that is empowered, or "cathected," by the psyche). Derrida announces enthusiastically in "Freud and the Scene of Writing" that Freud's *Project for a Scientific Psychology* is dependent "in its entirety upon an incessant and increasingly radical invocation of the principle of difference" (*Writing* 205). So Freud is already alert to the importance of difference, one of Derrida's key terms, as early as the mid-1890s. Yet Freud, alas, is not a Derridean. Derrida remarks that all Freudian concepts, "without exception, belong to the history of metaphysics" (197). He wants to claim Freud as support for his theory, to make him a champion of difference, yet at the same time he is reluctant to grant Freud the status of an enlightened champion of deconstruction. Freud must remain a mystified metaphysician, so that Derrida can unmask him: his blindness enables Derrida's insight.

Leaving the *Project for a Scientific Psychology,* Derrida shifts to a second text by Freud. In Freud's brief, intriguing "Note Upon the Mystic Writing Pad," composed three decades after the *Project* (in 1925), Freud relies on the metaphor of writing in order to describe the workings of perception and memory. The mystic writing pad, marketed as a novelty, consists of a wax tablet covered by a sheet of wax paper and, on top of the paper, a celluloid sheet. One writes on the celluloid sheet and then erases the writing by pulling apart the layers of the writing pad, so that the pad can be used afresh. The traces of what one has written are, however, retained on the wax tablet. Freud remarks that the celluloid sheet resembles conscious perception, which is continually fresh, and the wax tablet unconscious memory, full of traces of the past.

Derrida argues that Freud turns to the mystic writing pad in order to solve the original dilemma of the *Project:* the difference between perception and memory. The *Project* argued that some neurons are permeable (capable of receiving and retaining impressions, so that they become agents of memory) while others are impermeable (the agents of perception, rather than memory). The difference between memory neurons and perception neurons, Derrida points out, is like the difference between a sheet of paper (which conserves its traces forever but is quickly filled up) and an erasable celluloid sheet (which can be used forever but retains nothing). Freud describes an apparatus that, as Derrida puts it, reconciles "a perpetually available innocence," the stream of constant, fleeting new perceptions, with "an infinite reserve of traces," the storehouse of memory (223). The writing pad brings together two aspects of our being: the infinite depth of meaning that is remembering and the ever-renewed surface of life that is perception (224). The wax slab, which retains all traces, resembles the unconscious: a timeless reservoir of significance, without beginning or end.

There is a problem in Freud's essay, according to Derrida. Freud idolizes the unconscious, a place where (in Derrida's description) "nothing ends, nothing happens, nothing is forgotten" (230). Freud wants the permanence of the unconscious trace to be a kind of heaven of memory, a way of anchoring our being. Derrida, who argues against the Freudian idea of the unconscious as the permanent archive of our existence, insists that the trace is fragile, transitory, and death-ridden. "The Freudian concept of trace," Derrida announces, "must be radicalized and extracted from the metaphysics of presence which still retains it (particularly in the concepts of consciousness, the unconscious, perception, memory, reality, and several others)" (229). Freud's problem is that he wants the trace to be permanent, a way of ensuring the self: a desire that shows him to be a member of the metaphysical club. Therefore, Derrida argues, we must move beyond Freud, in order to understand that "the trace is the erasure of selfhood, of one's own presence, and is constituted by the threat or anguish of its irremediable disappearance" (230). "An unerasable trace" of the kind that Freud dreams of "is not a trace, it is a full presence, an immobile and uncorruptible substance, a son of God, a sign of parousia" (230).

Derrida, in these remarks, turns Freud into a religious devotee, one who attaches himself to the metaphysical idea of parousia: the full presence of a divine, because immortal, substance. (In Freud's case, this substance is the unconscious mind.) Derrida thus paints Freud as a thinker who clings to a metaphysical version of being. The unconscious, where nothing is lost, establishes its meaning triumphantly and for all time. Derrida prefers to emphasize the unstable and transient character of the trace, the writing that constitutes us: this is his challenge to Freud.

Derrida argues, then, that Freud holds on to the untenable idea that meaning is a permanent, monumental presence. Freud cannot accept its true fragility: therefore, he invents the traumatic cultural histories he describes in *Totem and Taboo* and *Moses and Monotheism*. In these works, Freud traces our civilization back to ineradicable traumas, founding events whose significance, though buried, cannot be evaded—the murder of Moses, the eating of the primal father by his sons. Freud insists on the reality of such hypothetical origins, in part because they embody a foreign presence that challenges our usual notions of morality and selfhood. We do not like to think of the source of conscience as being hidden in that long-repressed memory, our murder of the father.

Here we encounter a strange, contradictory turn on Derrida's part. Derrida, in spite of his criticism, also recognizes the persuasive power of Freud's idea that trauma entails the persistence of a stark alien presence within the self, frustrating our wishful sense of who we are. Derrida acknowledges Freud's notion of trauma when he turns to the Hebrew prophets, invoking them at the very end of "Freud and the Scene of Writing." In doing so, he reveals his allegiance to Jewish tradition as a possible means of escaping from the double binds that metaphysics, and its attendant skepticism, imposes on him. The Hebraic will be for him, as for Lévinas, an alternative to the preoccupation with sterile philosophical definition. The Jewish religion, in which the giving of the law is an unacceptable shock, spurring rebellion and betrayal, posits the traumatic as the kernel of our sense of reality. In Lévinas, the trauma is the face-to-face; in Freud, the events of psychosexual life. But both, according to Derrida, participate in a Jewish tradition for which meaning is prophetic, violent, and ineradicable.

Trauma is the outside force that breaks the hold of the metaphysics-skepticism model, according to which each presence becomes an absence and the work of the trace undoes what it claims to preserve. At the conclusion of his essay on Freud, Derrida opposes an Egyptian concept of writing to a Jewish one, the Egyptians being the metaphysicians and the Jews the prophets. The Egyptians think that writing has been given to humans as a benign storehouse of memory, like the wax slab of the mystic writing pad. For the Jews, by contrast, writing is imposed by God, painfully and fatefully. Moses bestows the law on them in the face of their great, stubborn resistance. For Derrida, Freud's sense of pain, of historical trauma, plays the central role in generating meaning (a point on which Freud followed Nietzsche). Whether or not the Israelites killed Moses, as Freud surmises, the giving of the Ten Commandments was unquestionably an occasion for frantic rebellion. And, in the story told by Exodus, the rebellion was violently suppressed. After smashing the tablets of the law, Moses tells the Levites to "slay brother, neighbor, and kin": three thousand people (Exodus 32:27–28).

Derrida realizes that Freud's interest in the violent origins of the law is in the line of the Hebrew prophets rather than the Egyptian scribes. Here Derrida forecasts his interest in Plato's *Phaedrus*, with its myth of the Egyptian invention of writing (discussed next chapter). He writes, "God, the Egyptians believed, had made man a gift of writing just as he inspired dreams. Interpreters, like dreams themselves, then had only to draw upon the curiological or tropological storehouse. They would readily find there the key to dreams, which they would then pretend to divine" (208). In this passage, Derrida makes dream interpretation among the ancient Egyptians sound like a rather amiable con game, one controlled, like writing itself, by a priestly sect. Perhaps, Derrida hints, psychoanalysis resembles this Egyptian practice in its deck-stacking priestcraft: a way of inventing the truth that it pretends to find, a crooked divination. Derrida makes us wonder, for a moment, if he intends to class Freud among the Egyptians, the deceptive readers of dreams (or at least to cast him as an ambitious Hebrew Joseph).

In turning from Egypt to ancient Israel, Derrida tacitly admits that Freud is not a self-serving deceiver, intent merely on finding what he wants in a dream or symptom. Though stacking the deck is surely, at times, a key Freudian practice, Freud was not the clever fraud that polemicists like Frederick Crews accuse him of being. Rather than conveniently producing meaning, Freud submits to it and struggles with it. Like a prophet, he announces the hard truth imposed on him. Freud had a near-religious sense of his vocation. He was surrounded by recalcitrant audiences ready to deny his claims to knowledge and turn a deaf ear to his truths. Freud in his integrity, like Moses and the prophets, bears the unavoidable Word.

In keeping with Freud's harsh, exalted sense of his message, Derrida in "Freud and the Scene of Writing" counters the Egyptian idea with passages from Ezekiel and Numbers. In chapters 2 and 3 of the book of Ezekiel, the prophet is told by God to eat a scroll covered with "lamentations, dirges, and woes" (*JPS*). Ezekiel opens his mouth, swallows the scroll, and finds it sweet as honey. This sweetness contrasts with the bitter rebelliousness of the children of Israel. The latter are repeatedly described in Ezekiel, chapter 3, as a *beit meri,* or house of rebellion. The book of Ezekiel puns on *meri,* "rebellion," and *mar,* "bitterness," when Ezekiel himself, despite the sweetness of the scroll, finds himself stunned and disheartened by the bitter prophetic mission imposed on him. Hearing the strident beating of angels' wings and the roar of their chariot's wheels, Ezekiel reports, "A spirit seized me and carried me away. I went in bitterness, in the fury of my spirit, while the hand of the LORD was strong upon me" (Ezekiel 3:14). The bitterness that Ezekiel feels corresponds to the constricted, compulsive character of his enforced vocation. The Lord opens his mouth, makes him speak. But the Israelites, a frustrate, resistant tribe, will probably not listen: so God warns the unhappy Ezekiel.

Numbers, chapter 5, also devotes itself to bitterness. The chapter describes the punishment for adulterous women. The priest is instructed to administer a "curse of adjuration" to the woman: a gruesome magical treatment that, if she is in fact guilty of adultery, will render her sterile. The words of the curse, which contain the name of the Lord, are put down in writing and then dissolved in a "water of bitterness," which the woman must drink.

Derrida brings together the Numbers and the Ezekiel passages because both propose that writing is a *pharmakon:* a magical, ambiguous potion capable of both cursing and blessing. (Freud's account of his own trimethylamine dream in *The Interpretation of Dreams,* in which he swallows a printed chemical formula, must also be on Derrida's mind here.) The trial by ordeal of the woman in Numbers, as she drinks the curses of the law—to be either stricken with sterility if she is guilty of adultery, or freed from suspicion if she is not—is matched by Ezekiel's intake of the scroll that is both sweet and bitter, combining the rapturous holiness of the exultant angels that surround him with the grim reminder that the Israelites will not heed his prophecy. Both the adulterous woman and Ezekiel find themselves yoked unwillingly to a command: God's writing is for them a harsh law. Even in cases of actual adultery, few women would, one presumes, have become sterile as a result of drinking ink. Yet the *idea* of sympathetic magic, effected by writing, remains.

Freud's image of the mystic writing pad—a mere toy, a trivial mechanism—may seem far removed from the baleful religious scenes of the Hebrew scriptures. Writing proves potent in the Bible. It curses and empowers mightily, and its effects cannot be revoked. In Freud, by contrast, the unconscious, depicted as writing, forms a vast, unruly collection of traces, with plenty of room for revision. This description sounds like the Egyptian idea of writing. And Freud, whose enthusiasm for ancient Egypt culminates in *Moses and Monotheism,* with its shocking insistence that Moses was an Egyptian, does rely prominently on hieroglyphics as a figure for the dream-work. Yet, as Derrida somewhat covertly recognizes at the conclusion of "Freud and the Scene of Writing," Freud's Word is much closer to the Hebrew scriptures than to Egyptian magic. Freud suggests that there is a traumatically disturbing, original factor within the self: something not of the self's making, imposed on it and yet utterly characteristic of it. It is like the law imposed by God on the Israelites, the origin of the strange superego that inhabits us.

As Harold Bloom and others have powerfully argued, Freud's writings are the closest thing to scripture that the modern age has produced. Laying down the hard laws of our reality, Freud seems to command us as Moses did. His authoritative explanation of our condition wins out over the schemes of normative religion, Marxism, and Whiggish progressivism.

Knowing Freud's authority, Derrida comes to terms with the force of the Freudian mythos in "Freud and the Scene of Writing," in spite of his efforts earlier in the essay to suggest that Freud is a mere captive of metaphysics and that his idea of the unconscious provides a source of wished-for logocentric stability. At the end of his essay, Derrida's invocation of the Hebrew scriptures' prophetic rigor allows Freud to transcend conventional logocentric philosophy and assume the mantle of authority as the thinker of those crucial concepts, trauma, anxiety, and repression.

Derrida remains ambivalent about Freud. He proves unable to dissolve Freud's unique institution, psychoanalysis, into the ocean of metaphysical resemblances. But he is equally unable to enlist it as a partner in deconstructive analysis. Deconstruction, unlike psychoanalysis, is a furtive science. It patiently unravels the texts of the past rather than creating a new way of thinking and a new institutional discipline, as Freud did. Yet in his apocalyptic moments Derrida reaches out for an extreme vision, a total break with the past, in a way that Freud never imagined doing.

Derrida's "Freud and the Scene of Writing," like his 1963 lecture on Foucault and "Structure, Sign and Play," first became known to a wide public in *Writing and Difference*. In that collection Derrida does his best to take the measure of his philosophical ancestors: in some cases, to defer to them; in others, to overcome them. These figures—including Husserl, Freud, Foucault, Lévi-Strauss, Lévinas, Bataille, Antonin Artaud, Maurice Blanchot, and Edmond Jabès—present different levels of influence on the Derridean approach.

The central drama of *Writing and Difference* concerns the other of philosophy: a rival element that, by remaining opposed to philosophy, allows it to define itself. This rival takes various forms: in Artaud, the radical, instinctive gestures of the theatre of cruelty; in Foucault, madness; in Bataille, the sovereign force of extreme passion; in Jabès, rabbinical commentary; in Lévinas, the face of the other. (As we have seen, in Freud the thought of trauma provides such an alternative.) All these thinkers seek to escape from, or at least provide an alternative to, the reign of logocentrism. By investigating their projects, Derrida hints that his familiar counterposing of skepticism and metaphysics has proven inadequate. Rather than puncturing (and exaggerating) metaphysical pretension in his skeptical manner, he seeks an alternative to arguments over metaphysics: an outside, a new reality.

Not all these figures are equally successful, in Derrida's eyes. In his drama of influence, he will show a marked preference for Jabès and Lévinas, the two thinkers who occupy themselves intensely with the Jewish tradition, over the other writers featured in *Writing and Difference*. As with his treatment of Freud, which ends in respect for Freudian authority and in serious invocation of the Hebrew Bible, Derrida calls on Judaism in order to rise above the narrower problem of voice and writing that occupies him in the *Grammatology* and *Speech and Phenomena*. In the *Grammatology*, Saussure's and

Lévi-Strauss's empiricism is declared naïve, as is Husserl's supposed attachment to the voice in *Speech and Phenomena.* In *Writing and Difference,* by contrast, the empirical stances of Freud and Lévinas point to a challenging truth, not an illusory trap.[8]

The reader senses an affinity between Derrida and Jabès, who meditates on the Jews as the people of the book, the people of writing. (Writing is Derrida's "God term," as Kenneth Burke would put it.) And Lévinas presents a challenge to philosophy, including Derrida's way of doing philosophy, that Derrida finds himself forced to recognize: Lévinas insists on the real presence of other people. Bataille and Artaud, not to mention Foucault and Lévi-Strauss, receive far harsher treatment at Derrida's hands than the admired Jabès and Lévinas.

Derrida placed first in *Writing and Difference* an essay reprinted from a 1963 issue of *Critique,* one of the earliest written of the pieces in the book. In this essay, "Force and Signification," Derrida sets himself apart from structuralism, the dogma of the previous generation. "Force and Signification" sets the tone for *Writing and Difference* with its headlong energy and its stream of almost ecstatic prose. The essay stands halfway between philosophical reflection and the flamboyant polemic of a poet-prophet.

The opening paragraphs of "Force and Signification" are giddy with triumph over structuralism. Derrida lauds the structuralists' achievement as "an adventure of vision" (*Writing* 3), but at the same time he accuses them of weakness. In their attention to form, Derrida charges, the structuralists neglect the force that stands behind sign making, the enormous strength of meaning itself. This neglect demonstrates, as it turns out, the structuralists' own lack of force—and their status as mere critics rather than creators. "*Form* fascinates,"

Derrida writes, "when one no longer has the force to understand force from within itself. That is, to create. This is why literary criticism is structuralist in every age, in its essence and destiny" (4–5).

Derrida here develops the opposition he had sketched so fluently in "Genesis and Structure," his early essay on Husserl (also reprinted in *Writing and Difference*). In "Genesis and Structure," as noted earlier, Derrida set Husserl's interest in the force of origins against his attention to the structures of thinking and perceiving. These two sides of Husserl cannot be harmonized, Derrida suggested. In "Force and Signification," origin—here interpreted as the creative force that makes meaning—wins out over structure, in definitive fashion. (Similarly, in Freud, traumatic origin persists; and in Lévinas, the unmistakable moment of the face-to-face.)

Derrida's opening note of Olympian coldness in "Force and Signification," his claim of superiority to structuralism, raises an obvious question. If he does not resemble the weak structuralist critics who attend to form alone, how does he distinguish himself from them? Derrida derides the "diminished ardor" of the structuralists, their "cries of technical ingenuity or mathematical subtlety" (5). So what does he have to offer instead? The structuralists' arguments are an empty city, a mere "skeleton," Derrida asserts. He himself brings life, under the name of force. How will he prove his strength, his alliance with creative power? Derrida here assumes for himself the prophetic address he associates with Freud in "Freud and the Scene of Writing" and with Nietzsche in "Structure, Sign and Play."

For his advantage over structuralism, Derrida relies on Maurice Blanchot: the spare, ascetic writer of essays and *récits* (that is, fictions) who raised the image of the void to spiritual centrality. A favorite mise-en-scène in a Blanchot story is the dire meditation in an empty room, undertaken by a faceless character left alone with the pain of memories. Blanchot's stripped-down writings evoke an "essential nothing," "the blind origin of the work in its darkness" (8). "Only *pure absence*," Derrida judges from the case of Blanchot, "can *inspire*" (8).

Derrida goes on in "Force and Signification" to enlist two more writers in his campaign against structuralism. He cites the "book about nothing" dreamt of by Flaubert: a text of total purity in which radical emptiness would define the place of literature. And Derrida adds for good measure Artaud's stark confession. Artaud remarked, "I made my debut in literature by writing books in order to say I could write nothing at all" (8). The push toward expression is anguished, terrifying, because it begins and ends in nothing.

For Artaud himself, artistic expression finished in madness and utter isolation. Derrida devotes an entire essay in *Writing and Difference* to the primitive manner of Artaud, who, he writes, believed in "the metaphysics of flesh which determines Being as life" (179). Artaud exhibited his howling body to an audience ready to savor his avant-garde theatrics, his fits of onstage frenzy. But Derrida is a creature of the study, not the theatre; and finally, Artaud is of limited use for him. (In 1998, however, Derrida, about to give a talk on Artaud's drawings at a conference held at Irvine and encountering a malfunctioning microphone, decided to shriek his lecture to a bewildered audience of six hundred people: his homage to Artaud.)

In "Force and Signification," Derrida depends on Blanchot, Flaubert, and Artaud for his image of writing as an apocalyptic and challenging endeavor. He explains that the provocation of such writing, unlike the word of the creator God in

Genesis, gains strength from the push and shove of rival meanings: from, as he calls it, the equivocal. Writing is, remarks Derrida, "A power of pure equivocality that makes the creativity of the classical God appear all too poor. . . . Writing is the anguish of the Hebrew *ruah,* experienced in solitude by human responsibility" (9). There is a notable ambivalence here: does Derrida want to enlist the Jewish God in the deconstructionist cause or not? The ruah is the breath of God at the beginning of Genesis, moving on the face of the waters. Here Derrida wrestles with the Hebrew God of his youth, and steals this God's power for literature: for the solitary excess of a Blanchot-like ascesis, and for an idea of human responsibility borrowed from the existentialists. (Continuing the religious motif, Derrida follows these sentences with a comparison between the anguish-ridden adventure of writing and the prophetic ordeal of Jeremiah.)

Derrida in "Force and Signification" manifests his force by fanciful pen thrusts. His equivocation, the source of power he claims for writing, makes it at times hard to tell whether he is advancing a real argument or merely playing the sublime, and sublimely ridiculous, philosopher. He is capable of invoking both Moses and Nietzsche's Zarathustra in order to herald the Derridean revelation: "It will be necessary to descend, to work, to bend in order to engrave and carry the new Tables to the valleys, in order to read them and have them read" (29). Derrida, at the ready age of thirty-two, stands supremely confident and ambitious, trying on the role of prophet and law giver. He smiles at his own pretension and coaxes forth thundering pronouncements. "Force and Signification" is an astonishing piece of creative writing, for a philosopher, for anyone.

"Force and Signification" begins *Writing and Difference*

by harnessing together the superb and haughty traditions of avant-garde polemic, existentialist bravado, Blanchot's matchless asceticism, and the prophets of the Bible. As we have seen, Derrida's point is to claim force for himself, against what he sees as the limp outworn clarity of structuralism. He follows this first essay with another attack, the treatment of Michel Foucault already discussed ("Cogito and the History of Madness"). Derrida is in a much quieter mood as *Writing and Difference* continues with his thoughtful, admiring essay on Edmond Jabès, author of *The Book of Questions*. Jabès's volume, which appeared in 1963, is a Talmudic rumination on Jewishness, time, and writing. Jabès exposes, writes Derrida, "a powerful and ancient root," "an ageless wound": the Jewish connection between memory, trauma, and the "passion of writing" (64). For Derrida, following Jabès, the Jews are not merely in history; they *are* history. "The only thing that begins by reflecting itself is history. And this fold, this furrow, is the Jew" (65).

Jabès, Derrida argues, shows that the situation of the Jew is exemplary. And the Jew is also the poet: bound and yet freed by language's demands on him, the man who painfully questions his own nature, his future, and his past; who questions the Law as the Law questions him. Yet the poet and the Jew are not completely synonymous. "There will always be rabbis and poets," close to one another yet incapable of being fully united (67). One might add that there will always be rabbis and philosophers, and the division between them. For all his Talmudic ingenuity, Derrida remains a free philosophical spirit, rather than a pious Jew who trusts in the covenant.

Derrida's tentative, inquiring relation to Zionism appears in his essay on Jabès. The holy book, as Jabès describes it, is written anywhere that the Jew wanders; place becomes a high, enabling metaphor. Derrida comments: "When a Jew or a poet proclaims the Site, he is not declaring war. . . . The site is not the empirical and national Here of a territory. It is immemorial, and thus also a future. Better: it is tradition as adventure" (66).

"Tradition as adventure," rather than the "national Here of a territory": with his beautiful definition of Jewish learning and writing, Derrida separates himself from the triumphalist praise of the Israel that had survived destruction, and unexpectedly increased its geographical dominion, in the Six-Day War. (Though the essay on Jabès dates from several years earlier, it was republished in 1967, the year of the Six-Day War: a fact that casts a new light on these sentences.)

For Derrida, Jewishness does not take place within history, as a narrative of war, exile, and cultural achievement, but *at the source* of history—seen as the bewildering separation between God and man. In the garden of Eden there was no history; when God turns away from his creation, historical time begins. (This idea reads like a transposition into religion of Derrida's point about Husserl in relation to Joyce: Joyce wanders within history, whereas Husserl asks a more basic question about the origin of historicity; see chapter 1.) Here we have the underlining of origin, of a traumatic starting point, common to Derrida's readings of his Jewish sources, from Freud to Lévinas to Jabès. The feeling of being abandoned, even rejected, by God is basic to the Hebrew Bible. Derrida writes that Moses's breaking of the stone tablets of the law "articulates, first of all, a rupture within God as the origin of history" (67). Beginning with the Flood, God at times turns his back on his chosen people, repenting of his generosity. "God is in perpetual revolt against God," Jabès writes (cited 68). The division within God consists of his combination of tender sympathy for the Israelites and angry withdrawal from them. Experiencing God's periodic revoking of his favor gives Judaism the freedom to begin its own history, in longing for the God who has turned away.

Derrida refers to his commentary on Jabès as "pitiful graffiti" (74): a loving scribble in Jabès's margins. Of all the essays in *Writing and Difference*, the one on Jabès is indeed the most purely adulatory, without the admixture of critique that characterizes the others. It is certainly far different in tone from the overt assault on Foucault or the anxious struggle with Lévinas in the same book. Derrida allows himself to be, simply, a disciple of Jabès.

As the Jabès essay rises to its heights, Derrida gives way to his fondness for apocalyptic drama. He speaks of (without defining) an "original illegibility," which is "incommensurable" both with the reasonable logos and with the opposite of the logos (whatever the latter may be). "The Being that is announced within the illegible is beyond these categories, beyond, as it writes itself, its own name" (77). This Being sounds like Derrida's honest idea of God, surpassing the bounds of the metaphysical-skeptical paradox. He concludes by invoking Blanchot once again and by signing his own chapter as Reb Rida: a pun on the name Derrida. With this self-nicknaming, Derrida joins in the rabbinical conversation that Jabès invented: *The Book of Questions* consists of a series of Talmudic questions and answers by fictional rabbis.

Derrida a rabbi? Jabès remarks in *The Book of Questions,* "To every question, the Jew answers with a question" (cited 67). It is a familiar thought. Continual inquiry—unsettled, questing, and yet centered on a supremely canonical text—remains the practice of Jewish learning. "Turn it and turn it, for everything is in it," Rabbi ben Bag Bag says of the Torah in the magnificent wisdom tract *Pirke Avot,* a major source for Jabès. Derrida too focuses on certain sacred texts: not the books of Moses but the books of Hegel, Heidegger, and Husserl. His way of probing and turning the books he loves is, arguably, rabbinical.

At the very end of *Writing and Difference,* after its climactic demolishing of Lévi-Strauss in "Structure, Sign and Play," Derrida writes a coda calling up once again the imaginary rabbis who populate Jabès's *Book of Questions.* The very last two words of *Writing and Difference* form a new signature, "Reb Derissa": another rabbinical alter ego for Derrida. (*Riss,* meaning "rift" in German, is a term from Heidegger.) Clearly, Derrida clings to something in Jabès that seems to him more exalted than the logocentric philosophical tradition he so energetically dismantles.

We are seeing, again, the clash between Derrida's religious and philosophical inclinations: between his alliance with a prophetic tone derived from the Tanakh, or Hebrew Bible, and his focus on the metaphysics-skepticism debate. Philosophy dominates *Writing and Difference,* as it does the other two books of 1967, *Speech and Phenomena* and *Of Grammatology,* along with most of Derrida's work for the next twenty years. But after that point, beginning in the late 1980s, Judaism returns. In *Writing and Difference,* Jewishness already incites the philosopher's fascinated attention. For Derrida, Jabès represents a way of thinking decidedly different from, even alien to, the Western logocentric tradition.

The most intense struggle with a precursor in *Writing and Difference* occurs in Derrida's long, wrenching essay on Emmanuel Lévinas, who explicitly chooses Jewishness over philosophy. At seventy pages, the chapter on Lévinas is the most substantial one in *Writing and Difference,* and it shows the greatest degree of admiring effort on Derrida's part.

Lévinas, born in Kaunas, Lithuania, in 1906, learned Hebrew, Russian, and German as a child, and he had a strong knowledge of Jewish tradition. In 1923 he traveled to Strasbourg to study philosophy. Five years later, he moved on to the University of Freiburg, where he got to know a young, ambitious professor of philosophy named Martin Heidegger. In Freiburg, Lévinas was, like Heidegger, an enthusiastic student of Husserl. But he gradually turned from Husserl, disappointed with the narrowness of phenomenology, its seeming distance from life. Much of Lévinas's thought became an argument with Husserl and Heidegger, who shared an emphasis on the isolated human consciousness. Both Husserl and Heidegger, Lévinas charged, neglect our relations with other people, especially the disruptive, disturbing encounter with those in need, the face-to-face. This encounter is the crucial experience invoked in Lévinas's writings, and it proves central for Derrida as well.

The decisive experience of Lévinas's life was the destruction of Europe's Jewish population during World War II. Lévinas himself, in the French army during the war, was taken captive by the Germans and protected by his status as a prisoner of war. His wife and daughter survived the Nazi onslaught, but the rest of his family in Lithuania was murdered in the death camps. For Lévinas, the Shoah raised the question of an evil so sure of itself that it could bravely proclaim its mission. Stalin's Communism used torture to extract false confessions from its victims, but such lies were not necessary to the Nazis: their will to persecute, and to kill, was unashamed.

In 1961 Lévinas published his great work *Totality and*

Infinity, a wide-ranging, mythopoeic critique of the premises of Western philosophy, particularly its devotion to solitary thought and its avoidance of the other: the individual human being, whether stranger, neighbor, or friend, who demands a response from us, and on whose behalf we are called to account. *Totality and Infinity* made Lévinas a major figure in European thought: an intense, difficult critic of philosophy's goals and premises.

Derrida's essay on Lévinas, entitled "Violence and Metaphysics" and positioned halfway through *Writing and Difference,* is the toughest, most intricate part of the book: its real center. In "Violence and Metaphysics," Derrida eloquently demonstrates Lévinas's importance for the debate between philosophy and religion. Derrida means with that title to underline the way that metaphysics, the tradition of Western philosophy, violently opposes itself to nonphilosophy. (One of Derrida's more noticeable trademarks, from the sixties on, is his use of the word *violence* in a metaphorical sense.) Greek thought aims to conquer the world, exiling anything that cannot be recognized or categorized by reason. But violence also appears in the encounter that Lévinas focuses on as the basic experience left out by Greek philosophy: when the face of a stranger in trouble breaks in on us, making an unavoidable appeal and interrupting our complacency. We are confronted by the other in an almost brutal way—a way that strikes home.

Lévinas takes up the significance of the Hebrew word *ger,* which means at once foreigner, stranger, and neighbor. In the Torah, the Israelites are commanded by God to care for the ger in their midst: they have an obligation toward those who are unconnected to them by religious or national ties. This obligation feels unconditional, the response to a cry of need.

Derrida first considers Lévinas's reaction against Husserl

in light of the importance Lévinas places on the stranger, the other. For Lévinas, Husserl provides the culmination of philosophy's tendency to reduce life to the status of an object: mere material perceived by the senses and then remembered or imagined by the solitary mind. Husserlian phenomenology studies how things appear to the calm, meditative eye of the thinker. But what if the thinker's identity is jarred by the sudden presence of another person, who makes a demand more immediate and more vital than the philosopher has reckoned with? Suddenly the world is not an object of study, but an invading, and a personal, presence.

As "Violence and Metaphysics" continues, Derrida discusses Lévinas's critique of Heidegger. Heidegger does have an active conception of social life in his philosophy, but only as what he calls "Being-with" (*Mitsein*). It is the "with" that Lévinas objects to: Heidegger focuses on situations where we live easily in the company of others. Instead of this casual solidarity of everyday life, Lévinas aims at the far more dramatic, even piercing, encounter with the other, the face-to-face. When someone appears to you in terror or in need, this is not mere arm's-length, passing companionship of the kind that Heidegger describes. Instead, you are made drastically vulnerable to, and responsible for, another person. As Derrida summarizes him, Lévinas has accomplished a thoroughgoing polemic against the inclination of metaphysics, of reason itself, to ignore one thing not usually dreamt of by philosophy: the instant and pressing ethical relation with other human beings.

The driving theme of Derrida's Lévinas chapter in *Writing and Difference* is the way that Lévinas, attempting his escape from philosophy, breaks through into a rough empiricism with a boldness that both impresses Derrida and makes him rather nervous. The face of the other supplies a brute fact that cannot be explained away by any amount of metaphysical footwork. Elaborate theories of morality, calculations based on prudence, fairness, and social utility: all are decimated by the primal presence of another human whom we are responsible for simply because he or she is *there,* and suffering.

Derrida struggles with Lévinas's emphasis on the face of the other. He twists and chafes against the idea that there is a real presence, a face, that argues by its very existence against philosophical abstraction. Derrida's antilogocentrism is more subtle than Lévinas's in that Derrida sees no alternative to the reign of concepts imposed by Greek philosophy and continuing through Husserl and Heidegger. (Lévinas protests such subtlety, seeing in it the mark of evasion.) Instead of pointing to an outside of metaphysics or to something beyond and before metaphysics, like Lévinas's face of the other, Derrida wants to shake metaphysics from within: to identify a factor that destabilizes reason and renders it contradictory.

Lévinas, Derrida writes, must presuppose what he criticizes: Western philosophy. The Jewish tradition to which Lévinas adheres was in fact influenced by Greek philosophy. Hellenized Jews were active for centuries in Alexandria. The Platonized Gospel of John was written under the influence of the Hebrew Bible. Athens and Jerusalem are, in this sense, entangled: they cannot be firmly distinguished.

There is, though, a good argument against any attempt to entwine Athens with Jerusalem, to assert (with St. Paul, and with Joyce's *Ulysses*) that "jewgreek is greekjew." Ethics presents itself to most of us in the West, whether we are Christians, Muslims, Jews, or none of the above, as the inheritance of the Torah. The Hebrew Bible enjoins us to care for the widow and the orphan and not to murder our fellow man: regulations that Socratic reason tends to erode. The obligation suggested by Mosaic law meets its opponent in the philosophical tradition, which has often undermined such religious demands. The covenant cannot, after all, be made rational. There is nothing more absurd than the honoring of father and mother above other humans, many of whom are, to any objective (that is, philosophical) eye, worth far more than one's parents.

In his essay on Lévinas in *Writing and Difference* Derrida tacitly acknowledges the autonomy of Jewish ethics, its separateness from philosophy. Lévinas's demand to attend to the person before you comes from outside philosophy: it is a form of religious empiricism. Empiricism recognizes the brute reality of the world, the things themselves, as opposed to the abstraction usually emphasized by philosophy. And so the empirical sense, in its rough immediacy, presents a kind of antiphilosophy. The philosopher tends to see empirical reality as a challenge, along with the primitive ethical demands of scripture that emphasize this reality (the poor widow at your door, the crying orphan).

Here Derrida shows his difference from a thinker like Hegel, for whom there is, in effect, nothing outside of philosophy. Hegel understands empiricism as a partial, limited perspective, ripe to be superseded by Hegel's own idealist position. For Hegel, quarreling perspectives must be understood as interdependent, as pieces of a puzzle—but pieces that become essentially worthless once the puzzle is complete. In *The Phenomenology of Spirit*, successive steps in the history of philosophy are assimilated and rendered obsolete by Hegel and his readers. For Hegel, then, empiricism stands for a moment in the story of philosophy as it moves toward its triumph; not, as Derrida presents it, the recognition of a world that challenges philosophy from outside.

Derrida writes that empirical Jewish ethics, Lévinas's ethics, "contests the resolution and coherence of the logos (philosophy) at its root, instead of letting itself be questioned by the logos" (*Writing* 152). Is this Jewish other a genuine outside, then, unlike Foucault's madness or Artaud's theatre of cruelty: a true representative of the force that Derrida has failed to discover in structuralism? Does Lévinas strike at the origin of history and experience, instead of merely reflecting on our ways of conceiving experience? To answer yes to these questions would be to become a Lévinasian, and that Derrida is not yet ready to do, not for another twenty years. But he acknowledges Lévinas's work as a crucial questioning of his own mostly Greek project of deconstruction.

Derrida has no answer to the Lévinasian question, only an intrigued impulse to brood over it. "Are we Jews? Are we Greeks?" he asks. "We live in the difference between the Jew and the Greek, which is perhaps the unity of what is called history. We live in and of difference, that is, in hypocrisy, about which Lévinas so profoundly says that it is 'not only a base contingent defect of man, but the underlying rending of a world attached to both the philosophers and the prophets'" (153). As both Jews and Greeks, we remain divided between these two terms, both of which live profoundly within us.

Derrida's essay on Lévinas shows him at his best: ready to acknowledge a thought other than his own and to present it in all its strength. Derrida's treatment of Lévinas is in this respect noticeably different from his readings of Plato, Saussure, Rousseau, Austin, and Husserl, which show them to disadvantage so that Derrida himself may claim victory.

Derrida, then, gives Lévinas his due. His adoption of Lévinas's ideas in the 1990s might have been predicted decades earlier by a canny reader of *Writing and Difference*. But for the next two decades, Derrida continues on his basic course as a skeptical unraveler of logocentrism, relatively unconcerned with Lévinas's emphasis on ethics.

Less than a year after the appearance of *Writing and Difference, Of Grammatology,* and *Speech and Phenomena,* an epochal event occurred, one that Derrida, like every other French citizen, and especially every intellectual, was forced to reckon with. This event was the student revolt of May 1968. The students hurled a vivid protest against the sterile, stagnant university system; the cramped and repressive living conditions in their dormitories; the seeming uselessness of their education. They succeeded in blockading the streets of the Latin Quarter and in shutting down the Sorbonne. Classes were replaced by a communal free-for-all consisting of endless insomniac debates over politics and revolution.

Led by "Red Danny," the young firebrand Daniel Cohn-Bendit, the students of May '68 seemed to be winning. French workers, suffering under a low minimum wage, joined them in a general strike. For a few days in May, it looked as if the French government might be brought down by the combined action of the workers and the students. By the end of the month, however, the strike had dissolved: the majority of the French people stood by their leader de Gaulle who, in a decisive speech, forcefully invoked the need for public order.

In October 1968, just a few months after the upheaval on the streets of Paris, Derrida traveled to America to present a talk at an international colloquium on philosophy and anthropology in New York. The lecture, later included in Derrida's *Margins of Philosophy* (1972), is entitled "The Ends of Man." It is one of Derrida's most eloquent and influential statements of his place in philosophical tradition. In the course of his talk, Derrida casts a reflective eye on the revolt of May '68, as well as on the wider scene of global politics.

Derrida begins by addressing the encounter between philosophy and politics, as he was compelled to do in that turbulent year. After expressing what he calls his "agreement, and to a certain point my solidarity," with critics of the war in Vietnam, Derrida alludes to recent events: *les evènements*, the student revolution in France. Like Hegel hearing the cannons from Napoleon's victory at the battle of Jena as he finished the *Phenomenology*, Derrida notices history on the margins of his work. "The writing of this text," he remarks, "I date quite precisely from the month of April 1968: it will be recalled that these were the weeks of the opening of the Vietnam peace talks and of the assassination of Martin Luther King. A bit later, when I was typing this text, the universities of Paris were invaded by the forces of order—and for the first time at the demand of a rector—and then reoccupied by the students in the upheaval you are familiar with" (*Margins* 114).

On the one hand, Derrida makes his sympathies with the students clear by using the phrase "invaded by the forces of order." On the other, he rather anxiously backs away from making any definite statement of political solidarity with the rebels of May. Derrida continues, "This historical and political horizon would call for a long analysis. I have simply found it necessary to mark, date, and make known to you the historical circumstances in which I prepared this communication" (114).

In an interview given in 1991, Derrida remarked, "I was not what is called a soixante-huitard [sixty-eighter]. Even though I participated at that time in demonstrations and organized the first general meeting at the time at the École Normale, I was on my guard, even worried in the face of a certain cult of spontaneity, a fusionist, anti-unionist euphoria, in the face of the enthusiasm of a finally 'freed' speech, of restored 'transparence,' and so forth, I never believed in those things" (*Points* 347). While supporting the students, Derrida was appropriately wary of their utopian ebullience, which saw world-changing political import in an outpouring of excited speech. The students, Derrida implied in his 1991 interview, had inherited the logocentric idea that language can be utterly decisive and self-aware, a "transparent" expression.

In spite of Derrida's criticism, confessed many years later, "The Ends of Man" shows, in a rather covert manner, that Derrida has a positive interpretation of May 1968. For him, the student revolt points a way beyond logocentric humanism (beyond the ends of man). The events of 1968 nourish Derrida's prophetic inclination.

Derrida intends his title to suggest the conclusion or overcoming of the humanist tradition. Sartre had also allied himself with the striking students. But Derrida makes us reflect on whether Sartrean activism was reaching its apogee in the late sixties or instead breathing its last. Derrida implies that there might be a posthumanist era on the horizon, that the revolution of the sixties might bring into being a new consciousness, one that would render passé both Sartre's Communism and Raymond Aron's liberalism. Derrida hints, then, that he understands the antilogocentric import of 1968 as Sartre does not.

If there was an antihumanist aspect of the '68 revolt, it must be linked with the name Michel Foucault. Foucault, earlier than Derrida, had heralded a "beyond" of the human. For Foucault, it was irrelevant to think in terms of man's essence or dignity. Foucauldian man is simply material (though at times recalcitrant material) for ideological transformation. The technology of "disciplinary formations," visible in madhouses, prisons, hospitals, and similar institutions, determines our poor being and consciousness. Cherished values, human rights: from a Foucauldian perspective, these are simply fantasies that have nothing to do with the harsh reality of history.

The sixty-eighters gathered inspiration from Nietzsche, Foucault's favorite philosopher, as well as Bakunin, Marx, and Mao. The striking students of Paris inscribed a Nietzschean slogan, "Soyez cruelle!" (Be cruel!) on their barricades. Instead of speaking as Sartre did in the name of freedom, they cited historical inevitability, the revolution: the call of the future, which would transfigure us in frightening, exhilarating ways we could hardly predict. In 1970, Foucault himself manned the barricades at the University of Vincennes, enthusiastically throwing stones down at the police. A few years later, Foucault would applaud Khomeini's Iranian revolution because it furnished another sublime spectacle: the masses urged into ceaseless activity.

In 1979, when the Shah was overthrown, Foucault cared only that the people were displaying fanatic revolutionary energy. It did not matter whether a just or unjust order was being born in Iran. Foucault later reconsidered his enthusiasm for Khomeini's revolution. But he had revealed that he, like Sartre, had a strong inclination to place his trust in the collective rather than the individual, and in the sheer force of history, no matter how violent. (This inclination against humanism and toward mass violence for its own sake, common currency among French intellectuals from the 1930s on, has been expertly diagnosed by the historian Tony Judt in his book *Past Imperfect*.)

Derrida does not mention Foucault in "The Ends of Man." But he clearly has him in mind: he wants to compete on the revolutionary territory that Foucault had marked out. Despite his diffidence about expressing outright enthusiasm for the student revolt of May, one senses that Derrida might not have minded being cited along with Foucault and Nietzsche on the students' banners.

"The Ends of Man" is devoted in large part to Heidegger's "Letter on Humanism" of 1947, his critique of Sartre. Sartre had famously announced that "existentialism is a humanism." Heidegger, in a long, fascinating essay directed to his student Jean Beaufret, who would later become Heidegger's ambassador among the French intellectual classes, took Sartre to task for his belief in "man," *l'homme*.

Sartre understands man as an essence, with (as Derrida puts it) "no origin, no historical, cultural, or linguistic limit" (*Margins* 116). What Sartre relies on, according to Derrida, is "nothing other than the metaphysical unity of man and God, the relation of man to God, the project of becoming God as the project constituting human-reality. [Sartre's] atheism changes nothing in this fundamental structure. The example of the Sartrean project remarkably verifies Heidegger's proposition according to which 'every humanism remains metaphysical,' metaphysics being the other name of ontotheology" (116).

Derrida in "The Ends of Man" aligns Sartre's bad humanism with the "anthropologistic reading of Hegel, Husserl and Heidegger" (117) prevalent in postwar French thought, notably in Kojève's lectures on Hegel's *Phenomenology*. Kojève's central point, his interpretation of the master-slave dialectic in Hegel, invokes the existential angst of an individual confronting death. Arguing against Kojève, Derrida wants to reclaim these three thinkers, Husserl, Hegel, and Heidegger, for an antihumanist and antimetaphysical program, even though their works are tied to humanism. We must read them more deeply and thoroughly, deconstruct them: then the antilogo-centric kingdom will be unveiled. (There is, however, no hope for poor Sartre, unlike the three Germanic H's.)

Existentialists see the end of man, his telos or goal, in his finitude: his mortality. The absurdity of a life curtailed by death provides the necessary occasion for heroic idealism, Sartre suggests. If we face the meaninglessness of our lives, apparent in the limits imposed by mortality, we can make significance out of nothingness. On this point Sartre has been swayed by Heidegger. Heidegger speaks in his early master-work *Being and Time* of Dasein's anxiety before its own death, a mood that spurs resolute decision making.

Derrida will have none of such angst-ridden bravado. Rather, he values the contrasting aspect of Heidegger shown in the later "Letter on Humanism." In place of humanism's direction toward man (shown in *Being and Time* as well as in Sartre's work), Heidegger now points us toward Being. Heidegger explicitly criticizes Sartre, and implicitly his own earlier work, in the "Letter." He describes Being as the inde-scribable factor that is always furthest away from man yet al-ways near too, and strangely inaccessible. Being remains per-manently different from beings, the various entities in the world. It cannot be identified with any specific being, any per-son or thing, although it is somehow present everywhere as an "unobtrusive governance" (cited in *Margins* 131).

Heidegger, much to Derrida's delight, proves especially attentive to the connection between Being and language. "Lan-guage," Heidegger writes, "is the house of Being in which man ek-sists by dwelling, in that he belongs to the truth of Being, guarding it" (cited in *Margins* 131). But Derrida also has a prob-lem with Heidegger's rhetoric on the question of Being, and especially with his reliance on certain key metaphors. Heidegger speaks of man as the shepherd of Being. He invokes the house of Being, as well as the revelation of Being, its coming to light. Heidegger implies that Being and man are proper to each other, that they belong together. But, Derrida asks, "is not this security of the near what is trembling today, that is, the co-belonging and co-propriety of the name of man and the name of Being, such as this co-propriety inhabits, and is inhabited by, the language of the West, such as it is buried in its oikonomia, such as it is inscribed and forgotten according to the history of metaphysics, and such as it is awakened also by the destruction of ontotheology? ... This trembling," Derrida concludes, "which can only come from a certain outside—was already requisite within the very structure that it solicits" (133). The house that metaphysics built is shaking, if not collapsing; all our cherished ideas of the human have been questioned. And the shaking comes from within, from metaphysics itself.

But, as Derrida admits, the "trembling" of traditional ideas also comes from a "certain outside," not just within the erudite texts of philosophers. The radicals of the sixties, in France as well as America, proclaimed their challenge to what Derrida calls "the language of the West" and amplified it to an earsplitting volume. Throwing out books and traditions in favor of chemically induced ecstasy, sexual release, and free expression, these liberated spirits could scarcely have cared about rereading Heidegger.

Derrida gestures only hesitantly toward that "certain outside," the history of his day. For a phrase or two toward the end of "The Ends of Man," he does try to rouse himself to a concern with "military and economic violence." In the last two pages of his essay, he borrows ideas from none other than Foucault. Derrida makes the familiar Foucauldian point concerning "the force and efficiency of the system that regularly change[s] transgressions into 'false exits'" (135). Derrida here follows Foucault in his suspicion of the liberationist, utopian element of the counterculture of the sixties. The grim, inescapable system cannot be overturned. But it can be rendered absurd, cast in a radical new light. Derrida winds up his essay by calling on Foucault's favorite deity, the overman of Nietzsche, who dances joyously on the grave of conventional pieties.

We have escaped Heidegger for the more daring and iconoclastic Nietzsche. Heidegger, in the series of Nietzsche lectures he gave in the midst of World War II, vainly tried to imprison Nietzsche in the tradition of metaphysics: Derrida sets him free. "His laughter then will burst out," Derrida says of the overman. "He will dance, outside the house, the *aktive Vergesslichkeit,* the 'active forgetting' and the cruel (*grausam*) feast of which the *Genealogy of Morals* speaks. No doubt that Nietzsche called for an active forgetting of Being: it would not have the metaphysical form imputed to it by Heidegger" (136). Derrida gives us this faintly barbarous picture of a Nietzschean escape from metaphysics in order, once again, to join ranks with Foucault, for whom Nietzsche is the god of the unimaginable future: of the exciting, threatening, apocalyptic—and impossible—hope for escape from all that imprisons us. Derrida, at the end of "The Ends of Man," underlines the radical derring-do of his tone by dating his text "May 12, 1968," a crucial day of the Paris students' rebellion. He concludes by hoisting his essay directly over the revolutionary bonfire.

"The Ends of Man" is dramatic in its ambivalence. As so often, Derrida seems to have it both ways, stirring us with a sublime, drastic image—the Nietzschean overman dancing at his cruel feast—and, at the same time, reminding us of the need for Talmudic focus on the cherished writings of his favorite thinkers. But by the end of the sixties, Derrida's concern with tradition was beginning to appear old-fashioned. In the midst of the storm, the metaphysics of the great philosophers seemed to many to be less relevant to the fate of the West than Mao's little red book, Che's aphorisms or, for that matter, Jimi's screaming guitar.

III

Plato, Austin, Nietzsche, Freud

I n the sixties Derrida became aware of the futility of playing the skeptic, as he had done in his early critique of Husserl. Instead of restricting his role to deflating metaphysics, which, as he saw it, assumed a universe governed by the commanding self-consciousness of a thinking subject (Derrida's charge against Husserl), Derrida turned to Jewish tradition and, at different moments, to Nietzsche in order to stake a far wider claim for his philosophy. He wanted to unveil a new world—though this world's contours remained unclear. He assumed a prophetic tone in his treatment of Lévinas and Jabès, suggesting that an ethical demand connected to Judaism was somehow implicit in the deconstructive project.

In the seventies Derrida proved unable to sustain his prophetic emphasis. The youth culture had failed to accomplish a revolutionary transformation of society; Derrida's new, muted tone may be a response to this larger defeat. In his discussions of Plato, Freud, and Austin, which I will consider in this chapter, Derrida's depictions of writing are far less apocalyptic than they were in the late sixties. Writing becomes a sign of the flux of the world, neither good nor bad in its essence. Its function, for Derrida, is to underline the randomness of our lives, and the undependability of meaning. Although Derrida in his reading of Nietzsche suggests a liberating role for writing, this liberation is cryptically described. In pursuit of such freedom, Derrida launched into avant-garde play with language in 1974's *Glas* ("death knell" in French), a collage of quotations from and commentary on Hegel and Jean Genet that flaunts its discontinuous, sometimes opaque style.

Derrida's core theme in the seventies is resistance to psychology. He refuses the intertwining of the psyche and philosophical thought that lies at the heart of the thinkers he studies. In this chapter, I give extensive portraits of Plato, Freud, and Austin, and to a lesser degree of Nietzsche, in an effort to show what Derrida decides to ignore in their work. It is necessary to grasp the larger projects of these thinkers in order to see how Derrida slights their ambitions. In each case, he asserts the importance of writing and rejects that of the individual soul. He scants the life we live with others in favor of textual abstraction.

The impersonality of Derrida's concept of writing means that he must deny the validity of any psychological emphasis he finds in his chosen authors. Both Plato and Austin base their (quite different) philosophical projects on our nature as social beings, dependent on the give and take of shared words. In this they resemble Freud, whose work depends on a therapeutic dialogue between analyst and patient. The involvement with the fact of dialogue and the influence of personality on meaning, shared by all four of the writers discussed in this chapter, distances them from Derrida's own inclinations. He must, therefore, avoid their most significant aspect in order to assimilate them.

Plato's commitment to absolutes, his need to define concepts in a rigorous and universally applicable way, makes him, in Derrida's eyes, an arch-metaphysician. By addressing Plato in his work, Derrida tackles his exact opposite: the philosopher who believes that truth, justice, and virtue are stable, definable entities. Derrida takes aim at Plato the logocentrist.

But this picture of Plato is far from accurate. Plato's use of a literary form, the dialogue, indicates that his thought relies fundamentally on conversation and on the dramatic irony that goes along with conversational interaction. Instead of the dogmatist that Derrida sees in him, Plato is an artist of human character; he looms as the most literary of philosophers, the one most interested (along with Nietzsche and Søren Kierkegaard) in psychological portraiture. It is Plato's profound interest in the psyche that Derrida deliberately misses, as he misses it in Austin, Nietzsche, and Freud.

I will first try to give Plato consideration in his own right, as I have with Husserl and Freud, before addressing Derrida's treatment of him in his renowned essay on the *Phaedrus,* "Plato's Pharmacy" (1968). Because Derrida gives relatively short shrift to so many of the major emphases of the *Phaedrus,* I will provide a rather substantial account of Plato's dialogue. Attending to the parts of Plato's *Phaedrus* that Derrida slights will enable us to understand the limits of the deconstructionist perspective. I devote more space to Plato than to Derrida's other philosophical ancestors because Plato remains, for Derrida as for us, the ultimate source of Western thought.

Plato is often thought of as the father of philosophy. There were thinkers before him, of course: not just his beloved mentor Socrates but also the dark and obscure Heraclitus and the deeply puzzling Parmenides. Plato's breadth and richness are unrivaled in Greek philosophy or any that followed. His intricacy makes for seductive power. Bothered and intrigued by the dialogues, we plunge into them, get to know them better—and they begin to inhabit us.

Plato is also the most dramatic of philosophers. He says almost nothing in his own voice, with the exception of several letters of disputed authenticity. (The most famous, the Seventh Letter, recounts his failed effort to educate his student and later the tyrant of Syracuse, Dionysius, in philosophy.) All is dialogue in Plato: brilliant, witty, touching, and complex. From fourth-century Athens to the present day, readers have pored over the *Republic,* the *Symposium,* the *Phaedrus,* and other dialogues, searching them for clues to Plato's opinions. But the answers are to be found not in Plato's definitive intentions, supposing these were available, but instead in the individual reader's experience of the dialogues, with their dramatic twists and turns. He asks: What kind of soul are you, reader? How do you respond to the drunken gate-crashing of the handsome Athenian general Alcibiades, who bursts into the *Symposium* and recalls his attempt to coax Socrates into seducing him both intellectually and erotically? Are you shocked or pleased by the challenge to Socrates' authority? Do you approve of, or are you disgusted by, the proposals of Socrates in the *Republic:* the ideal city that features coed naked gymnastics, equal rights for men and women, and the potential for incest among boys and girls raised not by their parents but in a collective nursery?

As we read Plato, our responses matter above all else. He provokes our thinking by making us dwell on our feelings about the characters and ideas of the dialogues. The *Republic* depicts an ideal state that at times looks more like a cross between a Communist reeducation camp and a kibbutz gone badly wrong; we are by turns enthralled and repulsed by it. By pushing our reactions to the extreme, Plato teaches us about our motives and interests and challenges us to develop them further, under the tutelage of philosophy.

Derrida's reading of Plato ignores this psychological dimension: the way that Plato makes us aware of our reactions to his work, in order to instruct us. Derrida remains intent on proving that Plato is a nostalgist who yearns for the perfect presence of truth. Unable to achieve this perfection, Plato, in Derrida's view, rails against our fallen world, which obstructs the realization of philosophical ideals. The same ignorant mob that sentenced Socrates to death controls political life. If the philosopher could conduct a dialogue within his soul and contain it there—if he could dwell always in the serene empyrean realm of ideas, unsoiled by the corrupt world of the city—then his dream would be achieved.

Does Plato have such a fantasy? Does he want to purge the city, in retaliation for its execution of Socrates, so that only an elite mini-society of philosophers would be left? I argue that he does not. Plato knows that the soul, the object of his study, cannot be made pure. Neither can the city. Both social life and the individual psyche are places of struggle, in his view. In this sense, Plato is the precursor of Freud, with his tripartite model of the mind composed of id, ego, and superego. In Freud, each of the three psychic agencies strives for dominance, and this war is never won. Our natures remain mixed, the self a territory in dispute. Plato has a similar three-part division of the soul in his *Republic:* appetite; manly courage or enthusiasm; and reason, the high will to knowledge. In the *Phaedrus* the scheme is simplified. Here Plato divides us in two, into a beastly and a godlike desire. The wrestling match between these two opposing forces is vividly depicted in the rapturous centerpiece of the *Phaedrus,* the myth of the charioteer.

"Plato's Pharmacy" is an extended essay, over a hundred pages long, first published in *Tel Quel* in 1968 and reprinted in Derrida's book *Dissemination* (1972). In "Plato's Pharmacy" Derrida devotes not a single sentence to the myth of the charioteer, probably Plato's best-known fable about what human beings are like. Instead, he dwells on the subject of speech and writing in Plato's dialogue, epitomized in the obscure myth of Theuth near the end of the *Phaedrus*. As he so often does, Derrida here takes a small, overlooked section of a text and argues that it is all-important. Derrida does not touch the crucial center of Plato's dialogue, only its fringes.

Along with the *Symposium*, the *Phaedrus* may be Plato's most sparkling, fascinating dialogue. There are two drives within us, says Socrates: two sources of self, two ruling principles. One of them is an inborn desire for pleasures; the other is worthy opinion informed by knowledge (*epiktetos doxa*). Good judgment guides us; desire drags us down. For Plato, this remains the most fundamental fact about us, as souls: we are split in two. But the split is far from simple. Socrates' definitions seem to struggle against each other. Socrates defines eros as "the irrational [*aneu logou*] appetite that has gained power over the judgment [*doxa*] urging one toward the right thing." This appetite is "forcefully driven by the desires akin to it in its pursuit of the body's beauty, winning in the contest, and taking its name from its force—it's called eros."[1] (Socrates here puns on *eromenos*, "beloved," and *erromenos*, "forcefully" or "violently" [238b–c].) Eros wins out against judgment or doxa, against the accepted opinion that shows us the right thing to do.

In order to understand love in its madness, Socrates remarks, you have to know what the soul is like. The soul resembles a charioteer with a pair of winged horses, one of them noble and obedient and the other ornery, recalcitrant. The noble horse strives upward, toward the region of the gods and the heavens beyond them: a place immune to worldly damage where ecstasy and calm prevail. But the bad, unruly horse leans downward, toward the earth. The soul, poised between them, steers.

The encounter between lover and beloved, erastes and eromenos, is a struggle between a desire for sex and a sublimated desire to engage in philosophy. Socrates explains: "[The beloved's] desires are similar to his lover's, but weaker: to see, touch, kiss, and lie down with him; and indeed, as one might expect, soon afterwards he does just that. So as they lie together, the lover's licentious [*akolastos*] horse has something to suggest to the charioteer, and claims a little enjoyment as recompense for such hardship; while its counterpart in the beloved has nothing to say, but swelling with confused passion it embraces the lover and kisses him, welcoming him as someone full of goodwill, and whenever they lie down together, it is ready not to refuse to do its own part in granting favors to the lover, should he beg to receive them" (255d–256a). Plato's language is full of sexual energy. The soul, under the magnetic influence of the form of the beautiful, begins to molt, melt, and sprout eager wings. The wrestling match among our conflicting impulses goes on. When the beloved is finally ready to acquiesce in the lover's passion, the charioteer, with the aid of the good, noble horse, resists the impending sex act "with a reasoned sense of shame." If the lover and the beloved succeed in staving off sexual fulfillment—if "the better-ordered elements of their minds get the upper hand"—then they will pursue philosophical lives, lives of sublimated passion. This result sounds like a victory for the higher self, the aspect of us devoted to knowledge rather than sensual enjoyment. But note that it is not a liberation from the contentious, lustful element in our souls, but rather a constraining of it. "Having enslaved that part through which evil attempted to enter the soul," lover and beloved become free for contemplation.

According to Socrates in the *Phaedrus*, the wild, threatening force of sex is "enslaved" by the virtuous man, not destroyed (256b). We are not mixed equally and never will be. Crucially, though, the friction between the parts of the soul, in the *Phaedrus* as in the *Republic*, leads to the passion that we need to pursue wisdom. Without passion, without the fight of the higher against the lower impulses, we would never seek love—or philosophical knowledge. For Socrates, love, like philosophy, expresses the restless contention of a divided self. This is what Socrates means when he says that philosophy is the work of eros, amazing and frightening in what it reveals. In both love and philosophy, the fight within us shows us who, and what, we are. And we are more surprising to ourselves than we would have thought, resembling the strange creatures of myth.

In the great set piece of the *Symposium*, Diotima's speech, the rapture of perfect knowledge is intensely yearned for—and unattainable. Diotima is a mystic witch who instructs Socrates in the ways of desire that animate the universe. In the *Symposium*, she ends her lecture to the admiring, bewildered sage of Athens with a thrilling climax: five pages of unrivaled beauty on the pure shining excitement of the Idea. At the end of Diotima's speech, we look down from Plato's Everest. The whole world lies transfigured below us, now that we have glimpsed the sheer irresistible beauty of philosophy. Knowledge is electric, a drive that transforms the world by launching our whole being toward an ecstatic, tantalizing vision of beauty.

The *Phaedrus,* like the *Symposium,* is about love and rhetoric—and philosophy. In both dialogues, Plato stages his praise of philosophical desire against sophistic rhetoric. The sophists of Athens marketed the skills required to seduce an audience, whether the audience was a beloved or a crowd of voters. Recent critics wish to bring Socrates close to the sophists he criticized, the purveyors of low persuasion. But for Plato's Socrates philosophy is an erotic art, not a sophistic one. Plato tells us the difference between sophistic rhetoric and philosophy. The distinction between speech and writing that Derrida emphasizes is simply not the focus of the *Phaedrus.* Whether speeches are spoken or written, only one thing matters about them for Plato: are they the instruments of sophistic persuasion or of its opponent, philosophy?

Philosophers, unlike sophists, prize the inward agon— fierce mental debate—and find it intrinsically rewarding, because it leads to truth. The soul as Plato depicts it in the myth of the charioteer is all about struggle. As such, it answers the vision of base calculation that the rhetorician Lysias and his fan Phaedrus give us at the beginning of Plato's dialogue, in the speech of the nonlover who aims to win over an eromenos just as prudent and self-serving as himself. In the myth of the charioteer, even baseness—the reckless, raging desire centered in the bad horse—proves spirited rather than calculating. The masters of rhetoric, simply put, are nonlovers: firmly on the side of calculation and opposed to the fervent impulses of thought as well as feeling. Socrates is against sophistic rhetoric because rhetoricians prize self-possession and manipulation over the madness that every enthusiast, whether lover or philosopher, must yield to.

I will offer some thoughts as to why Derrida is so unconcerned with the difference between rhetoric and philosophy, so obviously a main concern in Plato's dialogue. But first I will try to give Derrida his due in my reading of "Plato's Pharmacy," a philosophical essay full of high terms and dazzling in its style. Derrida derives his title from Plato's reference to the *pharmakon,* a Greek word that means both "medicine" and "poison." (The double meaning is appropriate enough, since given the state of the medical art in fifth-century Athens, gulping down a curative potion could be a risky proposition.)

Socrates uses the word *pharmakon* to describe writing. And writing, Derrida argues, is presented by the *Phaedrus* in the myth of Theuth as both a cure for faulty memory and a poisonous, corrupting substance. We tend to rely on the written word as a substitute for living memory. According to Socrates, writing down one's thoughts about philosophical matters amounts to generating an insufficiently vital series of formulations. The written record remains far removed from real philosophy, the energetic conversational thrust and parry that Socrates shows in his dialogues when he subtly instructs or forcefully skewers his opponents viva voce. But Plato, unlike Socrates, writes it all down—and he draws our attention to this paradox.

Derrida links the pharmakon to the related word *pharmakos,* meaning "scapegoat": a term that Plato never actually uses in his dialogue, but one that, Derrida implies, he must have in mind, since Socrates became the scapegoat for Athens. (And since writing is Socrates' own whipping boy: for Plato depicts him as the immortal champion of conversation.)

Plato cherishes the dialogue form because it allows him to show that knowledge takes the form of a conversation. Faced with a written text, we can ignore it, put it aside, or remain bored or ignorant. But when questioned by a person, we must answer—or be exposed in our evasions. Derrida makes the case that Plato's attempt to exalt speech over writing must fail. Writing has to win, Derrida argues. The dialogues are books, after all; we are reading them. The truth, Plato announces, is "written in the soul." The philosopher finds it necessary to use the image of writing, rather than speech, for the highest thing he can evoke: truth.

The *Phaedrus* constitutes a "trial of writing," Derrida claims (*Dissemination* 67). As far as Plato is concerned, writing loses against speech, the living word that Socrates, who never wrote anything down, remains loyal to. But in Derrida's book, writing is the necessary victor. Only after writing appears can we understand the difference between it and speech, and know the way these two opponents are entwined with, or parasitic on, each other (101). In his way of living and talking, Socrates embodied virtue (*arete*). But his example lives only because Plato wrote so much about him.

Let us take a closer look at Derrida's complex argument in "Plato's Pharmacy." Derrida tells us he will pick out for us the "hidden thread" of Plato's dialogue (65). This thread leads to a more far-reaching conclusion than Derrida's preliminary idea (that Plato, because he writes, must make speech yield to writing). For Derrida, the *Phaedrus*'s covert message, which Plato himself remains unconscious of, is that speech also actually *is* writing: that all our expression is an ambiguous creature divided against itself. The voice, with Plato's aid, proclaims its own superiority over the written word, but this boast cannot be sustained. What if these two seemingly opposed entities, speech and writing, are in fact the same thing? In that case, Derrida argues, Plato's effort to distinguish writing from speaking must fail.

Socrates tells the story this way, close to the end of the *Phaedrus*. He has heard about an Egyptian god named Theuth, "the first to discover number and calculation, and geometry and astronomy, and also games of draughts and dice; and, to

cap it all, letters." Theuth presents his marvelous new invention, writing, to Thamus, the King of Egypt. Socrates continues: "When it came to the subject of letters, Theuth said, 'But
this study, King Thamus, will make the Egyptians wiser and
improve their memory; what I have discovered is a drug [phar-
makon] of memory and wisdom.'"

King Thamus is less than impressed by the god Theuth's
ingenious novelty. "Most scientific [*tekhnikotate*] Theuth," he
says,

> You, as the father of letters, have been led by your
> affection for them to describe them as having the
> opposite of their real effect. For your invention will
> produce forgetfulness in the souls of those who
> have learned it, through lack of practice at using
> their memory, as through reliance on writing they
> are reminded from outside by alien marks, not
> from inside, themselves by themselves: you have
> discovered a drug not of memory but of remind-
> ing. To your students you give an appearance of
> wisdom, not the reality of it; having heard much, in
> the absence of teaching, they will appear to know
> much when for the most part they know nothing,
> and they will be difficult to get along with, since
> they will have become seeming-wise rather than
> wise. (274b–275b)

Socrates, commenting on the Theuth story, presents a parallel between painting and writing. He remarks to Phaedrus:

> Writing has this strange [or surprising, *deinon*] fea-
> ture, which makes it like painting. The offspring of

painting stand there as if alive, but if you ask them something, they preserve a quite solemn silence. Similarly with written words: you might think that they spoke as if they had some thought in their heads, but if you ever ask them about any of the things they say out of a desire to learn, they point to just one thing, the same each time. And when once it is written, every composition is trundled about [*kulindeitai*] everywhere in the same way, in the presence both of those who know about the subject and those who have nothing at all to do with it, and it does not know how to address those it should address and not those it should not. When it is ill-treated and unjustly abused, it always needs its father [that is, its author] to help it; for it is incapable of defending or helping itself. (275d–e)

Derrida exaggerates the hapless, homeless character of writing, pushing Plato's account of it much further than Plato himself does. Writing "rolls this way and that," Derrida proclaims, "like someone who has lost his rights, an outlaw, a pervert, a bad seed, a vagrant, an adventurer, a bum. . . . Wandering in the streets, he doesn't even know who he is, what his identity— if he has one—might be, what his father's name is" (*Dissemination* 143).

This is picturesque but inaccurate. Writing, as Socrates indicates, depends on its father in times of need: that is, an author must answer for what he has made, his text. Derrida's image of writing as amnesiac and homeless invents a stark contrast, one that enables him to portray Plato—quite implausibly—as an enemy of all written expression. Writing undermines what Derrida sees as Plato's basic interest in crystal-clear, absolute perfection. Derrida remarks that, for Plato, "The immortality and perfection of a living being would consist of it having no relation at all with any outside. That is the case with God" (101). And the philosopher, devoted to a pure, imageless knowledge, would be a kind of God. Yet this Greek sage, though called the divine Plato by centuries of readers, neither wants godhead nor believes that he can attain it. He knows we are impure, by nature. Derrida's picture of Plato is far from the much more complex real thing.

Penelope Deutscher, a loyal Derridean, accurately summarizes Derrida's derogatory version of Plato when she writes that "Plato's debasement of writing implies his idealization of a thoroughly spontaneous, immediate, undeterred, therefore non-'inscribed' knowledge, or thought. Derrida exposes this ideal as an impossible phantasy."[2] Deutscher's, and Derrida's, description is valid only for Platonism, and a rather simple-minded Platonism at that, not for Plato himself. As I will argue, and as the best readers of the *Phaedrus,* Charles Griswold and Giovanni Ferrari, also point out, Plato does not debase writing in his dialogue.[3] Instead, he protests the misuse of writing, specifically by sophists and allied rhetoricians. He does so in order to define what philosophy can offer, how it distinguishes itself from the crowd-pleasing speech-maker's art.

Derrida claims that for Plato books are "foreign to living knowledge" (73). Plato tries to dominate writing and subordinate it to speech, by "inserting [writing's] definition into simple, clear-cut oppositions: good and evil, inside and outside, true and false, essence and appearance." Finally, Derrida gives this paraphrase of Plato's point: "In truth, writing is essentially bad" (103). The pharmakon leads readers astray (70–71). And Plato, writes Derrida, desperately wants to get back on track, separating the true from the false, dividing lucid consciousness from the unclarity of poetry, dreams, and myth. Banishing writing, as the Egyptian king perhaps should have done, would bring us this lucidity.

But Socrates clearly says in the *Phaedrus,* in a passage Derrida overlooks, that there is nothing reprehensible about the written word as such, only about writing poorly or irresponsibly (as Lysias has done in his wretched speech praising the nonlover). Socrates remarks, "This much, then, is clear to everyone, that in itself, at least, writing speeches is not something shameful. . . . But what is shameful, I think, is speaking and writing not in an acceptable way, but shamefully and badly" (258d). Socrates repeats *aiskhron,* "shameful," the same word he applied to the behavior of the bad horse in the myth of the charioteer. Like the chariot of the soul, writing can turn in either a good or a bad direction. In itself, though, writing is a neutral vehicle, just like speech.

Plato underlines the fact that we are responsible for the acts of rhetoric we commit, whether in speech or in print. To reflect on this fact is to move from sophistic training to Platonic philosophy, with its psychological insight: we have begun to address the state of our souls. Derrida, by implying that the use and destiny of writing cannot be controlled, gives the sophist an excuse and lets the blame for any corruption in practice fall on the medium itself. The Derridean sophist would claim that the vagrancy of writing, the supposed instability of written meaning, absolves the writer of the duties of authorship. Writing's shifting nature allows the sophistic rhetorician to evade the philosopher's demand that speechmakers not corrupt an audience, incite ruin, or inflame low passions. In making this case, the sophist pleads, unconvincingly, a merely technical innocence.

The opposition between philosophy and other persuasive uses of words thus proves to be the organizing polarity of the *Phaedrus,* not the opposition between speech and writing, as Derrida claims. Whether someone prefers the rhetoric of the courts of law and the political arena or the conversational ways of philosophy tells us something about this individual's soul: so Plato's *Phaedrus* becomes a means to the reader's self-knowledge.

In contrast to Plato's philosophical psychology, the opposing art of the sophist requires from its audience a certain degree of ignorance. The *Phaedrus* suggests that sophistic rhetoric's esteem for its be-all and end-all, effectiveness, requires the separation of technique from belief. You can either be taken in by a seduction speech or marvel at the mannerisms that the rhetorician-seducer uses. But in order to be taken in, you must not notice the manipulation. Phaedrus, at the beginning of the dialogue, is in awe of Lysias's speech, a nonlover's attempt to seduce a beautiful boy by claiming that he is superior to the lover. But Phaedrus does not for a moment believe in Lysias's argument. The implied point is that if you know Lysias's rhetorical tactics, you can protect yourself from his art. The sophist's ideal is to deceive his audience, and to teach his technique to similar deceivers. The sophist resembles a magician who convinces a credulous audience by means of concealed expertise. When the expertise is revealed to a connoisseur like Phaedrus, the persuasive power is lost. Plato, by contrast, draws a firm line between philosophy and mere deception, even when he advocates a deception like the *Republic*'s noble lie; the reader of the dialogues, who is meant to be puzzled by the relation between dialectics and mythmaking, can never be simply taken in by such a lie.

The sophistic rhetorician's distinguishing of technique

from belief, so that the more you know how the persuasive trick is done the less you are taken in by it, is anathema to Socrates. In this respect, Socrates stands at the opposite pole from the sophist. What you discover about Socrates' techniques, his irritating, enrapturing ways of trapping and fascinating his interlocutors, makes you an interlocutor yourself, unable to tear yourself away. The way he works seems occultly but definitely related to what he works on: subjects like desire, justice, and the self. You want to discover the connection between method and manner, if there is one. The more curious you get about the intimate relation between Socrates' subject and his way of discussing it, the more involved you become in philosophy—and in psychology, since you are now aware of the responses of your own soul.

When we finish a Platonic dialogue like the *Phaedrus*, we find it hard to decide what we were seduced into. It is certainly not a particular, definable act, like giving up one's body to a lover (or nonlover) or casting a vote for a defendant's guilt or innocence. Instead, we return to our reading, our thinking and being perplexed. *That* is the seduction—and its desired result. This effect explains why Socrates prizes rapturous enthusiasm, along with a hint of erotic obsession, as the way of philosophy. Philosophy too is a kind of love, rough and refined, able both to yield and to pursue.

Speech as mere entertainment, or mere instrument, with easily measurable effects, provides a well-known game: its master is the sophist Lysias. Socrates plays a very different game. His words, occurring once on a hot day in Athens, turn out to be written in our souls, passing remarks by a well-known stranger that remain indelibly there whenever we talk about beauty or desire. Derrida's effort to instill a straightforward contradiction into Socrates' discourse fades away, outshone by the radiant, many-colored light of the *Phaedrus*. Instead of wishing for simple and unambiguous speech, as Derrida claims, Plato studies the psyche in its nuances. But Derrida eliminates this psychological dimension from his portrait of Plato.

The early seventies were a time of significant changes for Derrida. His father, Aimé, died in 1970; the next year, he returned to Algeria to teach for a few months at the University of Algiers. Now in his forties, he was becoming increasingly well known in France, part of a set of exciting cutting-edge theorists. But, as always, Derrida resisted being assimilated to any group. In 1972, he broke with *Tel Quel* and its editor, Philippe Sollers, over the journal's Maoist politics. He had long felt alienated from the doctrinaire leftism of French intellectual life, evident in *Tel Quel*'s Communist proclamations. Now he separated himself more explicitly from his colleagues. In 1971 and 1972, Derrida taught at Oxford and at Johns Hopkins. He was expanding his intellectual reach to include not just ancient Greek and modern German thought but also contemporary approaches to philosophy in the English-speaking world.

From Plato, Derrida turned to another of his influences, this time a current rather than an ancient figure, and one associated with Oxford, where he was teaching: J. L. Austin. Like Plato, Austin is a psychological thinker in the broad sense: preoccupied with what we say and how we say it because, in his view, our conversation tells us who we are. As in the case of Plato, Derrida decides to overlook this aspect of Austin, instead seeing in him the wish for univocal meaning typical of the logocentrist.

In August 1971, three years after "Plato's Pharmacy," Derrida delivered, at a conference in Montreal, a lecture called "Signature Event Context." Though he briefly discussed Husserl, Derrida's emphasis was on the work of Austin, one of the ancestors of what has become known as analytical philosophy. (Many prefer to think of Austin as an ordinary language philosopher rather than an analytic philosopher; the two schools are related, but the ordinary language philosopher is less influenced by logical method and more committed to conversational evidence than the analyst.)

Since the early seventies, if not earlier, the study of philosophy has been divided into two camps. One of them is the group of Continental philosophers (including Derrida) who base their work on an intense familiarity with European philosophers from Plato and Aristotle to Hegel, Heidegger, and Husserl. The other is the analytic school; their approach is sometimes called Anglo-American philosophy, since it first took root in the English-speaking world.

Analytic philosophers devote themselves with precision to a series of problems, frequently definitional ones. What is a person? and what is an action? are typical subjects for the analytic philosopher, who often adopts an iconoclastic attitude toward the centuries-old tradition of metaphysical speculation. Ludwig Wittgenstein, a central figure for analytic and ordinary language philosophy, insisted that he was incapable of reading Aristotle, because Aristotle was simply wrong. Such a stance toward a classic philosopher would be unthinkable in the Continental school. Though Derrida makes Plato's *Phaedrus* shallower and more one-sided than it is, he still regards it as central: such a canonical text demands discussion. Continental philosophy pores over the tradition, regarding it as the necessary, inevitable home of thought. Austin, by contrast, often suggests that he wishes to dispel a confusion caused by the mistaken ideas of earlier philosophers, ideas that Austin tests against the practices of everyday life. Perhaps, he may suggest, some of Plato's or Aristotle's or Kant's ideas just don't work. For the Continental philosopher, the question of what works—what passes the tests of ordinary life and ordinary language—usually does not arise.

Austin is perhaps Derrida's strangest choice for an interlocutor. Straitlaced and meticulous, a model of the restrained Oxford don, he was best known for developing the theory of the "performative utterance": the idea that our sentences do things in the world more often than they describe the world, as he put it in his lecture series "How to Do Things with Words" (1962). Austin's laconic seductiveness, practical and understated, couldn't be further away from Derrida's pull-out-the-stops hyperbole, his spectacular proclamations of the end of man and the monstrous, ineffable specter of futurity.

Derrida's strategy against Austin in "Signature Event Context" is to claim that Austin's modest hemming concealed an authoritative, even dictatorial penchant for drawing the boundaries of legitimate speech. Austin, however, is really interested not in laying down the law but in testing the weight of our particular actions. We do things with words so that we can excuse, avoid, or subtly revise the meaning of our deeds. Derrida proves indifferent to this provocative ethical face of Austin's work: its character as a psychological analysis that tells us about ourselves, and specifically about our wishes to evade or misrecognize our actions. Instead, he sees in Austin only a typical metaphysician's wish to prove the reliability of the conscious ego's words and thoughts.

The mild-mannered Austin with his pipe, tweeds, and horn-rimmed glasses was in fact a philosophical revolutionary. A code-breaker for Britain during World War II, he often headed for the nursery when he visited a friend's house, because children's play was one of the best sources of material for philosophy. If the archetypal philosophical idealist was the pre-Socratic Greek Thales, so absorbed by the heavens that he fell into a ditch, then Austin willingly descended into the ditch: the valley of our rich, self-contradictory everyday behavior. Austin's influence in legal study has been great, since he examined so many concepts that the law holds dear, including the involuntary, the intentional, and the accidental.[4]

Austin displays a bemused, inquisitive rigor in his philosophical essays. He believes in the power of circumstances to govern the words we use, rendering them effective or not. He remarks, "We may plead that we trod on the snail inadvertently; but not on a baby: you really ought to look where you are putting your great feet" (*Papers* 194–95). "Of course," he adds, "it was (really), if you like, inadvertence." But this plea works only for more trivial situations (as with the snail); it is not going to be allowed here, with the crushed baby in full view.

Austin's diagnosis of the occupational disease of philosophers focuses on their desire for the "incorrigible statement," something that will be true under all circumstances. (The rest of us share the disease at times; philosophers are not merely misguided, but usefully representative.) In his essay "A Plea for Excuses," for example, Austin remarks that philosophers think they know what they mean when they speak of performing an action. In fact, they tend to reduce all action to the (apparently) simplest cases. (Simple cases make bad law.) Austin writes that we assimilate actions "one and all to the supposedly most obvious and easy cases, such as posting letters or moving fingers, just as we assimilate all 'things' to horses or beds" (*Papers* 179). In this way, Austin kicks against the ideas and universals that philosophy so often trades in. He is, before Derrida, a critic of metaphysics. Derrida, who knows this, still attributes to Austin the prejudices of a metaphysical thinker.

Derrida argues in "Signature Event Context" that philosophers, including Austin, characteristically and wrongly see writing and speech as communication. In Derrida's essay, this word, *communication,* bears a metaphysical burden. It implies the conveying of content (meaning) by means of an apparatus (tongue movements or pen movements, say) and the delivering of this content to an addressee. Philosophers, according to Derrida, want to reliably transport meaning by keeping it controlled, tied to its proper context. Language, in their view, is merely an instrument. Signs are used to carry meaning from the speaker's mouth to the ears of an audience: from the writer's script to the reader's eyes.

Derrida disagrees with this idea, which he attributes to Austin and to philosophy in general.[5] For Derrida, writing is not to be thought of as communication, the stable transporting of meaning; and neither, therefore, is speech, which he considers a subset of writing. What he calls the iterability of words, the structure of repetition and variation that makes words signify, prevents context from being pinned down. In different situations (or cultures, or periods of history), the same words will have widely divergent meanings.

What then does Derrida want of Austin? (as Stanley Cavell puts the question in his essay on the two thinkers).[6] Derrida is intrigued by Austin's category of the performative, which seems to "beckon toward Nietzsche" and to break with metaphysics (*Margins* 322). But then Derrida takes back his compliment. As it turns out, Austin does not divorce himself from metaphysics at all. Derrida charges that Austin is a logocentrist who believes that meaning requires a clear, conscious intention on the part of the speaker (323). Here is Derrida's statement of the point (which is, as we shall see, rather unfair to Austin): "For a context to be exhaustively determinable, in the sense demanded by Austin, it at least would be necessary for the conscious intention to be totally present and actually transparent for itself and others, since it is a determining focal point of the context" (327).

Derrida asserts that Austin lets "the category of intention govern the entire scene and the entire system of utterances" (326). But Austin does not ride intention in this way; far from it. Instead, he suggests that self-interested moralizers exploit intention as an excuse, when in fact it is circumstances that govern meaning (rather than the speaker's consciousness). Here is Austin, near the beginning of *How to Do Things with Words:* "One who says 'promising is not merely a matter of uttering words! It is an inward and spiritual act!' is apt to appear a solid moralist standing out against a generation of superficial theorizers. . . . Yet he provides . . . the bigamist with an excuse for his 'I do' and the welsher with a defense for his 'I bet.' Accuracy and morality alike are on the side of the plain saying that *our word is our bond*" (*How to Do* 10).

If the circumstances are appropriate, then one actually gets married by saying the required words: a performative utterance. As Austin wittily (and strangely) puts it, "When I say, before the registrar or altar, etc., 'I do,' I am not reporting on a marriage, I am indulging in it" (6). Appropriate circumstances include standing before a judge, priest, ship's captain, or similar figure, having a marriage license handy, and so on. If one is already married, or one is an actor playing the bride or groom in a stage play, the ceremony "misfires" (as Austin terms it).

Consciousness does play a role, but a circumscribed one, in determining appropriate conditions for the marriage ceremony. If you are deluded enough not to know that a marriage is occurring at all—say, if you have been drugged or brainwashed by your potential spouse—then this lack of awareness, imposed against your will, can indeed be grounds for an annulment. But you cannot squirm out of a marriage by claiming that you didn't really mean to get married, or weren't paying attention (even if these things are true). Instead, like Touchstone in *As You Like It,* you must hope for a truly serious glitch: a ceremony performed so badly that it proves invalid.

Derrida claims that Austin does not properly consider the crucial status of the misfired or infelicitous, the way the botched cases make the successful ones possible. In fact, both Austin and Derrida assert the pervasiveness, the central importance, of misfiring. But misfiring means something different for each of them. For Austin, as Cavell writes, misfired cases and the excuses tied to them hint at the "unending vulnerability of human action, its exposure to the independence of the world and the preoccupation of the mind" (*Philosophical* 53). In Derrida, by contrast, the seemingly marginal misfired cases prove central because they show that context is drifting and indefinable. Any wedding could turn out to be a stage play, any groom a bigamist. (Such possibilities have stocked the skeptic's arsenal since Descartes: those people on the street might be automata, Descartes suggests in his *Meditations.*) One cannot, therefore, according to Derrida, attain the specific local description, the accurate account of a particular situation, that Austin trusts in (or longs for).

Derrida is wrong to claim that Austin believes in the power of conscious intention to define situations. This misreading may not matter, however. The real quarrel between the two thinkers lies in a somewhat different place: Derrida simply doesn't believe in situations, and Austin does. For Austin, where we find ourselves instructs us as to who we are. Austin

often describes cases in which we try to get away with something; such cases end by reining us in: suggesting how, and to
what, we are obligated.

Derrida rebels against such obligation. For him, the author or speaker of a statement is not provably bound to the
statement. Our word is *not* our bond, Derrida boldly asserts
(*Margins* 328). (Again, he is a classic skeptic in this regard.)
Yet, as Austin would point out, in an ordinary way, and in a
legal way too, we have to be tied to what we say. It is not a very
effective excuse to say that our words were simply out of our
hands, or our mouths. The endless human inventiveness in the
field of excuses suggests to Austin that finessing responsibility
is one of the main things we do.

Derrida, convinced that responsibility as a concept must
be metaphysical and therefore flimsy, decides not to care about
it. But for Austin one is responsible if the circumstances render one so; there is nothing metaphysical about the question.
(Austin adds that responsibility is not an apt criterion in all
cases; it too can become a canard [*Papers* 181]. Each instance
demands judgment.)[7]

None of Austin's questions involving our habitual, unavoidable ways of judging ourselves and our actions are of
philosophical concern to Derrida. Rather, he tends to charac-
terize them as metaphysical illusions, inescapable yet insubstantial. Austin's aim of clarifying words and ideas by submitting them to the practical test of ordinary life seems worse than
futile to Derrida, for whom the ordinary, as he confesses in
"Signature Event Context," is not a viable concept at all.

Austin, who died a decade before Derrida's lecture on
him, was not able to answer his deconstructionist opponent.
But "Signature Event Context" spurred a heated reply by a follower of Austin, John Searle. Derrida then answered Searle in

an essay of over a hundred pages entitled "Limited INC." The gap between analytic and Continental philosophy only became wider as a result. As in the case of Derrida's later exchange with the philosopher of hermeneutics Hans-Georg Gadamer (discussed in the next chapter), the two opposing sides seemed to be talking past each other.

Derrida's avoidance of psychological criteria provides an unexpected key to his battle with Austin. Austin's philosophy of ordinary language depends on assessments of character: the character of situations and of the actors involved in them. As in the case of Plato, the state of the soul plays (rather surprisingly) a central role in Austin's thought. If we were all easily irresponsible, determined to bend the rules to our own whims, then ordinary language would bear no weight at all. But it demonstrably does. In Austin's vision, when we abide by conventional limits, we do so because these limits tell us who we are. When our ingenuity succeeds (when an excuse works, for example) and when it rewards us with thoughtful implication, it stands apart from the false ingenuity of the merely manipulative, which, like Lysias's sophistry, is bound to be seen through sooner or later. There is something truly convincing, and therefore reliable, about the exemplary excuse, something that tells of the depth of our lives in language.

Along with Plato and Austin, Nietzsche was a major figure for Derrida in the early seventies, an influence to be reckoned with. Whereas Derrida cast the other two as the champions of logocentric stability, Nietzsche was his inspiration: the daring thinker who put philosophy itself in question. Nietzsche's commitment to intellectual adventure proved indispensable to Derrida. Nearly a hundred years before Derrida, Nietzsche had sailed beyond the furthest reaches of earlier thinkers, disclosing new and unprecedented philosophical seascapes. Nietzsche, like Plato, plays the rebel psychologist among philosophers: he specializes in detecting the personal motives of the great thinkers as they build their theories. Derrida finds no use in such psychological insight; instead, he focuses on the liberating potential of Nietzsche's words. By the early seventies, Derrida is no longer resoundingly prophetic, as in his treatments of Nietzsche a few years earlier; but he does continue to see in Nietzsche a new freedom.

In 1973, in an anthology entitled *Nietzsche aujourd'hui* (*Nietzsche Today*), Derrida published "The Question of Style," an essay derived from his contribution to a Nietzsche conference at Cérisy-la-Salle the previous year. Derrida retitled his piece *Spurs: Nietzsche's Styles* when it was issued in book form several years later. Derrida had finally turned his attention to the German thinker who was to dominate French philosophy in the 1970s, as Marx, Hegel, and Heidegger had dominated it in previous decades. Heidegger, especially, was still a name to conjure with in the bookstores and cafés of Paris, but Nietzsche's star was rising. Derrida aided this ascent, as did his friend Sarah Kofman, a brilliant young philosopher, and the influential theorist Gilles Deleuze. A celebrated essay by Foucault, "Nietzsche, Genealogy, History," also played a role in the canonizing of Nietzsche as the most radical of spirits. David Allison's anthology *The New Nietzsche* (1977) gathered many of these pathbreaking French interpretations and presented them to an eager American audience.

The complicated nature of Nietzsche's opinions shows up in the many-faceted, even contradictory, way that later eras inherited his thought. Nietzsche, in the years between his death in 1900 and the end of World War I, was adopted as a hero by readers of radically divergent political leanings, from anarchists and socialists to right-wing nationalists. He also, strangely enough, became a favorite author for feminists.[8] Nietzsche's canonization by the Nazis (an unlikely fact, given his opposition to anti-Semitism) was vigorously combated in France by Georges Bataille and Pierre Klossowski, whose writings prepared the way for the later image of Nietzsche as poststructuralist saint.

Derrida in *Spurs* brings to the fore the question of Nietzsche's styles. Nietzsche has always been known as the most dazzling of writers among the philosophers, the most seductive in his rhetoric. In his practice of style, Derrida argues, Nietzsche identifies with women, whom he depicts as inherently seductive creatures—for better and for worse. Derrida adeptly overcomes the image of Nietzsche as a misogynist, an image that had dogged his reputation virtually from the beginning. This, after all, was the man who wrote, "From the beginning, nothing has been more alien, repugnant, and hostile to woman than truth—her great art is the lie, her highest concern is mere appearance and beauty" (*Beyond Good and Evil* section 232). Derrida revealed that Nietzsche was elusive and thought provoking on the question of "woman," as on every other issue that he touched.

Woman as Nietzsche sees her is not merely a shallow, deceptive figure who exists to tempt men into straying from the truth (although she is also that, at times, in his work). Her seductiveness is, for Nietzsche, a virtue. She cannot be pinned down, and this is why dogmatic metaphysics takes such pains to denounce her. She shows up the limitations of the old-fashioned, conventional philosopher (Nietzsche's frequent target). The philosopher cannot deal with woman for the same reason that he cannot deal with poetry, or with artistic illusion. Both woman and art pose a permanent challenge to philosophy's stodgy belief in the accessibility of knowledge, the achievement of certainty. In her role as the Dionysiac artist, freely manipulating appearance and reality, woman escapes all the clumsy denunciations that philosophers, from Socrates on (and including Nietzsche himself at times), cast at her.

What Nietzsche sees as woman's disregard for truth becomes her triumph over the philosophers, who cling to ponderous, inflexible ideas of certainty. Feminine deception turns out to be more actively in the service of life than the dogmatic philosopher's rigid beliefs. Life itself is a woman, Nietzsche announced: a shimmering, ever-changing being whom one loves because of her exciting and unreliable nature.

Freud remarked that Nietzsche might have had more self-knowledge than any other man of the nineteenth century. Derrida in *Spurs* is careful to note Nietzsche's advanced consciousness of his own sensibility, his addiction by turns to both nuance and brutal hyperbole. But Derrida's governing emphasis is on the uncontrollable nature of Nietzsche's oeuvre, the way it far exceeds the original intentions of its author.

Nietzsche's psychological insight has a limit, according to Derrida: he cannot understand himself, because "Nietzsche" is merely a name attached to a vast series of words. Here is Derrida's familiar skepticism again, poised against the image of Nietzsche as a personality. But now the skepticism has been turned inside out, so that (Derrida implies) it has freeing imaginative potential. "I have forgotten my umbrella," scribbled on a random scrap of paper, was one of the seemingly trivial statements found among Nietzsche's effects after his death. What if, Derrida suggested, all of Nietzsche's work could be compared to "I have forgotten my umbrella," a remark whose context we remain utterly ignorant of? Even such an incidental note to oneself may have untold significance (in Nietzsche's case, as in ours). This reliance on the

fragmented and the cryptic as the basis for imaginative newness seems relatively thin. (In later years Derrida suggests that
the secret of the inmost self is similarly cryptic and therefore
resistant to analysis.) Derrida seems to have lost conviction in
the Nietzschean overman, praised in "The Ends of Man" a few
years earlier: the overman has yielded to a humble umbrella.

In *Spurs* Derrida makes much play with the idea of the
umbrella, which unfolds its fabric in order to protect, perhaps
even to disguise. In this way, Derrida brings this modest object
close to Nietzsche's image of woman as a goddess-like being
wrapped in illusory veils. But the umbrella is also phallic, hard
and aggressive. This is the potentially dominant aspect of
the feminine that Nietzsche feared. Women seemed to him
tougher than men, more knowing.

Here we must swerve back to psychological reading and
recognize that Nietzsche remains bound to his peculiar anti-
feminine pathology. In his madness, Nietzsche poignantly declared that "'I' is every name in history," implying that his own
perspective, his discipline of strong reading, colored all he saw;
but also, conversely, that every individual, throughout all
history, has a similarly strong perspective. Nietzsche cannot
be removed from his personal bias and translated into an impersonal theory. In an important sense, the bias makes the
thought.

Derrida's reading of Nietzsche influenced Sarah Kofman, a fellow member of GREPH, the informal organization
of philosophers that they and others had formed in 1975. Kofman was a gifted philosopher who, afflicted by suicidal depression, was to kill herself at the age of sixty, on Nietzsche's
birthday. Her first book on Nietzsche, *Nietzsche and Metaphor*,
appeared in 1972, the same year as the Cérisy symposium
where Derrida delivered the lecture that became *Spurs*. Her

second volume, *The Enigma of Woman*, released in 1980, amplified Derrida's work, establishing the study of gender in Nietzsche as a crucial field for Continental philosophy.

Derrida and Kofman together pioneered an approach that allowed Nietzsche, in his creative originality, to question Freud, rather than to be reductively subjected to Freudian categories. Nietzsche the misogynist feared the castrating woman, the joyless feminist who, he insisted, ought to be raising children rather than penning angry polemics. But Nietzsche's fear of feminism did not prevent him from celebrating woman at other points in his work as a creature who is inherently much stronger and more enlightened than her male opponent. Nietzsche was, then, both misogynist and antimisogynist.

In line with his reading of the woman question in Nietzsche, Derrida treats the philosopher's opinions in other areas as exploratory and often self-contradictory. Derrida sides with Nietzsche's wild streak, the philosopher's Dionysian proliferation of images and stylistic gestures, against Heidegger's staid Apollonian effort to pin Nietzsche down and identify him with two central ideas, the will to power and the eternal return.

Yet slighting the programmatic aspects of Nietzsche, as Derrida does, has its price. In 1968, in the conclusion of "The Ends of Man," Derrida had invoked Nietzsche's overman as a figure who promises the "active forgetting of Being," homelessness, and a nonplace beyond metaphysics. But Nietzsche actually conceives of the overman as the prophetic bearer of a new relation to our lives, a way of teaching humanity to conceive a new beauty, not a way of estranging us from the world as Derrida suggests.

Seeking a new era, Nietzsche aims to vanquish the self-hatred that he claims was established by the Christian idea of the self and its morality. For Derrida, there is no particular distinction between one Western religion or culture and another: all are colored by metaphysics and logocentric prejudice. He therefore fails to grasp the point of the Übermensch's striving. In Derrida the only strife is the impossible effort to cross over to the outside of an all-encompassing system that has "always already" existed. Nietzsche, by contrast, has a firm sense of historical possibility, of how one god replaces another. He therefore understands the political role of the philosopher as Derrida does not. He also underlines the character of the philosopher, who reacts in a personal, motivated way to earlier epochs.

Nietzsche wants a new world in which artistry can take up its rightful place. But this world can only be the work of a philosophical lawgiver with a harsh message: a prophet of order. Such prophecy is very different from Derrida's prophetic tone (in, for example, "Structure, Sign and Play," which, as we saw last chapter, draws on Nietzsche's pronouncements). Derrida delivers a liberating or messianic message, generously (or vaguely) defined. Nietzsche, by contrast, wants a new political order, a world governed by a reimagined system of values.

Nietzsche is, ultimately, interested in imposing meaning, rather than merely following the scattershot, exhilarating sweep of it. To suggest, as Derrida does, that "I have forgotten my umbrella" might occupy the same status in Nietzsche's oeuvre as *Thus Spake Zarathustra* is to fly in the face of the author's own strong will, his intended vision. Uncomfortable with a regime of values that exacts suffering from us by making us deny our own natures, Nietzsche wants a new world that will serve life. Mere dispersal of meaning is not enough.

When he considers Nietzsche's view of women, Derrida

finds a more profitable subject, since Nietzsche knows that here he cannot assert his vision. He finds himself defeated by the sheer foreignness of women, by the labyrinth of the other's sensibility. In recognizing Nietzsche's troubled relation to the feminine, Derrida does Nietzsche studies a great service. Yet here, too, Derrida misses an important aspect of Nietzsche. In *Spurs,* Derrida envisions a Nietzsche identified with the "affirmative woman," a figure who knows no difference between lies and truth and who rejoices in illusion. The "affirmative woman" becomes, for Derrida, a near-messianic character capable of replacing the Übermensch: a notion that inspired a generation of French feminists. But the figure of woman praised in *Spurs,* and by writers like Hélène Cixous and Luce Irigaray, offers a release from responsibility, rather than the new vision of responsibility that Nietzsche championed. Unconstrained by beliefs and values, she represents a spectacular aesthetic freedom, but one that Nietzsche considered too ungovernable to be part of his wished-for future.

As Derrida himself half-admits, such adoration of a utopian femininity remains at the furthest pole from Nietzsche's own attitude, which envisioned the formation of a regime ruled by a strict (if radically innovative) hierarchy, the work of the philosopher-prophet. In claiming that Nietzsche's occasional identification with women is basic to his philosophy, Derrida takes a liberty: he subordinates Nietzsche's actual announced program, his core sense of his mission, to the wilder regions of his text. In this way, he avoids the knowledge of Nietzsche's character, which finally favored rule, not anarchy.

In 1980 Derrida returned to Plato in his book *The Post Card: From Socrates to Freud and Beyond.* In this work, Derrida tries his hand for the first time at creative writing: a bold but failed attempt. Derrida discovered the postcard of his book's title in the Bodleian library at Oxford. It reproduces a thirteenth-century picture of Plato and Socrates with the two sages rather peculiarly positioned. The stately, poised figure labeled "Socrates" sits at a desk, absorbed in writing. Behind him is an anxious little man, "plato," who is poking Socrates in the back with his finger. The image reverses the well-known fact that Socrates wrote nothing, whereas Plato's works were voluminous. Excited by his find, Derrida bought a stack of the Socrates-Plato postcards and proceeded to write breathless, fragmented love letters on them. The postcards were dated from 1977–79 and sent from New Haven, New York, London, Oxford, and the other familiar haunts of Derrida's academic career. The text of these letters became the nearly three-hundred-page opening section of *The Post Card,* called Envois.

The Post Card, written more than a decade before the internet era, is, in effect, a blog *avant la lettre.* Derrida fills his book with tightly veiled personal references that only the addressee of the postcards (presumably his wife, Marguerite) could understand. *The Post Card* is unusually frustrating, even by Derrida's standards. (Future generations will no doubt be mystified by Richard Rorty's judgment that in this book Derrida achieves an "incredible richness of texture" rivalling Proust, Joyce, and Sterne.)[9] At one point in *The Post Card,* Derrida gives us a feckless image of impossible desire: "When I receive nothing from you I am like a dying tortoise, still alive, on its back. You can see it erect its impotence toward the sky" (*Post* 109). The Derridean tortoise points its wilting, ineffectual logos at the heavens inhabited by the immortal philosophers: such is Derrida's joke against himself. (He evidently has in mind the tortoise that supports the world in Hindu and Stoic cosmology.)

Derrida, commenting on the medieval picture of Socrates writing with Plato standing behind him, explores the
possibility that Plato is sexually molesting his revered mentor:
"For the moment, myself, I tell you that I see *Plato* getting an
erection in *Socrates'* back and see the insane hubris of his prick,
an interminable, disproportionate erection . . . slowly sliding,
still warm, under *Socrates'* right leg" (18). In addition to
sodomizing Socrates, Plato, we are told, is riding a skateboard
(17); also, he is a tram conductor (17); and finally, he "wants to
emit . . . to sow the entire earth, to send the same fertile card to
everyone" (28). "Imagine the day," muses Derrida, "when we
will be able to send sperm by post card" (24).

Derrida's fantasies may seem infantile or merely random,
but they bear a relation to the Platonic idea that philosophy
sows a seed of truth in the listener or reader. Socrates, whom
Plato saw as the father of his discourse, his logos, has become
a source of wisdom inherited by everyone who reads and seriously ponders the Platonic dialogues. Derrida also alludes to a
passage in Plato's Second Letter (a text whose authenticity is
disputed) in which we are told, "There is not and will not be
any written work of Plato's own. What is now called his is the
work of a Socrates grown young and beautiful." Plato wants,
then, to become Socrates; or, perhaps, he wants Socrates and
himself to be a single person. (Derrida, disappointingly, pretends to see this desire of Plato's as a wish for revenge on
Socrates: this is a parody of psychology rather than the real
thing.)

Derrida's *Post Card* presents an idiosyncratic version of
philosophical esotericism, and as such it responds to Plato.
There is a long tradition that Plato's true teaching consists not
in his published writings, stunningly beautiful as they are, but
rather in the hidden lore passed down orally among his disci-

ples. But Derrida's esotericism, a seedy half-opaque series of glimpses, remains far removed from Plato's. In *The Post Card,* a book that implicitly argues against Plato's desire for beauty and permanence, it is not the ideal that counts, but rather the transitory: the trash and ephemera of the moment. Thus we receive the bewilderingly intimate but at the same time strangely abstract and unmeaning details that Derrida hands over in his meandering text. Derrida's pursuit of distraction stands starkly against Plato's noble desire for immortal children, the offspring of mind (164–65).

The mammoth *Post Card* encompasses not just Plato and Socrates, but also Freud. When Derrida turns from Plato to Freud, he makes a connection between two thinkers who do their work in the space between myth and reason, between the aura of religion and the stringent work of philosophical reflection. Both are fundamentally concerned with the human psyche. But with Freud, as with Plato, Derrida substitutes the impersonal workings of language for the thinker's psychological insights.

In his treatment of *Beyond the Pleasure Principle* in *The Post Card,* Derrida opts for a championing of the unconscious, with its powerful current of regressive force that frustrates the conscious ego, over the drama of the individual psyche. This interpretive choice forces Derrida to ignore the most interesting and relevant aspect of Freud's *Beyond:* the debate that Freud pursues between, on the one hand, the regressive or conservative character of drives and, on the other, the push toward development on the part of both societies and individuals.

Beyond the Pleasure Principle, published in 1920, is one of Freud's major metapsychological works. In it, Freud advances the concepts he needs to explain the psyche: eros, repression, the death drive, and the pleasure and reality principles. Freud begins by mentioning a puzzling fact: that the victims of traumatic neurosis, including the so-called war neuroses, return time and again in their dreams to the original disruptive event, the trauma that has ruined their lives. Instead of avoiding trauma, they seek it out and repeat it in imagination. Haunted by images of battlefield carnage, mutilation, and violence, the soldiers of World War I posed a severe test for Freud's ideas about the mind as a wishful mechanism. Freud, as he began writing, recognized this obstacle in the way of his theory of the psyche. According to Freud, wish fulfillment is our main psychic strategy: we recast experience so that it gives us pleasure rather than pain. Dreams, for example, are wish-fulfillment devices, as Freud triumphantly announced in his monumental *Interpretation of Dreams* (1899).

The mind, according to Freud's early theory, is a massive "rewrite" machine, editing out or revising anything unpleasant. Only when reality unavoidably steps in do we reluctantly agree to negotiate with it. So the baby, Freud says in the *Interpretation of Dreams,* busily hallucinates satisfaction when its mother's breast is temporarily unavailable; the infant's lips mime sucking gestures as it smiles with beatific satisfaction. But eventually the power of wish fulfillment runs out. As the baby becomes suddenly, ravenously hungry, the allure of the illusory breast fades and real need intrudes. With luck, the mother's actual breast comes back in response to her infant's wails. Reality proves to be better, after all, than mere fantasy.

Beyond the Pleasure Principle transforms the wish-fulfillment scenario of the *Interpretation of Dreams.* In the *Interpretation,* the infant was able to make the mother return as a supplier of nourishment. Renewed crying gets the breast, which is demonstrably superior to fantasy. In *Beyond,* by contrast, Freud describes a way of making the mother return as a source of symbolic satisfaction rather than an answer to actual need.

Freud has been observing a small child, he tells us (in actuality his grandson Ernst, one and a half years old). "This good little boy," Freud writes, "had an occasional disturbing habit of taking any small objects he could get hold of and throwing them away from him into a corner, under the bed, and so on. . . . As he did he gave vent to a long, drawn-out 'o-o-o-o,' accompanied by an expression of interest and satisfaction" (*Beyond* 13). Freud soon realizes that the baby's "o-o-o-o" stands for the German word *fort* (gone), and that "the only use he made of any of his toys was to play 'gone' with them" (14). (Parents will recognize in Freud's description the energetic interest on the part of small children in making things, including themselves, disappear.)

The game then acquires another stage. "The child," Freud writes, "had a wooden reel with a piece of string tied round it. . . . What he did was to hold the reel by the string and very skillfully throw it over the edge of his curtained cot." This disappearance is accompanied by the baby's customary "fort." But when he pulls the reel back out of the cot, making it reappear, he utters a new word: *da* (there). Freud notes that the reappearance of the reel causes more satisfaction than its disappearance (14).

Freud's fort-da game has occasioned much commentary. Often, it is taken as the core scene of Freud's *Beyond the Pleasure Principle,* its last word. Derrida takes it as such, and spends most of his time reading the fort-da episode, at the expense of the rest of Freud's book. But Freud in fact has some ambivalence toward the fort-da game: he doubts its capacity to explain human symbol making.

In *The Post Card*'s discussion of Freud's fort-da scenario, Derrida remarks, "The child identifies himself with the mother since he disappears as she does, and makes her return with himself, by making himself return without making anything but himself, her in himself, return. All the while remaining, as close as possible, at the side of the PP which (who) never absents itself (himself), and thus provides (for himself) the greatest pleasure. . . . He makes himself disappear, he masters himself symbolically . . . and he makes himself reappear henceforth without a mirror, in his disappearance itself, maintaining himself like his mother at the other end of the line" (*Post* 319). Derrida reads baby Ernst's game as a triumph: the infant has become the master of symbolism, maneuvering himself and his mother in tandem.

But according to Freud, the fort-da game has its limitations. As he notes later on in *Beyond*, the repetition of an experience of satisfaction (like the return of the reel to the baby's grasp) is not enough (*Beyond* 51). The infant will progress to the effort to make a baby of its own to give to the mother, a project that, "carried out with tragic seriousness, fails shamefully" (22). The infant's desire to become mature, to be a little parent himself, cannot be mere repetition; it is not regressive. A more sophisticated form of satisfaction is being aimed at, as we develop our childish ideas of grown-up success. The baby's incorporation of the mother in himself, celebrated by Derrida, must inevitably prove partial. The mother is a separate being, and the child must seek to please her (which boys rather implausibly attempt to do, as Freud notes, by trying to make a baby for the mother). She is not merely symbolic, despite Derrida's implication.

Freud notes that although they repeat what has made an impression on them in real life, children "abreact the strength of the impression [that is, discharge it through action] and, as one might put it, make themselves master of the situation. But on the other hand," he adds, "it is obvious that all their play is

influenced by a wish that dominates them the whole time—
the wish to be grown-up and to be able to do what grown-up
people do" (16). In the phrase "on the other hand" lies much of
the concealed drama of *Beyond the Pleasure Principle.* The infant produces his own satisfaction via the fort-da game. But
instead of finding satisfaction in satisfaction, he demands (we
demand) more: newer, more complicated forms of achievement. Wanting to be a grown-up means intuiting that there
are adult forms of self-punishment and self-reward, beckon-
ing from a realm beyond the easier pleasures and pains of
babyhood. Becoming the master of presence and absence, in
the manner of the baby playing fort-da, is no substitute for
becoming grown-up. The fort-da game is not, then, the definitive instance of our ways of creating meaning, as Derrida
claims it is.

The impulse to maturity is basic in Freud. Late in *Beyond
the Pleasure Principle,* Freud quotes Goethe's Mephistopheles
on the force in humans that "presses ever unconditionally
onwards [ungebändigt immer vorwärts dringt]" (51). Framed
by neurotic resistance and repression, the ambitious personality wants not greater quantities of pleasure but, like Goethe's
Faust, more sublime and difficult ones. Wish fulfillment has
yielded to a higher aim: a push toward the less accessible, more
finely rewarding goals.

Freud cannot explain such ambition, but he knows that
it poses a problem for any theory that bases itself on repetition.
He therefore introduces a new element that battles against the
regressive leaning of the death drive, its wish to restore an earlier state of things: the wish for the new. This wish he calls eros,
the drive that opposes death. Eros in *Beyond the Pleasure Principle,* and elsewhere in late Freud, begins in sexuality. It aspires
restlessly to the achievement of more complex forms of social

organization, greater plurality and sophistication. Freud's eros is, in essence, the force of human development.

We do not have Freud's essay on sublimation; he destroyed what he wrote of it. Sublimation, which would account for why we often prefer harder and more complex forms of symbolic satisfaction to easier ones, was Freud's greatest stumbling block. The problem of sublimation is related to a question concerning the therapeutic process, which works (when it does) through the patient's conviction of having made progress, of having figured something out. Progress in therapy takes the form of increased knowledge, rather than mere recovery of a lost source of pleasure. In effect, knowledge becomes a new cause of enjoyment; and more sophisticated knowledge satisfies more strongly, or convincingly. Therapy requires a basic form of sublimation: thinking and talking about a problem rather than acting it out for neurotic satisfaction. Derrida's treatment of Freud, by ignoring the question of why and how Freud's therapy works, skirts the issue that was always central to him. If we fail to attend to it, the point of Freud's discovery is lost.

It is telling that Derrida brings Plato and Freud together in *The Post Card*. The two are in some ways similar. Plato and Freud are united by the fact that both founded disciplines or institutions: philosophy and psychoanalysis. Writing on both, Derrida slights the institutional aspect of their thought. That is, he fails to consider Plato's overriding concern with the (usually unwelcome) place of the philosopher in his society. And he rarely mentions Freud's role as the champion of psychoanalysis, surrounded by a hostile world that clings defensively to smooth pieties and outworn creeds.

Because he neglects their sense of disciplinary mission, Derrida also neglects another bond between Plato and Freud,

their shared emphasis on education. Both look toward the
improvement or development of the individual. The therapeutic bent of both thinkers, their wish for a movement upward toward psychic health, stands in contrast to Derrida's
own emphasis on the static, seemingly interminable continuity of certain paradoxes: the infection of speech by writing, the
corruption of mastery by dispersion of meaning, and the interruption of the self-assured ego by randomness.

According to Derrida, Freud's work pictures our memory, and therefore our experience, as an *archive*, a jumbled cat-
alog vulnerable to constant breakdowns, interruptions, and
confusions. (This argument forms the center of his later book
on Freud, *Archive Fever* [1995].) In the form of the archive, the
unconscious stalks us, looming insidiously behind all our accounts of ourselves and obstructing our hope for coherent,
verifiable selfhood. Derrida is right about the corrosive power
of the unconscious in Freud. But he ignores the fact that
Freud's aim was not to destroy the force of all narratives by
submitting them to the unconscious, but rather to distinguish
among our stories of ourselves. Freud as therapist encouraged
the possibility of a (necessarily fictive) coherence, which he
identified with health: a strong story of the self.[10] We decide
that certain accounts, or tales, define our identity. And in
doing so, we submit such stories to the imaginative equivalent
of reality testing.

As I have pointed out, Austin, Plato, and Nietzsche, as
well as Freud, adhere to accounts of the self's motives. For each
of these thinkers, what we expect from and demand of others,
as well as ourselves, determines the truth of our words and actions. This diagnostic aspect present in all four authors proves
uncongenial to Derrida because it implies that strong meanings have a basis in personality, in the peculiarities of self-

definition. Plato's boy-loving rhetorician, Austin's bigamist or welsher, Nietzsche's manipulative woman: all are minor case studies essential to these thinkers' arguments. Instead of focusing on the motives ascribed to such characters and on our reaction to them, Derrida emphasizes writing itself (in Plato), "woman" herself (in Nietzsche), and the prevalence of misfiring (in Austin). In his consideration of Freud, Derrida declares that the network of unconscious signification, rather than the individual's grappling with meaning, is Freud's great discovery. There is a pattern here: with Freud, as with the others, Derrida elides the question of character in favor of the workings of différance, a force that stands behind and outside us. He avoids the core, psychological insight.

Despite Derrida's implication, all narratives cannot, and should not, be seen as equally dubious in the face of the unconscious or the random disseminations of writing. Philosophers from Plato to Freud have staked the very identity of their thought on the role of a powerful and capable narrative: a self-making that can be proven fit, the work of what seems like necessity. Such a story is Plato's myth of the charioteer; and such is Freud's account of eros and death. In both, psyche and philosophical impulse are joined. Derrida's separation of the two comes at a cost.

IV

Gadamer, Celan, de Man, Heidegger

"America is deconstruction." Derrida's pronouncement certainly seemed to be true in the 1980s, when he spent much of his time lecturing in the United States. He would land on a Saturday afternoon at JFK and be met by his Yale colleagues Paul de Man and J. Hillis Miller. An enthusiastic visitor to New York, he loved Brooklyn Heights and Poets' Alley in Central Park. And there was the desolate, stirring landscape of Laguna Beach, where he lived while teaching at the University of California at Irvine. Invoking Central Park together with the southern California coast, Derrida wrote, "Almost out loud I speak to all the poets in Poets' Alley, cousins of my friends the birds of Laguna Beach" (*Counterpath* 101–2). The 1980s were in many ways the most eventful decade of Jacques Derrida's life, marked by his transatlantic evangelism on behalf of deconstruction—and by the posthumous scandals surrounding the careers of Paul de Man and of Heidegger.[1]

The eighties began for Derrida with a major disappointment. He had been nominated for a prestigious chair at the University of Nanterre, where he would have succeeded the famous pioneer of hermeneutics Paul Ricoeur, who was retiring. (Derrida had been Ricoeur's assistant at the Sorbonne in the early sixties.) But the support for Derrida was not unanimous, and Alice Saunier-Seité, the French minister of education, denied him the position (and, in fact, abolished the chair). This failure stung Derrida, who dwelled bitterly on his rejection until his death. He felt ostracized by the French university system, which refused to give him the kind of professorship he deserved (he was considered for other such positions after Nanterre, only to be turned down). His response was to reorient his academic life around North America rather than Europe. He had been teaching at Yale for a few weeks every year since 1975; he now increased his presence in America, lecturing across the United States. When J. Hillis Miller moved from Yale to Irvine, Derrida went with him. At the same time, he began teaching at New York University. Derrida was still preoccupied with European thinkers, but his professional life had shifted to the new world.

In this chapter I focus on Derrida's encounters with three of the European figures who drew his attention in the 1980s, as he settled into his new role as ambassador of advanced thought, sent by the Continent to America: Hans-Georg Gadamer, Paul de Man, and Martin Heidegger. All did their work during Derrida's own lifetime; one of them was his close friend. These three thinkers become test cases for Derrida's claim that there is something inalienable and mysterious about the self, apt to be violated by an outside interpreter's judgment. Gadamer's dependence on dialogue means, for Derrida, that he fails to respect the foreignness of the other person. (This is

the divide between Derrida and Gadamer in their readings of
Paul Celan.) With de Man and Heidegger, the personality of
the thinker himself is at issue. In refraining from judging de
Man and Heidegger, Derrida holds himself to a different,
higher standard than that of the popular press, which was
eager to expose their connections with Nazism. But Derrida's
refusal, eschewing psychological and ethical criteria, comes at
the cost of explanatory power. In the instance of de Man, Derrida is tempted to imagine a heroic inner life for his friend.
Giving in to this temptation, he inadvertently demonstrates
the impossibility of avoiding a myth of the self. Finally, Derrida cannot keep de Man's inwardness cryptic: he tells de
Man's life story.

       An important political event occurred in 1981. Czech po-
lice arrested Derrida in Prague, where he had gone to teach a
seminar that had not been approved by the Communist au-
thorities. With grim and ironic appropriateness, his Czech persecutors planted drugs on him while he was at Franz Kafka's
grave. Accused of drug smuggling, Derrida landed in a Czech
jail, where he was stripped naked, photographed, and threatened. Derrida, the Czech government knew, had actively
protested the Communist regime and had even organized a
group with the scholar Jean-Pierre Vernant and others, the Jan
Hus Association, in support of Czech dissidents. Still the rebel,
Derrida took a risky stand for the intellectual freedom of his
wife's homeland. He was released only after the intervention of
François Mitterand's government.

       The second important event of 1981 for Derrida was his
debate with Heidegger's most prominent disciple, Hans-Georg
Gadamer, that April at the Goethe Institut in Paris. Gadamer
was born in 1900, when Kafka was seventeen years old and
Queen Victoria was still alive. He grew up in Germany before

World War I and, after studying with Heidegger in Freiburg, became one of his nation's best-known philosophers. His lifetime would span the century: he continued writing well into his eighties and died in 2001 at age 101.

Gadamer was the world's leading philosopher of hermeneutics. Simply defined, hermeneutics is the study of interpretation. (The word derives from Hermes, the Greek messenger god.) And interpretation, according to Gadamer, is a kind of conversation: the development of understanding that occurs whenever two people talk to each other, or when a reader confronts a book.

Gadamer, in sharp contrast to Derrida, was practical in his rhetoric and his interests. His masterwork, *Truth and Method* (1960), can be readily comprehended by undergraduates. He insisted throughout his career that the desire to understand and to come to agreement with others is at the core of human life. Such an argument rankled Derrida, given the latter's emphasis on the distances implied in the words we speak. Derrida stayed rigidly opposed to Gadamer's idea that meaning unfolds gradually through the give and take of dialogue.[2] Instead, for Derrida, our statements remain fragmented and random, and we ourselves are therefore intractably aloof. (The de Man affair leads Derrida to his most pointed statement of this position.)

Gadamer's Paris speech in 1981 is a meticulous and expansive treatment of interpretation and understanding. Gadamer begins by asserting that "the ability to understand is a fundamental endowment of man, one that sustains his communal life with others and, above all, one that takes place by way of language and the partnership of conversation" (*Dialogue* 21). Gadamerian conversation is based on the temptation, to which most of us gladly yield, to compromise our habits and beliefs by becoming seriously involved with others. The willing exposure of self that occurs in such exchanges is for Gadamer the standing risk, and source of gain, of our existence. In Gadamer's account language is not about the truth or falsehood of propositions, as Derrida charges. Instead, our words aim at a sharing of insight.

Yet language, for all its commonality, Gadamer adds, "never touches upon the last, insurmountable secret of the individual person" (22). A main issue for Gadamer, then, is the difference between the common nature of meaning, built up by the conversation that joins us together, and the fundamentally elusive, even secret, identity possessed by every individual. This private identity cannot be fully comprehended in our language, but it nevertheless shows itself every time we speak. When he states that such a "last . . . secret" cannot be disclosed yet can be demonstrated in language, Gadamer distinguishes himself from Derrida, for whom the secret can neither be disclosed nor demonstrated.

Gadamer's speech from his debate with Derrida undertakes a careful examination of different cases of interpretation: reading a poem; interpreting the law; giving testimony in court; psychoanalyzing a patient. Gadamer shows himself attentive to the practical differences among such everyday situations in a way that is deeply foreign to Derrida and that poses an implicit challenge to him. As was apparent in his treatment of Austin, Derrida rebels against the power of context to define our words.

Gadamer's final example is that of the psychoanalyst and the patient. The analyst, Gadamer states, makes the patient's statements and actions intelligible by pulling rank: by going behind the patient's back and resorting to a subtext that explains what's really going on. This sort of decoding is an anomaly in interpretation, Gadamer insists. In particular, the patient's dream, which provides material for the analyst, occupies the opposite extreme from a literary work. In a poem or work of fiction, "every word 'sits' there in such a way that it appears almost without possibility of substitution, and in a certain way it really can have no substitute" (49). A successful artwork cannot be translated fully; it surprises even its author with a newness of meaning that resists ready summary. An artistic or literary statement, Gadamer claims, therefore stands in contrast to the words of a neurotic patient. The latter can and must be decoded in pursuit of an underlying meaning, as art cannot be without harmful reduction.

Gadamer's distinction between the case of the neurotic analysand and that of the writer might have stung Derrida, who was so adept at decoding the texts he chose to discuss, studying them for signs of logocentric bias. Derrida plays the analyst, and all of Western culture is his sick patient, afflicted with the disease of metaphysics. Gadamer implicitly asks whether Derrida is sufficiently ready to learn from the books he takes up: whether he is willing to let them instruct him, rather than merely inspecting them for symptoms.

Derrida's response to Gadamer in 1981 consists of a brief, disengaged series of comments. There is, perhaps, a hint of disdain in them. As Gadamer later said, Derrida missed the point of Gadamer's speech—as it seemed to Gadamer, deliberately. Derrida's remarks, made the day after Gadamer's lecture, were unusually abbreviated, lasting only a few minutes. In this speech, Derrida mainly claims that the Gadamerian idea of interpretive good will, the effort I make to understand a person's or a book's intended meaning, is bound up with Kant's notion of good will: the impulse to aim at unconditional moral values. Derrida, normally so generous, and prolix, in his comments on his interlocutors, treats Gadamer as if the two have little to say to each other. At least this is how Gadamer took Derrida's words.[3]

The debate between Gadamer and Derrida, which has often been called a nonencounter, founders on the gap between these two remarkable thinkers. Derrida constructs a version of Western thought in which consciousness wants to have meaning under full control (the logocentric imperative). Such control can only be broken, according to Derrida, by a realization of the radical, ungovernable drift of language. Metaphysics is answered by skepticism: or, rather, an image of it is answered, since skepticism has remade metaphysics for its own purposes.

For Gadamer, in contrast to Derrida, the philosophical tradition begins with and ultimately comes back to Socratic dialogue: a format in which conversational partners, even as they strive against each other, try together to establish a shared sense of an important subject (say, justice or virtue). We cannot lock up meaning, and we do not really want to. What we want instead is to subject ourselves to an ongoing process of discovery: the dialogue with a book or person that remains guided by a shared interest. Even the most obscure works of art enter into such a conversation with us, according to Gadamer. Despite Gadamer's hostility toward psychoanalysis, which is motivated by his wariness concerning displays of expertise, he believes in the therapeutic power of interpretation. The work of art knows, and imparts this knowledge without insisting on mastery (as the psychoanalyst does, according to Gadamer).

Gadamer's Heideggerian emphasis on the uncanny power of the work of art is not completely foreign to Derrida. Indeed, Derrida's essays on the poet Paul Celan share a patient angle of approach with Gadamer's dignified meditation on Celan, entitled "Who Am I and Who Are You?" But whereas Gadamer pictures Celan's difficult poetic texts asking questions of the reader and the reader answering back, Derrida underlines the self-sufficiency of Celan's hermetic language: the poet's barbed challenge to anyone who would presume to understand his work fully. Otherness for Derrida is not shared as in Gadamer but instead utterly foreign, frustrating the reader.

In Derrida's reading of Celan, then, the self remains cryptic and unspoken. The difference between Gadamer and Derrida on Celan sums up the gap between these two thinkers. Gadamer prizes understanding even in the most difficult circumstances; Derrida favors an avant-garde opacity that defeats us. Celan may let us into his work, but only to a degree, Derrida asserts. He uses his tough combination of foreign tongues, made-up words, and crystalline, spiky images as a shibboleth: a way of strictly controlling how, and to what degree, he may be read. Gadamer, by contrast, emphasizes the ways in which Celan reaches toward his reader. We grapple with shared hermeneutic tasks as we work in the bleak shadows that loom over Celan's poetry: the unprecedented devastation of World War II and the Shoah. What seems to be the relentless obscurity of Celan is, for Gadamer, actually an effort to speak and to be heard.

Gadamer seems to know Celan's sense of his own difficulty better than Derrida does. For Celan, difficulty is paradoxically an effort to connect to the world. Celan remarks in his Meridian lecture that the poem is like an individual, "alone and on the road": "The poem wants to reach the Other, it needs this Other, it needs a vis à vis. It searches it out and addresses it. Each thing, each person is a form of the Other for the poem, as it makes for this Other."[4]

Finally, Gadamer is truer than Derrida to the basic im-

pulse of a writer like Celan: his need for an other, for someone
he can reach toward and make understand. Derrida's more hermetic version of Celan occupies an important place for him; it
suggests that our most intimate identity is finally illegible,
closed off from knowledge. The insistence that we remain unknown means, once again, that the psyche is protected from
interpretation. Derrida resists psychology in defense of the (as
he sees it, necessarily hidden) person. The life story of Paul de
Man will put this Derridean idea to the test.

In the year 1984, Derrida later remarked, "I traveled and
wrote the most in my life" (*Counterpath* 209). "In barely a few
months there was Yale, New York, Berkeley, Irvine, Cornell,
Oxford (Ohio), Tokyo, Frankfurt, Bologna, Urbino, Rome,
Seattle, Lisbon ..." This was quite a fate for the young man who
had never spent a night away from El Biar, Algeria, until the
age of eighteen. Derrida's ceaseless travel schedule was, perhaps, compensation for the sense of provinciality he endured
as a teenager in North Africa.

Of all Derrida's travels during 1984, his trip to Yale was
the most significant. On this occasion Derrida gave a course in
memory of his dear friend Paul de Man, who had died in December 1983. As it turned out, de Man's posthumous fate, the
scandal that would surround his name a few years later, was to
prove a pivotal event, perhaps the most significant moment in
Derrida's career. The theme of the hidden self, alluded to in
Derrida's writings on Celan and in his nonencounter with
Gadamer, reveals itself fully in his readings of de Man.

Derrida's course on de Man took place on the top floor
of Harkness tower: one of the oldest and most fragile buildings on the Yale campus. A tiny, antiquated elevator spared
students and professors from the ascent up the long, winding
stone staircase. The faithful, de Man's and Derrida's, were

ready. Then Derrida began, speaking of course in French (later, he was to learn English quite well, but this was 1984). "*Le* mémoire . . ." Derrida intoned. "*La* mémoire; *le* mémoire."

Derrida was playing on two French words. The masculine noun, *le mémoire,* means essay; the feminine *la mémoire,* memory. The two things were opposed yet also somehow the same, since our memory depends upon a trace or marking, a note left in the mind. Derrida drew his theme of writing and memory from "A Note Upon the Mystic Writing Pad," the essay by Freud that he had, many years earlier, discussed in *Writing and Difference.* The wordplay with *mémoire* was a nervous verbal fiddling on Derrida's part, yet moving as well in its devotion to de Man. Derrida circled around the great critic's memory without quite touching him. In his reaction to the de Man of 1987, whose life had become a scandal, Derrida would more closely approach the question of de Man's inwardness: what he kept secret about himself, what he refused to make public. Forced to interpret what de Man concealed, Derrida would show the limits of his respectful caution before the hidden self.

Famous for his mild yet slightly scurrilous wit, de Man was also known as an unfailingly kind and helpful advisor. He had dozens of dissertation students at any given time, and he helped them into good positions all around the country. Most of all—and this was said in hushed, unbelieving tones—he was honored for never sleeping with his female students. Clearly, de Man was the exemplar of a higher morality.

The posthumous adulation of Paul de Man came crashing down when a Belgian student named Ortwin de Graef discovered in 1987, three years after de Man's death, that he had written collaborationist articles for the Belgian newspaper *Le Soir* during the Nazi occupation of that country. In one of the

Le Soir pieces, de Man speculated coolly about the consequences for Europe if it were to be deprived of its Jews: nothing bad, since the loss of millions of Jews would have no real effect on European culture. Derrida, electrified by the shocking news of de Man's willing proximity to Nazism, immediately began a campaign, conducted largely by telephone, to rally professors of literature and philosophy to the defense of de Man. For Derrida, journalists were the enemy. They hated real thought, and they would be eager to bring down de Man, one of our great thinkers, by exposing him as a Nazi sympathizer.

Newsweek did indeed publish a photograph of de Man next to one of marching storm troopers, and the fact that the youthful de Man was never a Nazi, but rather an author of pro-collaborationist articles, was forgotten by some journalists. David Lehman, a talented poet and critic, published a book, *Signs of the Times* (1988), in which he (implausibly and unfortunately) proposed an affinity between the methods of deconstruction and de Man's wartime apologetics for German fascism.

Derrida was determined to attack the journalists' treatment of de Man, mercilessly if need be, before they won the battle over deconstruction, which was de Man's legacy and his own. It is no exaggeration to say that, for Derrida, journalists were the real Nazis. Derrida makes this analogy explicit in the course of his lengthy essay on the de Man affair, "Paul de Man's War."

During this time, if you weren't with Derrida you were against him. Almost as soon as the scandal broke, he started a petition against the press coverage of de Man and energetically set about organizing a conference on the *Le Soir* articles. In a published essay, Derrida accused de Man's dear friend Harold Bloom of acting more reprehensibly than de Man himself in his writings for *Le Soir.* Bloom had suggested that de Man's wartime actions, being a matter of personal conscience, should not become the subject matter of petition drives and academic conferences. The dispute ended relations between Derrida and Bloom, who had previously been affectionate friends.[5]

The quarrel over de Man's legacy was more than merely an argument among his friends. By the time of his death, de Man had become a presiding figure in literary study. In the eighties, comparative literature at Yale was, in large part, a private canon engineered by de Man's charisma and kept in place by his amazing ability to secure teaching positions for his PhD students. Graduate students in comp lit, at least those under de Man's direct supervision, were encouraged to read Rousseau, Kant, Hölderlin, Hegel, Schlegel, Nietzsche, Heidegger, Wordsworth, Walter Benjamin—and not too much else. The focus was on certain touchstones in the works of these writers: the passages that demonstrated the "unreadability," or self-undoing capacity, of language. As with Derrida, skepticism was triumphant. De Man was selling a formula, one that was fairly easy to learn and reproduce. One's reading was meant to demonstrate a theoretical point: that it was impossible for language to make reliable claims about the world.

Before his death, de Man told at least one close friend that he knew that disturbing revelations about his past would be printed after he was gone; he wanted those he loved to be prepared for some disagreeable, even traumatic, news. He had reason to worry. De Man in his book *Blindness and Insight* had described the biography of authors as a "waste of time" (*Blindness* 35). At the time he wrote those words, he surely knew that the facts of his own biography, when they were eventually discovered, would change everything about the way he was read.

The lightning-quick German invasion of Belgium took place in May 1940. De Man's articles in *Le Soir* appeared shortly afterwards, between December 1940 and November 1942. De Man's uncle, Hendrik de Man, had been the leader of the Belgian socialist party. In 1940, after the Nazi invasion, he dissolved the party, bowing gladly to German control. "For the working classes and for socialism, this collapse of a decrepit world is, far from a disaster, a deliverance," Hendrik de Man wrote (*Responses* 159). The twenty-one-year-old Paul de Man joined his uncle's celebration of the German victory. In the course of his writings for *Le Soir,* which consist largely of cultural commentary and book reviews, he urged the acceptance of German domination and applauded the demise of liberal democracy as the necessary price for a renewal of Belgian national greatness. One de Man article, from March 1941, is overtly anti-Semitic, and it created great obstacles for de Man's defenders. In this essay, entitled "The Jews and Contemporary Literature," de Man sees the Jews as a "foreign force," alien to European culture even when they seem most assimilated: a classic anti-Semitic canard.

I was still at Yale, de Man's intellectual home, at the time of these revelations, and I remember the range of responses. A few students who had never liked de Man reacted to the news with cold satisfaction, but most were shocked. De Man had seemed so simpatico: generous, friendly, always with a sly twinkle in his eye.

At de Man's funeral service, held in January 1984 at the Yale Art Gallery, he was eulogized as, in effect, a saint of literary criticism. Barbara Johnson, the influential deconstructionist and student of de Man who had just been hired at Harvard (a watershed moment, since until then Harvard had been largely resistant to French theory), stated solemnly, "In a profession full of fakeness, he was real." Another professor, Ellen Burt, praised de Man as follows: "He had no time to waste being seduced, disquieted, or threatened by women" (*Signs* 143–44).

I was present at the memorial service for de Man, as were virtually all of the students and professors in Yale's comparative literature, French, and English departments. Many of us were struck by the fervent devotion, almost religious in tone, shown to the dead de Man by his disciples. They would carry his work on, in his memory; he had shown the way for all future reading. Derrida spoke, movingly, in French. He remarked on de Man's "generosity, his lucidity . . . the ever so gentle force of his thought: since that morning in 1966 when I met him at a breakfast table in Baltimore. . . . From then on," Derrida added, "nothing has ever come between us, not even a hint of disagreement" (*Yale* 323–24).

In stating that there had been no disagreements between himself and de Man, Derrida performed a tender revision of the historical record. As they met and chatted eagerly at that 1966 breakfast in Baltimore, during Derrida's first visit to the United States, Derrida and de Man learned that they had both been working on Rousseau's *Essay on the Origin of Language,* a little-studied text. The next year, 1967, Derrida would publish his epic reading of Rousseau in *Of Grammatology;* and de Man, in an essay that appeared three years later, would loudly voice his differences from Derrida.

In his eulogy, Derrida touchingly remarked on de Man's heroic good spirits in the face of death. He quoted from a letter de Man had written during his final illness, in which he remarked with cheerful self-possession, "All of this . . . seems prodigiously interesting to me and I'm enjoying myself a lot. I knew it all along but it is being borne out: death gains a great deal, as they say, when one gets to know it close up" (*Yale* 326). De Man's resolve in his last days was extraordinarily noble, capable of profoundly affecting even his severest critics.

Derrida concluded his speech at the funeral service with a story of de Man, Derrida, and Derrida's son Pierre "driving through the streets of Chicago after a jazz concert." De Man and Pierre Derrida were discussing the *âme* of a violin: the piece of wood that supports the bridge. In French *âme* is also the word for "soul"—and this was a soulful occasion. Derrida had not realized that his friend de Man was an "experienced musician":

> I didn't know why at that moment I was so strangely moved and unsettled in some dim recess by the conversation I was listening to: no doubt it was due to the word "soul" which always speaks to us at the same time of life and of death and makes us dream of immortality, like the argument of the lyre in the *Phaedo*.
>
> And I will always regret, among so many other things, that I never again spoke of any of this with Paul. How was I to know that one day I would speak of that moment, that music and that soul without him, before you who must forgive me for doing it just now so poorly, so painfully when already everything is painful, so painful? (326)

Despite the seeming lack of soul in de Man's criticism, his deliberately icy and clinical tone, he was a practitioner of music—like Socrates before his death, as recounted in Plato's *Phaedo*.

Derrida did not yet know in January 1984 that *âme*, "soul," had been an important word for the youthful Paul de

Man. In his *Le Soir* articles, de Man gladly evoked the passions of the *völkisch* heart, writing of "the Hitlerian soul and the German soul which, from the start, were so close together" (*Le Soir*, October 28, 1942). Perhaps because of this early misstep, he was later to avoid the language of the soul, thinking it naïve and dangerous.

Knowingly or not, Derrida in his funeral speech was echoing not just Plato and the young, pro-Hitler de Man, but also the distinguished Harvard professor Reuben Brower. At the beginning of the sixties, Brower tried to secure a professorship for de Man at Harvard, where de Man was already teaching in an immensely influential course: Hum 6, Brower's innovative introduction to close reading (or, as Brower called it, "slow reading"). Brower wrote in January 1960 to his colleagues Harry Levin and Renato Poggioli that "Paul has what I can only call *soul:* for him aesthetic and moral choices are not separable, he has some of the fine Gallic feeling that a critical position is a position of combat. This means of course that he is sometimes obstinate, sometimes 'prickly.' But aren't all good men 'prickly' at his age?"[6] A peculiar combination of battle-ready obstinacy and amiability characterized both Derrida and de Man, drawing the two friends together. Derrida's own combative nature appears more than anywhere else in his handling of the de Man affair.

De Man had counted upon the devotion of his friends during his long career in America, beginning with his arrival in the United States in 1948. While working as a clerk in a bookshop in Grand Central Station, he was adopted by the *Partisan Review* crowd, including Mary McCarthy and the *Partisan Review*'s editor, William Phillips. A letter from McCarthy to the poet Theodore Weiss at Bard College began de Man's career in the American academy. After the stint at Bard, de

Man moved (with the student he had married, the daughter of a U.S. Senator) to Boston. (He had left a wife and children in Argentina, apparently without obtaining a divorce [*Signs* 169–76].)

Assisted by Weiss's strong letter of recommendation to Harry Levin at Harvard, de Man in the mid-fifties became a member of Harvard's illustrious Society of Fellows, along with other future intellectual and literary stars such as Stanley Cavell, John Hollander, Donald Hall, and Noam Chomsky. De Man then taught at Cornell and, from the seventies on, at Yale. As Lehman's book attests, de Man endeared himself to his friends in the academy (many of whom were Jewish, incidentally). He was a true mensch: funny, good natured, quick witted, and without the least trace of pretension.

The rumor that de Man had been a collaborator during the war came up while he was at Harvard in the fifties. De Man sent a letter to Renato Poggioli, the director of the Society of Fellows, indignantly asserting that the accusation was utterly unfounded. He even hinted to friends that he had been in the Resistance during the war; though, with a hero's modesty, he refused to provide any details of his activities. (During the controversy over de Man's wartime writings, Derrida would fulfill this fantasy by implying that de Man must have been secretly resisting the Nazis in his writings.)

De Man's first book, the landmark volume *Blindness and Insight,* was issued shortly after his arrival at Yale: in 1971, when he was fifty-two. De Man was a late bloomer, but the rigor and subtlety of *Blindness and Insight* proved that he was a force in contemporary literary criticism, capable of redefining the field with his reflections on the American New Critics, the phenomenologist Georges Poulet, the Marxist critic Georg Lukács, and others. These critics' best moments, de Man argued, were made possible by the fact that they over-looked something central in the works they discussed. Such blindness made possible the critics' insights.

The centerpiece of *Blindness and Insight* is an essay on the reading of Rousseau by . . . Jacques Derrida. Derrida, de Man charges, constructs a naïve version of Rousseau, a Rousseau who didn't know what he was doing, so that Derrida himself can claim the upper hand as a knowledgeable, sophisticated interpreter. Derrida tries to show that he, unlike Rousseau, cannot be tricked by false oppositions between nature and cul-ture, or wholesomeness and decadence.

But was Rousseau really so unreflective, so easily deluded? De Man argues that he was not: the genius Rousseau was no fool. Moreover, de Man suggests in a telling aside, Derrida himself does not actually believe that Rousseau was a naïf. He has simply decided to portray him that way in order to bolster his argument. "Either [Derrida] actually misreads Rousseau," de Man writes with a grin, "or he deliberately mis-reads Rousseau for the sake of his own exposition and rheto-ric," thereby "deconstructing a pseudo-Rousseau," a much eas-ier target than the real one. "The pattern is too interesting not to be deliberate," de Man concludes of Derrida's interpretive maneuvers (*Blindness* 139–40).

According to de Man, then, Derrida had made Rousseau blind in order to generate his own insights. The blindness (to Rousseau's sophistication) was apparently Derrida's own, de Man surmised. And it was likely that Derrida wasn't in fact blind to Rousseau's true complexity, but just pretending to be. He merely wanted to secure an advantage over his chosen au-thor, who could be shown to be hamstrung by logocentric prejudice. De Man's suggestion may seem ungenerous, but it is largely accurate. The implicit claim to superiority over the author is in fact a common pattern in Derrida's readings, as we have seen.

As de Man sees it, Derrida knows what Rousseau also knows: that literary language is an effort to disguise the true nothingness of existence. The effort is a necessary one. As Nietzsche said, we need art so that we will not perish from the truth. But the truth, the terrible vacuity that is life itself, still looms. *Blindness and Insight* speaks of our movement "toward meaning as void" (*Blindness* 127). Yet de Man, as he evokes this bleak cosmology, manages to sound witty and cunning rather than grim. De Man's supremely knowing tone makes for a sense of excitement; the drama of his prose, though somewhat antiseptic at times, hints at a brave look into the abyss. For de Man, the meaningless nature of human existence is a given, a comedy that he approaches with a certain stoic cheer. He shares with Derrida this inclination toward seeing life as absurd; for both, the appearance of meaning is the product of a random force, signification.

Deconstruction, in de Man's version especially but also that of the early Derrida, begins to sound like a replay of existentialism at its height, without the existentialist's belief in human heroism. Life is meaningless, and we must say so. Whereas the existentialists suggested that the criminal and the madman provided a true glimpse into the vortex, deconstructionists preferred the staid, ascetic company of writers and philosophers. (Though Derrida in *Writing and Difference,* as I have noted, celebrated the mad author and actor Antonin Artaud as an authentic emissary from the kingdom of the absurd.)

Reading, as explored definitively in de Man's magisterial *Allegories of Reading* (1979), seems to be a strictly useless activity, the record of a self-undoing on the part of language. Yet de

Man, strangely, insists that reading is an essential practice, and his disciple J. Hillis Miller has even asserted that de Man's concept of reading is profoundly ethical.[7] Miller overreaches in this claim. Ethics requires a conception of the world as deserving, and requiring, our human response. But deconstruction falls prey to a dualism that makes any action we might choose indifferent, and therefore incapable of being judged. Language acts instead of us. For de Man there is the void of meaningless existence on the one side and on the other our language, which confronts meaninglessness (or, in its weak, wish-fulfilling moments, avoids it).

In its prizing of elite strategies, de Manian deconstruction claims that it is better to confront the universal emptiness than to turn away from it as the weak-minded do. If we are strong, we know that language, not we ourselves, is responsible for what we say and do. It is hard to avoid making a connection between such a theory and de Man's cover-up of his wartime actions. Whatever had been written then in a newspaper called *Le Soir* had nothing to do with the biographical entity named Paul de Man.

Derrida's sense of identification with de Man was so deep that, when the journalists attacked, he himself felt the wound. And he lashed out in response. In his essay on the de Man affair, Derrida was capable of writing the following sentence: "To judge, to condemn the work or the man on the basis of what was a brief episode, to call for a closing, that is to say, at least figuratively, for censuring or burning his books is to reproduce the exterminating gesture which one accuses de Man of not having armed himself against sooner with the necessary vigilance" (*Responses* 128). It was not exactly temperate, and still less appropriate, to compare the critics of an intellectual who collaborated with the Nazis to book burners and exterminators of Jews. But Derrida did exactly this. According to Derrida, it was not de Man but rather American journalists who had abandoned their "elementary duties," showing themselves allies of "the ignorance, the simplism [*sic*], the sensationalist flurry full of hatred" (128). These journalists were like "the worst totalitarian police" (152). They were not merely fascists, but also idiots: "Finding as always its foothold in aggressivity, simplism has produced the most unbelievably stupid statements" (154). Standing against the monstrous danger posed by the American press, Derrida asserted that deconstruction provided the means to "identify and combat the totalitarian risk" (155).

It is painful, as well as exhausting, to read through "The Sound of the Sea Deep Within a Shell: Paul de Man's War," the sixty-page attempt to exculpate de Man that Derrida wrote for *Critical Inquiry,* a journal of theory published by the University of Chicago, in January 1988. The more one reads, the more one winces at Derrida's desperate need for de Man to have been a resister of the Nazis rather than an eager sympathizer with them.

Derrida insists that de Man, in 1942, was in a state of "private torment" over the war (129), and was actually trying to do good, to defeat the Nazis. During his speech at a University of Alabama conference on de Man's journalism in October 1987, Derrida remarked, "What I begin to see clearly [in de Man's work for *Le Soir*] is . . . an enormous suffering, an agony, that we cannot yet know the extent of" (149). The problem for Derrida, of course, is how to get to a conclusion that goes so obviously against the evidence. So now, in the hour of need, deconstruction rides in, ready to do its intricate work.

In his *Critical Inquiry* piece, Derrida circles warily around a few of de Man's other articles before finally arriving at the make-or-break example, exhibit A for the prosecution: de Man's essay "The Jews in Contemporary Literature" (*Le Soir,* March 4, 1941). The essay seems, as Derrida remarks, to contain "an antisemitism that would have come close to urging exclusions, even the most sinister degradations" (142). Here, Derrida's use of the conditional tense works to soften the ground before the deconstructive assault. De Man's article "would have come close to urging exclusions": an amelioration of the piece's actual tone. Somberly, slowly, Derrida cites the conclusion of "The Jews in Contemporary Literature," with its reference to "a solution to the Jewish problem," to "the creation of a Jewish colony isolated from Europe," to the Jews as a "foreign force" alien to European culture.

Now Derrida stalls. He considers for a moment, suspending the drama like an orator before a breathless, rapt crowd. Could there possibly be a defense of the de Man who wrote such sentences? "Will I dare to say 'on the other hand' in the face of the *unpardonable* violence and confusion of these sentences? What could possibly attenuate the fault?" (142).

Yes, Derrida will say it, and boldly: on the other hand. On the other hand, in spite of all appearance to the contrary, de Man was not a collaborator, not a racist. He *resisted.* Derrida does not merely "attenuate" de Man's "fault," his collaboration. He eliminates it, turning it into its opposite, resistance. (Such is the deconstructionist's sleight of hand.)

Derrida then rapidly, surprisingly, shifts his ground: he suddenly insists that we do know what de Man meant. "The *whole* article," Derrida emphasizes, "is organized as an indictment of 'vulgar antisemitism.' It is, let us not forget, directed against that antisemitism, against its 'lapidary judgment,' against the 'myth' it feeds or feeds on" (143). De Man in "The Jews in Contemporary Literature," Derrida concludes, actually defends the Jews, striking out against a "'myth' . . . an 'error' and a 'very widespread opinion'": namely, anti-Semitism.

The obvious problem with Derrida's defense of de Man here is that the words and phrases he cites repeatedly from de Man's article—"myth," "error," "lapidary judgment," "very widespread opinion"—are applied by de Man not to anti-Semitism, but rather to the mistaken idea that the Jews have infected European literature. De Man aims to oppose the myth that European belles lettres are *enjuivées* ("Jewified"), not to combat anti-Semitism itself. To celebrate the fact that European letters have remained vital and healthy despite the presence of the Jews, this alien force in the heart of Europe, is hardly to provide a critique of anti-Semitic ideas. And to add to this, as de Man does, that Europe would hardly miss its Jews were they suddenly to disappear does not seem like an effective way of arguing for these Jews and against their persecutors.

But in Derrida's view de Man makes just such an anti-anti-Semitic argument. De Man has written an "uncompromising critique" of the Nazis—so Derrida claims, astonishingly. It is, of course, a subtle critique, as we might expect from de Man. He "preferred to play the role of the nonconformist smuggler," just like the members of the resistance (143).

But, the reader might object, de Man chose to write for a newspaper filled with crude propaganda against the Jews. Just look at the pages of *Le Soir:* the journal was filled with racist slurs. Yes, says Derrida, but really it is "as if his article were denouncing the neighboring articles, pointing to the 'myth' and the 'errors'" (144). The de Man article is "an anticonformist attack" (145); we know this because de Man was an anticonformist all his life, a noble, independent soul.

It gets worse. Derrida goes on to describe de Man in his 1942 essay as, of all things, actually praising the Jews. Referring

again to the conclusion of "The Jews in Contemporary Literature," Derrida writes the following astounding words:
"Without wanting to attenuate the violence of this paragraph
that for me remains disastrous . . . the manner in which he
describes the 'Jewish spirit' remains unquestionably positive"
(146). Unquestionably positive? Yes, because, in "their cere-
bralness, their capacity to assimilate doctrines while maintaining a certain coldness in the face of them," these Jews strangely
resemble (so Derrida concludes) Paul de Man himself.

As Derrida knew, the idea that the Jew coldly adopts a
point of view but doesn't believe it, doesn't feel it in his heart,
is one of the familiar clichés of European anti-Semitism.
Richard Wagner's book on the Jews in contemporary music,
which was surely a source for de Man, demonstrates the power
of this image.

De Man's article on the Jews is sophisticated and neutral
in tone, rather than propagandistic. (In this sense, it is indeed
distinct from vulgar anti-Semitism.) As Alice Kaplan writes,
"De Man does not angrily demand the expulsion of the Jews
from Europe, but rather refers to it in passing, as a likely development in the near future. He reassures the public that
should it happen—the assumption being that it may well
happen—the disappearance of the Jews wouldn't be bad for
Western literature. This is collaborationist 'realism' at its
worst" (275). If so many had not reflected neutrally, as de Man
did, on the possibility of a *Judenfrei* Europe, then the Shoah
might never have occurred.

Kaplan should have the last word on "The Jews in Contemporary Literature," since she has studied closely the anti-
Semitic French and Belgian collaborators of the Nazi era. (This
topic was Kaplan's dissertation project when she was de Man's
student in the 1980s; one can only imagine de Man's inward re-

action when she told him her choice of subject.) There were, Kaplan emphasizes, "a number of approaches to the anti-semitic genre—cultural, racial, historical—which in their very disagreements, give the appearance of a respectable 'debate.' What is more, all of them draw [as de Man does] on a critique of an 'incorrect' form of racist thinking that is beneath their dignity" (275). Louis-Ferdinand Céline, the great novelist who poured out rabid fantasies of massacring the Jews, was the frequent whipping boy of the sophisticated anti-Semites. The latter, in conferences and learned discussions about the Jewish "problem," legitimized racism as a dignified, judicious, and "scientific" field. With "The Jews in Contemporary Literature," de Man assisted in such legitimation.

Derrida persists in his argument that de Man had the fate of the Jews at heart instead of viewing this fate with indifference. Since de Man states that the disappearance of the Jews would have no consequences for the cultural life of Europe, Derrida's case is a hard one to make. Derrida does make the case, with a nearly dire insistence. And he goes on to suggest, even more desperately, that perhaps de Man did not write the most offensive parts of the article in question. Derrida surely knows that very few of his readers will be convinced that "The Jews in Contemporary Literature" is an act of resistance to Nazism and a praise of the Jews. So, Derrida speculates, maybe de Man didn't write the essay at all (or at least, not the bad, the *seemingly* bad, parts of it): "Who can exclude what happens so often in newspapers, and especially during that period and in those conditions, when editors can always intervene at the last moment? If that was the case, Paul de Man is no longer here to testify to it. But at that point one can say: supposing this to have been the case, there was still a way of protesting which would have been to end his association with the newspaper"

(147). Paul de Man, of course, *did* end his association with *Le Soir*. And that fact, Derrida muses, suggests that *Le Soir*'s editors must have inserted the apparent anti-Semitism into his article on the Jews. De Man must have resigned in protest against this interference.

Unfortunately for Derrida, de Man did not stop writing for *Le Soir* until more than a year after "The Jews in Contemporary Literature" appeared. He left the collaborationist newspaper at the end of 1942, just as the tide was turning and it looked for the first time as if the Germans might lose the war. (These facts go unmentioned by Derrida.) Derrida argues that de Man the anticonformist couldn't possibly have been guilty of "cynical opportunism" (147) in quitting *Le Soir* the moment that a German defeat started to seem likely. But, one may suggest, anticonformism is no necessary barrier to cynical opportunism—especially with a complicated character like Paul de Man.

Derrida proceeds to recount in his *Critical Inquiry* essay the way he sprang into action after hearing the revelation about de Man's wartime activities from Ortwin de Graef. With Samuel Weber, he decided to turn a colloquium scheduled for October 1987 at the University of Alabama, in Tuscaloosa, into a symposium on de Man's writings from *Le Soir*. Photocopies of the articles that de Graef had given Derrida in August, some twenty-five of the more than one hundred articles de Man wrote, were distributed to the participants.

In his talk at the Tuscaloosa conference, Derrida broods over de Man's silence about his collaborationist past. He remarks that "this man must have lived a real agony"; but "he explained himself publicly," Derrida emphasizes. "He explained himself publicly," Derrida repeats twice more, mantra-like. The explanation Derrida alludes to occurs in the letter responding to rumors about him that de Man wrote to Poggioli in 1955, during his Harvard years. In fact, Poggioli kept the letter secret in accord with de Man's request; it was hardly a public explanation. And hardly an honest explanation, either: in his letter, de Man called the suggestion that he had been a collaborationist a "slander." He had written for a newspaper in Belgium during the war, he told Poggioli, but had quit in protest over German censorship.

In his *Critical Inquiry* essay, Derrida agrees with de Man's self-description in his letter to Poggioli, writing bluntly that de Man "was aware of having never collaborated or called for collaboration" with Nazism (150). Though it is true that Derrida had not read all of de Man's *Le Soir* writings when he wrote this sentence—writings that continually applaud the German leadership of Europe and urge Belgians to acquiesce in it—he had read enough to make a more accurate judgment than this.

Why did de Man never speak openly of his wartime writings? In his *Critical Inquiry* piece, Derrida delivers two innovative reasons: it would have been immodest, even "pretentious" and "ridiculous"; and it would have been a waste of time. "[De Man's] international notoriety having spread only during the last years of his life, to exhibit earlier such a distant past so as to call the public as a witness—would that not have been a pretentious, ridiculous, and infinitely complicated gesture?" (150).

Well, *no*, one is tempted to answer. At any rate (Derrida continues), after de Man became famous, there was simply no time for such revelations. "I prefer," writes Derrida, "that he chose not to take it on himself to provoke, during his life, this spectacular and painful discussion. It would have taken his time and energy. He did not have very much and that would have deprived us of a part of his work" (150). In saying that he "prefer[s]" de Man's decision not to confess, Derrida applauds de Man for the very concealment that was most troubling to his readers, friends, and students. It was better to keep it secret, not to make a show of oneself, to endure alone the agony of living a lie.

This bizarre picture of de Man's heroic silence testifies to the distortions of mind Derrida suffered in the shock of the de Man affair. But it tells us something more significant, as well, about an inclination of Derridean theory: even as it protects the hidden self from public scrutiny, it opens that self for Derrida's idealizing imagination. Twenty years earlier, Derrida had assailed Lévi-Strauss for fantasizing about the Nambikwara: seeing them as innocents, happy in their paradise. Now, Derrida himself engages in a fantasy projection—onto Paul de Man. Derrida's struggle with the journalists who attacked de Man, depicted as quasi-Nazis in his prose, becomes de Man's equally strenuous battle with the Nazified journalism of *Le Soir*. Both Derrida and de Man are members of the resistance: de Man silently, Derrida more overtly.

At a key point in his *Critical Inquiry* essay Derrida leaps into a flurry of obscurities—but not without a plan: "Transference and prosopopeia, like the experience of the undecidable, seem to make a responsibility impossible. It is for that very reason that they require it and perhaps subtract it from the calculable program: they give it a chance. Or, inversely: responsibility, if there is any, requires the experience of the undecidable as well as that irreducibility of the other, some of whose names are transference, prosopopeia, allegory. There are many others. And the double edge and the double bind, which are other phenomena of the undecidable" (151). These sound like the words of a man in a panic trying to change the subject. But Derrida means something quite specific by them. He wants to show, first, how rhetorical tropes "seem to make . . . responsibility impossible" but in fact "give it a chance."

Derrida knows exactly what he wants to do here, and it is something crucial to his treatment of the de Man affair. He had always been a skeptic about human intention, conscious meaning, and empirical evidence. Now, however, he is troubled, to a much greater degree than before the revelations about de Man, by the pervasive skepticism he had advocated: a skepticism that would deprive us of the ability to assign responsibility, to judge others and ourselves.

A call to a new kind of responsibility, Derrida suggests here, occurs to those immersed in deconstructionist skepticism. He asserts, as usual, that the difficulty of assigning authorship and stable meaning to a text makes our individual burden for saying, writing, and doing what we do also very hard to assign—in fact, impossible. But Derrida then implies (and this is the innovation) that the recognition of this impossibility makes it all the more imperative to acknowledge the "irreducibility of the other." And this acknowledgment means embracing true responsibility—toward the unknown self of the other, which remains invisible to those who read and live without exercising the sympathetic imagination of the friend.

If Derrida, in his pain, sidesteps the effort of pronouncing a judgment on Paul de Man, he undertakes this avoidance out of respect for the inexhaustible enigma of another human being. It is this sense of the necessary unknownness of the other person that torments the survivor, the Algerian Jew who loved Paul de Man. The problem is that the obscurity of de Man's motives becomes in Derrida grounds for assigning to him a heroic inner life—an effort that must be seen as an evasion of the difficulty that de Man's example presents.

As the *Critical Inquiry* essay goes on, agitated, perturbed,

and snaking into pages-long footnotes, Derrida's denunciations become more and more bitter. As for the *Nation*'s piece
on de Man by Jon Wiener: "One shudders to think that its author teaches history at a university" (160). And, Derrida adds,
the "venomous but always moralizing attacks" of Tzvetan
Todorov, Derrida's old friend, are full of "mistakes, lies and
falsifications number[ing] about three out of every four alle-
gations" (163). Again Derrida makes it clear that, in his fantasy
of the de Man case, the reporters who charge deconstructionists with a nihilistic indifference to morality are the true Nazis:
"Those who toss around the word nihilism so gravely or so
lightly should, however, be aware of what they're doing: under
the occupation, the 'propagators' of dangerous ideas were
often denounced by accusing them of 'nihilism,' sometimes in
violently antisemitic tracts, and always in the name of a new
order, moral and right-thinking" (164). Derrida tells the errant
journalists: because you denounce nihilism, you resemble the
Nazis who also denounced nihilism—and they were violent
anti-Semites. The defense of a dead friend has rarely revealed
such insistent and troubled depths in the survivor.

Derrida's treatment of Heidegger's involvement with Nazism
has two features in common with his response to the de Man
affair: a rejection of the summary judgments enacted by the
press and the hinting at a hidden spirit of resistance within
the thinker in question, the saving element that can rehabil-
itate him. With both de Man and Heidegger, Derrida turns the
tables on the accusers. Genuine thought, he suggests, demands
that we refrain from the easy, decisive sentencing that journalism relies on.

During the same year as the de Man scandal, 1987, Derrida published a book on Heidegger, titled *Of Spirit*. The Hei-

degger book has a background in another scandal, this time concerning not a beloved friend but one of Derrida's idolized philosophical ancestors. During the 1980s Hugo Ott, a scholar from Heidegger's own University of Freiburg, was amassing material on the philosopher's involvement with the Nazis. At the same time, a writer named Victor Farias circulated a manuscript on Heidegger's connection with Nazism.

Farias's book came out in France in 1987, just after Derrida's *Of Spirit,* and led, as expected, to a storm of controversy. Farias, like Ott, accused Heidegger of having a far more thoroughgoing investment in the Nazi regime than had been realized. Ott's book was the more scholarly one by far: Farias's descended, at times, into crude, far-fetched innuendo. Both Ott and Farias argued that Heidegger was an open anti-Semite and a consistent supporter of Hitler's policies. Heidegger had assumed the rectorship of the University of Freiburg in 1933, but he shortly afterward resigned that position. After World War II, he depicted his resignation as an act of protest against Nazism. This was not the case. Recent research by the Heidegger scholar Emmanuel Faye has made us more aware than before of the depth of Heidegger's commitment, in his lectures of the thirties and forties, to Nazi racial theory. Indeed, years before the Nazi seizure of power, Heidegger had complained about the *Verjudung* ("Jewification") of German universities.[8] Heidegger, who referred in a lecture course given during the 1930s to the "inner truth and greatness" of National Socialism, remained a loyal Nazi. Until the end, Heidegger was convinced that the German-instigated war was the only way to save civilization from the twin menace of Bolshevism and crass American materialism.

In 1949, Heidegger made his only public allusion to the Shoah when he remarked that "agriculture today is a motorized food industry, in essence the same as the manufacture of corpses in gas chambers and extermination camps." Genocide and combine harvesters appeared to be equivalent evils to him. Whether it was Jews or stalks of wheat that were being massacred, the real point was the imposition of technology on daily life.[9]

Derrida's book, it is important to note, has an additional political background. *Of Spirit*, like Philippe Lacoue-Labarthe's *Heidegger, Art, and Politics* (1987), and like Derrida's resurrection of Marxism six years later in *Specters of Marx*, can be seen as an attack on the revival of liberal humanism in France. The publication of Aleksandr Solzhenitsyn's *Gulag Archipelago* in the early seventies had led to a resurgence of anti-Communist liberalism among French intellectuals. In opposition to this wave, which seemed to many to be insufficiently critical of the oppressions exacted by what Marxists call "late capitalism," Derrida in *Of Spirit* outlined the similarity he saw between Nazism and humanism. He suggested that Husserl and Paul Valéry, both of them convinced democrats and opponents of fascism, had an affinity with Heidegger, who had used Nazi rhetoric in his *Rektoratsrede*, his speech accepting the rectorship at Freiburg.

In the days when Communism dominated the universities and the intellectual life of France, Derrida had rebelled; he was a liberal who remained suspicious of revolution and left-wing authoritarian regimes. Now that liberal humanism was fashionable, Derrida, true to form, espoused Marx (as will be discussed next chapter) and compared humanism to Nazism— at exactly the moment when Marxism, exposed as a repressive sham, was heading for permanent defeat in Europe. Derrida was a contrarian to the end; he had found a new authority to resist.[10]

Derrida's remarks in "Philosophers' Hell," the *Nouvel observateur* interview that he gave shortly after the publication of his book on Heidegger, are troubling. He announces his wish to overturn the binary opposition between Nazism and non-Nazism. Derrida wants to see what is "common to Nazism and to anti-Nazism, the law of resemblance, the inevitability of perversion" (*Points* 185). He adds that liberalism, just like fascism, is predicated on a "voluntarist" and "metaphysical" discourse.

When Heidegger uses the word *spirit* in his rectoral address, Derrida remarks, "he engages in a voluntarist and metaphysical discourse that he will subsequently view with suspicion. To this extent at least, by celebrating the freedom of spirit, its glorification resembles other European discourses (spiritualist, religious, humanist) that people generally consider opposed to Nazism. [There is] a complex and unstable skein that I try to unravel by recognizing the threads shared by Nazism and non-Nazism" (*Heidegger Controversy* 269). When he treats Heidegger's most famous moment of association with Hitler's regime, his Rektoratsrede, as showing that Nazism is fundamentally similar to liberal humanism, Derrida rules out of court the more pressing question of how Nazism and liberalism differ from each other. Further on in *Of Spirit,* he credits Heidegger in his later career with a movement away from Nazism that Heidegger never in fact made.

The similarity between Derrida's treatment of Heidegger and his defense of de Man is apparent. In both cases, Derrida endows the suspect thinker with a secret critique of the anti-Semitic fascism to which he overtly subscribed. And his arguments about Heidegger are just as logically dubious and oblique as in the de Man case. Because Heidegger criticized humanism,

Derrida suggests, he was (really or covertly) criticizing Nazism, which is also a philosophy of the human, of "spirit."

Most fascinating for followers of Derrida's career is the very end of "Philosophers' Hell," in which Derrida unashamedly signals his wish to be taken as an engaged political thinker, like Sartre or Foucault. Referring to his two books of 1987, *Of Spirit* and *Psyche* (the latter containing an essay on Nelson Mandela), Derrida remarks, "And what if someone finds amusement in showing that these two texts on the soul and spirit are also the books of a militant? That the essays on Heidegger and Nazism, on Mandela and apartheid, on the nuclear problem, the psychoanalytic establishment and torture, architecture and urbanism, etc., are 'political writings.' But you are right, I have never been, as you said, a 'militant or engaged philosopher in the sense of the Sartrean or even the Foucauldian intellectual.' Why? But it's already too late, isn't it?" (*Heidegger Controversy* 273).

It was not too late. Derrida in 1987 was getting ready to man the political barricades, to steal back the audience he had forfeited to the engaged Foucault. He was also about to make an about-face, reclaiming the moral high ground he had lost in the de Man and Heidegger affairs. Ethics and politics would be Derrida's watchwords for the remaining seventeen years of his life, rather to the surprise of those who had followed the career of the arch-deconstructionist to this point.

V

Politics, Marx, Judaism

In the 1990s, as he neared the close of his life and his academic career, Derrida again sought an arena outside philosophy: a wider and more consequential place than arguments about the coherence of metaphysical texts could provide. His chosen term, increasingly, was politics. And the accent of Derrida's political writings was a prophetic one, full of commanding ethical import. He relied more than before on a Lévinasian view of our responsibility toward others. Derrida was no doubt reacting to his own role in the de Man and Heidegger scandals, when he failed to confront the political commitments of these two thinkers. Instead, Derrida suggested, what mattered was that they were alert to the real danger facing twentieth-century Europe: metaphysical humanism. Such avoidance of the actual political context of de Man's and Heidegger's careers in the 1930s and 1940s risked making Derrida seem irrelevant or even negligent, more interested in words and concepts than in historical reality.

The political turn in Derrida's work began shortly after the de Man and Heidegger affairs. In October 1988, Derrida gave a lecture at Cornell called "The Politics of Friendship"; he repeated it in December at a meeting of the American Philosophical Association. Friendship and politics were the subjects of his seminar at the Sorbonne the same year. The results appeared in a book, *The Politics of Friendship,* published in France in 1994 and translated into English soon thereafter. Alongside *The Politics of Friendship* came a book on Marxism, *Specters of Marx,* in 1993. Also in the early nineties, Derrida began to comment on the political future of Europe, in lectures reprinted as a book entitled *The Other Heading.* Derrida had always been diffident about politics, in marked contrast to the engaged Communists of the rue d'Ulm. But now, late in his life, he was becoming political with a vengeance.

The explanation for Derrida's leap into politics is manifold. First, the fall of Communism and the resulting transformation of Europe seemed to demand the response of major intellectuals. Second, Derrida increasingly felt the need to compete with the intensely politicized Foucault, whose star had been rising ever higher among American academics since his untimely death from AIDS in 1984. And third, the growing influence of a new style of criticism, the New Historicism, created considerable pressure on poststructuralist thinkers like Derrida to prove that their movement, for all its indulgence in rarefied wordplay, was responsive to history and politics.

Finally, Derrida was sensing the impact of the de Man and Heidegger affairs. His commentaries on de Man and Heidegger had implied that the skeptical powers of deconstruction could, and should, dissolve the differences that remain central to our understanding of what happened during World War II: the oppositions between democracy and fascism, between resistance and collaboration. At the same time, as we have seen, Derrida developed an elusive secret identity for de

Man, turning him into an enemy of Nazi anti-Semitism; and even Heidegger was said by Derrida to be questioning Nazism.

Derrida must have been taken aback by the blurring of ethical differences he had produced. His characteristic skepticism seemed insufficient to him, and, as before, he turned to the prophetic approach of Lévinas to attain a wider view. Derrida required a supplement, one that would enable deconstruction to approach politics from a moral high ground, rather than suggesting that political distinctions are merely relative and unreliable. Derrida had first discussed Lévinas in the mid-1960s in *Writing and Difference* (see chapter 2). Now, needing a cure for deconstruction's relativism, he returned to his friend's work.

Derrida's turn toward ethics near the end of his life was not, of course, merely a strategic decision about the waning prestige of deconstruction. He was growing old, and with the approach of death he was reminded of the responsibilities and memories that made up his life, like anyone's. Ethics meant seeing all this with a new seriousness. Before, he conceived the disappearance of the self abstractly. Now, however, the end was approaching in an all too foreseeable way.

The fate of Louis Althusser perhaps played a role as well in Derrida's new concentration on final things. After Althusser strangled his wife in November 1980, Derrida, his old companion from the École Normale, was one of the few who were allowed to visit him in the psychiatric hospital to which he was confined (and in which he wrote his very strange memoir). After he was released in the late eighties, Althusser could sometimes be seen on the streets of Paris, startling crowds by shouting at them "I am the great Althusser!"

In early 1989, Derrida's mother suffered a stroke, as a result of which she no longer recognized her son; he writes about the experience in "Circumfession," the rather cagey autobiographical essay he published in 1992. Derrida relates that when he asked his mother where she was in pain she responded, still able to speak a little, "I have a pain in my mother" (*Jacques Derrida* 23). Derrida's decision to write about his mother's stroke marked a departure from his previous reticence about his personal history. He was wondering whether deconstruction could accommodate a sense of the emotional life, its disappointments and even degradations, along with theories of signification and différance. Somewhat furtively, psychology was intruding into the sacrosanct space of Derridean thought.

But the main impulse of Derrida's thought in the nineties was toward politics rather than psychology. In May 1990, Derrida participated in a colloquium in Turin, Italy, on European cultural identity. He was joined by a group of well-known intellectuals, including Giorgio Agamben, a Nietzschean philosopher influenced by Derrida; the social theorist Agnès Heller, then teaching at the New School; and José Saramago, the left-leaning Portuguese novelist who was later to win the Nobel Prize. The time was right for such an event: the Berlin Wall had fallen, and with it the old division between East and West. The question of Europe's future was eliciting newly intense interest.

In his talk in Turin, Derrida looked back to Husserl's and Heidegger's writings of the 1930s: their reflections, from opposing political viewpoints, on the crisis of European civilization. He then invoked Paul Valéry's announcement in 1939 that "our cultural capital is in peril" (68). Valéry, Husserl, and Heidegger were writing on the eve of an unprecedented conflagration, a war that all three knew was coming. Derrida, by contrast, gave his lecture in the wake of a cold war that was now, surprisingly and mysteriously, over.

Derrida's guidance for the European future, as delivered in Turin, seems understated, even banal. "On the one hand," he remarks, "European cultural identity. . . . cannot and must not be dispersed into a myriad of provinces, into a multiplicity of self-enclosed idioms or petty little nationalisms. . . . But, on the other hand, it cannot and must not accept the capital of a centralizing authority" (38–39). (Derrida puns incessantly in his Turin lecture on capital—Latin *caput*—and head). The authority that Derrida speaks against would be a hegemonic source of control, which he depicts in Orwellian terms (39–40).

So Europe, Derrida argues, should be neither a mere collection of rival nationalisms nor a centralized structure with a single capital: "neither monopoly nor dispersion, therefore" (41). This neither-nor is seen by Derrida as an impossibility, which he then glorifies as "the experience and experiment of the aporia," "the possibility of the impossibility" (41). Through these ringing Kierkegaardian phrases, Derrida tries to endow his rather vague observations with a heroic cast. The core message of Derrida's Turin lecture is an exceedingly general caution against the dangers of both nationalism and transnational authority. He offers little practical sense of the main issue confronting Europe after the fall of Communism: how the appeal of self-isolating ethnic groups might be handled by governments charged to rise above, and to manage, such ethnic particularism.

In October 1989, Derrida gave a talk at the Cardozo Law School in New York for a colloquium entitled "Deconstruction and the Possibility of Justice." As in the case of the Turin symposium, the theme of the Cardozo lecture indicates that Derrida realized the danger to his legacy if deconstruction were to become merely a proficiency in the art of excuse making, as his *Critical Inquiry* defense of de Man seemed to suggest. Derrida proclaimed in his speech that, despite appearances to the contrary, deconstruction had always been fundamentally concerned with justice and ethics. "What one currently calls deconstruction, while seeming not to 'address' the problem of justice, has done nothing else while unable to do so directly but only in an oblique fashion. I say oblique," Derrida continued, "since at this very moment I am preparing to demonstrate that one cannot speak *directly* about justice, say 'this is just,' and even less 'I am just,' without immediately betraying justice" (*Acts* 237).

Derrida's game is clear. To the exact degree that deconstruction refrains from judging, it serves the ideal of justice. By contrast, those who make declarations about decisions or persons being just or unjust (as all of us do from time to time) prove that they have no real sense of justice. Deconstruction's seeming avoidance of the issue of justice, then, turns out to be exemplary of a higher morality. Derrida insists that deconstruction is not (as its critics claim) "a quasi-nihilistic abdication before the ethico-politico-juridical question of justice and before the opposition of just and unjust" (247). Instead, the difficulty of defining what is just marks the affinity of justice with deconstruction, which is also notoriously hard to define. The law can be cited and discussed; but justice is terminally elusive. If we merely do what is required by law, we are not truly being just. Justice is in excess of the law: it asks more of us than mere obedience to a set of rules. Justice—and deconstruction—calls us, Derrida announces, to "the sense of a responsibility without limits, and so necessarily excessive, incalculable" (247).

This point is where Lévinas enters Derrida's lecture—the Lévinas who never tires of stating the priority of the face-to-face encounter, the meeting with the stranger who is also one's neighbor. Derrida approvingly cites Lévinas's notion of "Jew-ish humanism" (so different from the humanism endorsed by metaphysics) and states that "the Lévinasian notion of justice" comes close to "the Hebrew equivalent of what we would per-haps translate as holiness" (250).[1]

As Derrida continues his discussion, his idea of justice starts to accumulate the swirling hyperboles that he earlier at-tached to his previous God-term, writing. Justice, Derrida writes in something close to an aria, "seems indestructible in its affirmative character, in its demand of gift without ex-change, without circulation, without recognition or gratitude, without economic circularity, without calculation and without rules, without reason and without theoretical rationality, in the sense of regulating mastery. And so, one can recognize in it, even accuse in it a madness, and perhaps another kind of mysticism. And deconstruction is mad about and from such justice, mad about and from this desire for justice" (254). "Jus-tice remains to come," Derrida proclaims, "it remains *by com-ing*, it *has* to come, it *is* to-come, the to-come, it deploys the very dimension of events irreducibly to come. . . . Justice," he adds climactically, "as the experience of absolute alterity, is un-presentable" (256–57).

In this passage, Derrida seizes upon the imagery of the Bible's Book of Revelation ("I come quickly," says Christ the bridegroom). He combines this emphasis with the more sub-tle Jewish messianism that one might have expected from him, given his revived interest in Lévinas: the idea that the mes-sianic age cannot be represented and that it defeats our usual notion of history. Messianic justice is all the more spectacular because it is "unpresentable" and "unrecognizable," utterly unexpected. Yet, as Derrida somewhat glumly concedes in his lecture, the fallen law that we know still exists alongside its utopian counterterm, justice. The messiah has not yet arrived (257).

Speaking to an audience of law students and professors, Derrida in his Cardozo speech avoids discussing whether particular laws are just or not (a crucial part of legal philosophy). Instead, for him, every law is in some sense unjust, since law by its nature cannot accommodate the transcendent stature of justice as an idea. Derrida's reliance on justice as an unfulfillable demand, a demand constantly made of us, marks his debt to Lévinas, who like Derrida remains decidedly anti-Kantian on this subject. (For Kant, justice is characterized by obedience to the law, if one has decided that the law is just.) Lévinas insists that the presence of a person in need, a victim of violence or oppression, stimulates not our sense of law but rather our sense of justice. The law, again, is inherently unjust: we tacitly endorse a certain degree of oppression by declaring (for example) that social inequality is inevitable. Our laws mandate, or at least permit, the existence of wars, prisons, and other social miseries. But when we come face-to-face with oppression, we cannot bear it: justice enters our consciousness. We have an instinctive—a true—reaction, and recoil before the rationality of the law. An empirical event, the face-to-face, determines this response, which is not to be understood by metaphysics.

For Lévinas, then, justice is an instinct, and it proves our humanity even when we turn away from it. The Mosaic commandment forbidding murder is at work deep within us, according to Lévinas. Even the Nazis had to tell themselves that they were exterminating vermin rather than other human beings, in order to avoid being confronted by the face of the neighbor. As the critic Susan Handelman points out, the Lévinasian face-to-face, in which the presence of another person "interrupts" and "shames" the ego, "disrupt[s] that free, autonomous self that through its reasoning and consciousness thinks it can construct the world out *of* itself, or know the world *from* itself."[2] In this manner, Lévinas throws down the gauntlet to philosophy, which has relied so often on solitary consciousness as the arbiter of meaning. Lévinas's critique of metaphysics, up to this point, is in line with Derrida's, but Derrida has (as I have pointed out) an attachment to the solitary, unreachable self. Derrida's political-ethical turn in the nineties coexists with an idea of privacy that Lévinas would never accept.

Derrida's main base of operations in the 1990s was still America rather than Europe. He continued teaching at Irvine, along with his friend Hillis Miller. (Other French theorists, notably Jean-François Lyotard, also visited Irvine during the decade.) At Irvine, Derrida gave both lectures for a large audience and more informal seminars to small groups of students whom he selected for admission to the class. One graduate student from Derrida's Irvine years, Michael Fox, remembers him as being warm and approachable in his seminars, open to conflicting opinions and frequently funny. But Derrida remained stiff and poised in front of his large lecture audiences: careful of his formulations, as if speaking for posterity.

At Irvine, Derrida was a stickler for the rules, refusing to admit to his class students who had not followed the proper registration procedures. At the Irvine student center café before his seminars, he was invariably accompanied by a small, attentive crowd of admirers. Surrounded by students who mimicked his turns of phrase and his arguments, Derrida kept his distance, making clear his dislike of their obsequious manner. "He performed for the sycophants, but he didn't really like them," Michael Fox recalls.[3] Derrida preferred independent-minded students, who were less likely to use him for the advancement of their own careers.

Derrida "was always the Jewish Algerian outsider," Fox remembers, in contrast to his rather patrician, Ivy League–bred disciple Hillis Miller. He made a point of his unusual origins. Once after class, during a discussion of scapegoating rituals, Derrida took a staid group of students by surprise when he swung his arm energetically in a circle over his head. He was miming his grandmother's performance of the *kapparot*, the rite of expiation performed by some Orthodox Jewish women during Passover in which their sins are transferred into the body of a chicken that is first waved in the air and then killed.

The year 1992 brought the "Cambridge affair": a dispute over whether Derrida ought to be granted an honorary doctorate by Cambridge University. While this minor drama did not match in intensity the turmoil over the legacies of de Man and Heidegger in the late eighties, it was nonetheless seriously disturbing to Derrida. Derrida had already received half a dozen honorary doctorates, from institutions such as Columbia University and the University of Louvain. But this time, Derrida's nomination for a degree set off a storm of protest from prominent philosophers.

A letter opposing Derrida's nomination for the Cambridge doctorate was published in the *Times* of London on May 9, 1992. It was signed by nineteen philosophers from a number of countries and institutions, including, most prominently, W. V. O. Quine of Harvard and Ruth Marcus of Yale (who had opposed his lectureship there). The letter asserted that "in the eyes of philosophers . . . M. Derrida's work does not meet accepted standards of clarity and rigour." The petition noted that enthusiasts for Derrida's work came almost exclusively from outside philosophy departments. Derrida, the authors announced, had made a career out of using "tricks and gimmicks similar to those of the Dadaists and the concrete poets."

The letter continued: "Many French philosophers see in M. Derrida only cause for silent embarrassment, his antics having contributed significantly to the widespread impression that contemporary French philosophy is little more than an object of ridicule. . . . Academic status based on what seems to us to be little more than semi-intelligible attacks upon the values of reason, truth, and scholarship is not, we submit, sufficient grounds for the awarding of an honorary degree in a distinguished university" (*Points* 420–21). In the end, Derrida prevailed and was granted the doctorate, winning a majority of votes from the Cambridge dons. The philosophers had lost. Derrida's academic audience was, by the nineties, far wider than his discipline could account for. And he was in the process of trying to widen it still more.

In April 1993, Derrida gave a two-session lecture at the University of California, Riverside, inaugurating a conference called, punningly, "Whither Marxism?" The lectures became *Specters of Marx,* published in France later in 1993. Quickly translated by Derrida's friend Peggy Kamuf, *Specters of Marx* appeared in English in 1994.

Why Derrida on Marx, in 1993? As Richard Wolin and Mark Lilla, two discerning critics of poststructuralism, have suggested, Derrida's constituency in literature departments was gradually deserting him for Foucault: a thinker who, unlike Derrida, was overtly engaged with history and politics. Foucault had recently died, adding to the "halo effect" that surrounded him and his work. By the early nineties, the New Historicism, influenced by Marx and Foucault, became the dominant force in English departments, especially in the fields of American studies and Renaissance literature. More than ever, professors of literature were "getting political," bent on finding the ideological clues that might be imbedded in novels or poems.

In this new light, Derridean deconstruction suddenly seemed an outmoded and trivial activity, a self-congratulatory way of playing with language. It became reckless, even unforgiveable, to ignore the one word that all must swear fealty to: History. "History," Fredric Jameson had asserted in his magnum opus, *The Political Unconscious* (1981), "is what hurts": the ultimate sign of the real. By being historical, scholars could prove they were doing something valuable, connecting themselves to the ordinary world of the people. All that theory would be put, for once, to political use, in an effort to explain and thereby combat the forces that rule us. "History," Harold Bloom remarked to a class in the mid-1980s, "is the shibboleth of your generation." Twenty-five years later, it still is.

Derrida implied his careful distance from the immediate passions raised by politics and history. His role in the de Man and Heidegger scandals showed the suspicion he cast on all those, especially journalists, who were eager to make judgments about the involvement of intellectuals with political events. They didn't know how to read; it was best just to reflect on the profound questions that de Man's or Heidegger's behavior might raise, rather than trying to judge it.

By 1993, Derrida's insistence on the minute details of a text, and the withholding of political judgment that went along with such focus, was becoming perilously old-fashioned. A new age had arrived in the academy: a return of political commitment, which often required that one find ideological fault with authors and their texts. It was time for Derrida to change his stripes, to become a political thinker. He needed a trump card. He found one in the one thinker who, before all others, represents the conjunction of philosophy and politics: Karl Marx. In fact, Derrida astonishingly stated in *Specters of Marx,* deconstruction had always been, in a way, Marxist. "Deconstruction has never had any sense or interest, in my view at least, except as a radicalization, which is to say also *in the tradition* of a certain Marxism, in a certain *spirit of Marxism*" (92). The Derrida who had resisted the Communist allegiances of Sartre and Althusser, and who had stood apart from the doctrinaire Marxism of the École Normale, was now accomplishing a strange reversal. He had become not just an enthusiast of Marx but a Marxist ally, straining to prove that Marxism and deconstruction shared the same spirit.

There was, of course, a problem with Marx in 1993. Hadn't Communism lost the Cold War? Yes, but the ideals of Communism (or of "a certain Marxism," as Derrida preferred to put it) remained. Marx, who had famously announced in the *Communist Manifesto* that a specter was stalking Europe, was still haunting us. (Punning painfully, Derrida referred to his project in *Specters of Marx* as a "hauntology" [10].) Of course, virtually all the predictions and methods of Marxist theory had failed, notably including the dictatorship of the proletariat and the abolition of private property. Marxism, while it lived, had been closely aligned with murderous authoritarianism.

Derrida honored the memory of the millions killed by Stalin and Mao, mourning their suffering at the hands of tyrants. But, he argued, this lethal history remained separate from the *idea* of Marx. And this idea was, for Derrida, the object of a powerful nostalgic attachment. As Richard Rorty sardonically commented, "By saying that there are many Marxes, and then leaving most of them aside, [Derrida] can preserve

'Marx' as a quasi-synonym of 'justice.'"[4] Derrida was, it seemed, still avoiding history.

Derrida, in *Specters of Marx,* jettisons virtually all of the specific characteristics of Marxism, in order to save Marx. As Richard Wolin points out, he ignores Marx's neo-Hegelian (that is, metaphysical) insistence that the proletariat is the representative class of modern times. He fails to attend to the entanglement of state ownership and bureaucracy that characterized Marxist regimes. The practical realism of Marx, his constantly emphasized planning for the revolution, is suppressed by Derrida, who prefers to see in Marxism a vague messianic promise of an unexplained future, "the democracy to come."

Derrida's democratic Marxist future carries the promise of magical transformation; he hopes for deliverance from the society of the spectacle and related cyber-maladies, as well as the imperialist world order and mindless consumerism.[5] The liberation suggested here remains merely mysterious rather than, as in Marx's own writings, practical in orientation (that is, dependent on revolutionary action). Derrida's intent is to save Marx, not to subvert him. But his blindness to Marx's concerns with class struggle and revolution makes Marx seem less, rather than more, insightful.

In *Specters of Marx,* Derrida tries out a fashionable mode of inquiry, familiar from neo-Marxist journals like *Social Text* and *October* and indebted to the theorists Jean Baudrillard and Paul Virilio. There is a touch of frenzy in the style. Consider this rhapsodic passage, taken virtually at random from *Specters of Marx:* "Entire regiments of ghosts have returned, armies from every age, camouflaged by the archaic symptoms of the paramilitary and the postmodern excess of arms (information technology, panoptical surveillance via satellite, nuclear threat, and so forth). Let us accelerate things. Beyond these two types of war (civil and international) whose dividing line cannot even be distinguished any longer, let us blacken still more the picture of this wearing down beyond wear. Let us name with a single trait that which could risk making the euphoria of liberal-democratic capitalism resemble the blindest and most delirious of hallucinations, or even an increasingly glaring hypocrisy in its formal or juridicist rhetoric of human rights" (80). The prophetic tone here takes on active scorn for the rhetoric of justice under "liberal-democratic capitalism": such rhetoric, Derrida tells us, is merely "formal or juridicist." As in his Cardozo lecture, Derrida suggests that there is a truer, messianic justice, antithetical to the workings of the law.

From time to time, Derrida salutes "those who are working . . . in the direction of the perfectibility and emancipation of institutions that must never be renounced" (84). But this obligatory nod to liberalism is in jarring contrast to the apocalyptic coloring that saturates *Specters of Marx.* The re-forming of institutions pales next to the ghostly techno-hell of the "so-called liberal democracies" with their "media tele-technology," which afflicts us in its "irreducibly spectral dimension" (53). Derrida had apparently lost his faith in liberalism.

To praise an apocalyptic Marxism and scorn the "so-called liberal democracies," as Derrida does, slights the fact that the struggle for political freedom, the fight against corrupt governments and corporations, is much easier in liberal democracy than in any other kind of society. As Wolin argues, Derrida in his Marx book, like Heidegger in his famous last testament, the interview with *Der Spiegel* released after his death, is looking for a god to save us: an unimaginable future that might transport us out of the degraded present. In *Spec-*

ters of Marx, Derrida's spectacular flights of doom-mongering crowd out any possibility of actual political discussion. He prefers to deliver vague prophetic fervor, instead of discussing in concrete terms what criteria we might use for assigning social resources, redistributing economic power, or arguing about just and unjust wars.

Derrida frequently interrupts *Specters of Marx* with meditations on the ghost in *Hamlet.* At times, he seems to be attempting a far-out deconstructionist equivalent of Hamlet's speculations: "The logic of haunting would not be merely larger and more powerful than an ontology or a thinking of Being (of the 'to be,' assuming that it is a matter of Being in the 'to be or not to be,' but nothing is less certain). It would harbor within itself, but like circumscribed places or particular effects, eschatology and teleology themselves. It would *comprehend* them, but incomprehensibly. How to *comprehend* in fact the discourse of the end or the discourse about the end? Can the extremity of the extreme ever be comprehended? And the opposition between 'to be' and 'not to be'?" (10). Thus Derrida, king of infinite space, incomprehensibly comprehends the extremity of the extreme. A cold cosmic wind whistles through Derrida's sentences; in his book on Marx, one sees his inspiration at low ebb.

Derrida continued to pursue his interest in justice. In January and February 1997, he gave a course in Paris (to be repeated at Irvine) on the theme of "Hostipitality." The tongue-twister title was meant to accommodate the sense of the Latin word *hostis:* both host and guest—and enemy as well. To be hospitable, Derrida announced in his course, "is to let oneself be overtaken . . . to be surprised, in a fashion almost violent, to be raped, stolen . . . precisely where one is not ready to receive" (*Acts* 361).

"Hospitality is the deconstruction of the at-home; deconstruction is hospitality to the other, to the other than oneself," Derrida proclaims (364). This exalted vision of hospitality Derrida derives in part from chapter 12 of Genesis, in which Abraham becomes a wanderer, leaving his homeland of Ur. The fact that Abraham is himself uprooted, Derrida argues, allows him to become a host to the angels who visit him (in chapter 18). The astonishing scene in which Abraham bargains with God over the fate of Sodom, arguing that the Lord should spare the city, is also an act of hospitality in Derrida's sense: a taking responsibility for the life or death of the other. The other's hope for survival may displace one's own interests. In a story like Abraham's argument over Sodom, "one becomes, prior to being the host, the hostage of the other," given over to the hope for the other's survival (365). (This theme is familiar from Lévinas.)[6]

Such a radical vision of self-sacrifice means sacrificing, as well, one's judgment about the moral choices made by others. If Sodom is about to be destroyed, this is no time to weigh the faults of its inhabitants. The extreme pressure that Derrida exerts here, by pointing to a situation in which utter destruction is threatened, allows him to avoid moral description (as he did in his treatment of de Man and Heidegger, who, like the Sodomites, might not have survived bombardment from the skies). But—one might answer Derrida—even in the midst of catastrophe, people make character-revealing choices; and one can demonstrate hospitality toward them without abandoning a sense of who they are.

Once again, Derrida sees justice as so urgent that it is inconceivable, surpassing our customary ways of judging actions. For him, justice requires potentially dreadful self-sacrifice. The melodrama of such martyrdom, being "raped" or "stolen" by one's guest, diverts him from a more realistic study of how we are actually bound together in social life. As psyches, and as citizens, we continue to evaluate one another. And such evaluation cannot be separated from our sense of what dealing justly means.

Derrida argues in his hospitality course, as he does in his Cardozo lecture and his 1998 speeches in South Africa about the aftermath of apartheid, that only what is unforgivable can truly be forgiven: precisely because it is impossible to forgive the unforgivable, and because it is in such impossibility that real forgiveness consists. True justice necessarily takes such paradoxical form—if it can be said to exist at all. "Forgiveness must therefore *do the impossible*," Derrida intones. "It must undergo the test and ordeal of its own impossibility in forgiving the unforgivable . . . the possibility, if it is possible and if there is such, the possibility *of* the impossible. And the impossible of the possible" (386). (In South Africa, Derrida went so far as to suggest that forgetting, rather than remembrance, ought to be the point of the Truth and Reconciliation Commission.) Ironically, Derrida the great opponent of metaphysics constructs a sublimely metaphysical ideal of justice.

Such abstraction required a countermovement, a return to concrete issues. In 2001, a book of conversations between Derrida and the psychoanalyst Elisabeth Roudinesco was published under the title *For What Tomorrow . . . A Dialogue.* In this book, Derrida continues his aggressive program of "getting political," delivering statements on pressing questions including capital punishment, racism and anti-Semitism, and the future of Europe. (Interestingly, Derrida, while condemning executions in the United States, takes no notice of the more widespread use of capital punishment in China. In the last few years of his life Derrida received several doctorates from Chinese universities and, as a frequent visitor to China, was enthusiastic about the popularity of deconstruction there.)

For What Tomorrow, though rather miscellaneous in form, is useful for the evidence it provides of the intense degree of adulation directed toward Derrida near the end of his life. He had become, in some quarters, a truly prophetic figure, uniquely qualified to pronounce on the moral and political questions of his era. In her preface to *For What Tomorrow,* Roudinesco recounts her decision to interview Derrida, despite the danger, as she describes it, of being struck mute by his eloquence: "His gifts as a speaker, the power of his arguments, his boldness regarding certain problems of our times—as well as the practical wisdom acquired from countless lectures given in every part of the world—threatened to take my voice away" (ix).

Roudinesco recovers her voice. She begins by comparing Derrida to Zola, calling him "the incarnation of the Revolution" (9) and informing him, "In short, I am inclined to say you have triumphed" (2). She then makes herself heard on the subject of the United States, a familiar piñata for French theorists. "Every time I go there I feel a terrible violence," she shudders (29). Why, one wonders? Guns, drugs, racism, capital punishment? No, actually, it's . . . smoking bans. (Derrida mildly responds that anti-smoking laws have also been passed in France.)

Roudinesco goes on to the subject of sex on campus and what Derrida calls the "microclimate of terror" that surrounds it in the United States. "Sometimes," Derrida remarks, a professor "risks being accused because he smiled, gave a female student a 'compliment,' invited her to have coffee, etc." Referring to "what everyone agrees to call 'rape,'" Derrida notes that "the most widely shared passion never excludes some kind of asymmetry from which the scene of rape is never completely erased—and even informs the lovers' desires" (31). Derrida's comment may be offensive to some, but at least he stops short of Foucault's advocacy of decriminalizing rape (because, Foucault argued, sexuality should not be subject to legal regulations). He even, with some hedging, admits that sexual harassment exists.[7]

In *For What Tomorrow* Derrida prides himself on his iconoclasm, reporting that "in the United States, at the law school of a Jewish university [Cardozo Law School of Yeshiva University], I used this word *genocide* to designate the operation consisting, in certain cases, in gathering together hundreds of thousands of beasts every day, sending them to the slaughterhouse, and killing them en masse after having fattened them with hormones" (73). But he seems, provocatively, to be in collusion with such genocide. Announcing that "I do not believe in absolute 'vegetarianism,'" Derrida (who was a devoted carnivore) added, "I would go so far as to claim that, in a more or less refined, subtle, sublime form, a certain cannibalism remains unsurpassable" (67).

Derrida's comments on meat eating and sexual harassment have a casual air. Clearly, these are not his main concerns. Jewishness, however, is such a concern. Derrida and Roudinesco devote a considerable portion of their discussion to the Jewish question. Derrida comments that "it is only *just today* that, along with others, I am overcome with vertigo before something that has lately become obvious to me: French society continues to welcome back the old demons, particularly in milieus and in public spaces that, I thought, were safe from them" (110). Derrida remembers being expelled from high school in 1942, subjected to "daily insults" in the streets, to "threats and blows aimed at the 'dirty Jew,' which, I might say, I came to see in myself" (109). "Anti-Semitism was always rampant there [in Algeria]," Derrida says to Roudinesco. "This is well known" (113). "Nothing for me matters as much as my Jewishness," Derrida remarks, "which, however, in so many ways, matters so little in my life" (112). (Derrida married a non-Jew and, like Freud, refused to have his sons circumcised: a fact that Derrida mentions in *Archive Fever*, his late book on Freud [*Jacques Derrida* 222].)

Derrida and Roudinesco go on to discuss Noam Chomsky's defense of Robert Faurisson. Faurisson was, and still is, a frequent presence at Holocaust denial conventions. He has written several books on what he calls the "swindle" of the Shoah, claiming that "Hitler never ordered nor admitted that anyone should be killed on account of his race or religion," and going on to state that "the alleged 'gas chambers' and the alleged 'genocide' are one and the same lie" (cited in *Rising* 63). Chomsky not only advocated Faurisson's right to claim that the Holocaust had never occurred; he also allowed his statement to be used as a preface to one of Faurisson's books. In his preface, Chomsky noted that Faurisson did not appear to be an anti-Semite, but rather an "apolitical liberal." Derrida defended Chomsky's championing of Faurisson, arguing that Chomsky was merely standing up for an "unassailable" right to speak. He went on to advocate the dismantling of Europe's laws against Holocaust denial: public shaming of Holocaust deniers, as occurs in the United States, should take the place of legal prohibition.[8]

The nineties were hard times for Jewish causes, in part due to the influence in the academy of two passionately anti-Zionist intellectuals, Chomsky and the Palestinian-American professor Edward Said. Both campaigned for the elimination of the Jewish state, alone among the nations of the earth; Israel's very existence was seen as the bearer of a unique evil.[9]

And they did not shrink from misrepresenting the history of the Arab-Israeli conflict to serve their cause. Derrida in his conversations with Roudinesco refers to "an anti-Israeli indoctrination that rarely avoids anti-Semitism" (117); and he sees in references to the so-called Jewish lobby "a clear token of anti-Semitism" (118). (Derrida, it is important to add, also showed great sympathy for the tragic situation of the Palestinians.) Shortly after Derrida's interview with Roudinesco, things would get much worse, with Arab fury unleashed in France in retaliation for Israel's war in the Palestinian territories. In April 2002 alone there were 400 anti-Semitic attacks in France; synagogues and Jewish schools were firebombed. French Jews were panicked, and many emigrated, aware that more French citizens sympathized with the Palestinians than with the Israelis.[10] As his conversation with Roudinesco indicates, Jewish identity was once again forcing itself on Derrida's attention, as it had done in the 1940s in Algeria.

Derrida was about to encounter a test case for his political and prophetic voice. The events of September 11, 2001, called out for a response from all philosophers and intellectuals. When Derrida heard about the fall of the World Trade Center towers he was in a café in Shanghai, on a lecture tour of China. Several weeks later, he returned to Europe, where he received the Theodor Adorno prize from the city of Frankfurt. He was ready to reflect on the significance of the terrorist attacks.

Shortly after the Adorno prize ceremony, Derrida flew to New York, where he observed the aftermath of September 11 and where he was interviewed by the Italian journalist Giovanna Borradori. The interview was later published as a book, *Philosophy in a Time of Terror* (which also included a conversation between Borradori and the German philosopher Jürgen

Habermas). Derrida's commentary on 9/11 is frustrating on several accounts. He begins with expansive speculation, dwelling especially on the phrase "major event" in relation to 9/11. "What is an event worthy of this name?" Derrida asks. "And a 'major' event, that is, one that is actually more of an 'event,' more actually an 'event,' than ever? An event that would bear witness, in an exemplary or hyperbolic fashion, to the very essence of an event or even to an event beyond essence? For could an event that still conforms to an essence, to a law or to a truth, indeed to a concept of the event, ever be a major event?" (*Philosophy* 9). Not surprisingly, all these Derridean questions remain open. (In an essay published in the *New York Times* a few days after Derrida's death, Edward Rothstein quoted with disapproval Derrida's ornate comment on the phrase "September 11": "The telegram of this metonymy—a name, a number—points out the unqualifiable by recognizing that we do not recognize or even cognize that we do not know how to qualify, that we do not know what we are talking about.")[11]

Derrida declares that the 9/11 massacre "will have targeted and hit the heart, or, rather, the symbolic head of the prevailing world order. Right at the level of the head (*cap, caput, capital, Capitol*), this double suicide will have touched two places at once symbolically and operationally essential to the American corpus" (*Philosophy* 95–96). Only a few weeks after the biggest terrorist assault in history, near the ruins of the site, stood Jacques Derrida, darting and punning in his fluent way.

After having wondered whether there is such a thing as an event, much less a major event, Derrida goes on to ask if there really are terrorists. "In the first place, what is terror? What distinguishes it from fear, anxiety, and panic?" (102). He concludes that "'terrorist' acts try to produce psychic effects

(conscious or unconscious) and symbolic or symptomatic reactions that might take numerous detours, an incalculable
number of them, in truth. . . . And does terrorism have to
work only through death? Can't one terrorize without killing? And does killing necessarily mean putting to death? Isn't
it also 'letting die'? Can't 'letting die,' 'not wanting to know that
one is letting others die'—hundreds of millions of human beings, from hunger, AIDS, lack of medical treatment, and so
on—also be part of a 'more or less' conscious and deliberate
terrorist strategy?" (107–8). So (apparently), if I neglect to
contribute to Doctors Without Borders, I'm a terrorist, comparable to the suicide murderer on a school bus who fervently
hopes to kill as many children as possible. (Derrida adds
that the members of the French resistance were also terrorists
[109].)

Derrida's determination to avoid supplying an overly
narrow definition of terrorism lands him in bleak, skeptical
confusion. If we're all terrorists, then nobody is. As in his Cardozo lecture and other commentaries of the 1990s, Derrida
prefers to invoke justice on an abstract level rather than con-
sidering its application to actual cases; and this abstracting
tendency leads to a lack of ethical discrimination. Most of us
would agree that the deliberate murder of noncombatants, including children, is a greater moral fault than turning aside
from instances of suffering. By demonstrating his lack of interest in such distinctions, Derrida deprives himself of the status he aims for: the renowned philosopher pronouncing on
the central ethical issues of our time.[12] At the apex of his ambition as a political intellectual, Derrida found himself ham-
pered by his unwillingness to engage in moral judgment.

During these same years Derrida was involved in the
making of a film about his life. In contrast to the conversations

with Roudinesco and Borradori, *Derrida,* released in 2002, does not devote much time to the themes of politics and justice. Its center of interest is not Derrida's political opinions but his idea of the cryptic, necessarily hidden self.[13] In 1995 Amy Ziering Kofman, who had attended Derrida's lectures at Yale and at the Sorbonne, decided she wanted to make a documentary film about him. Kofman, then living in California, proposed the film to Derrida after a lecture at UC–Irvine. After a long silence, Derrida scribbled a postcard from Paris expressing his approval, and they were off.

At least, this is what Kofman thought had happened. Derrida had actually written *no* on the postcard, but in his customary, very bad handwriting. In any event, the film was made, and it is a fascinating document. Derrida, though something of a dandy with his fashionable suits and flamboyantly styled hair, was noticeably uncomfortable being filmed. (In a memorable scene from the movie, we actually see Derrida at the hair salon, the stylist's scissors snipping away as Kofman recites a passage from one of his essays on Nietzsche.)

Not happy with how he looked on screen, Derrida was equally wary of having his thought misrepresented, as it had so often been by the media: he demanded that he be given final veto power over the movie. After the final cut had been made, he would get to see the movie first, and any scenes or images he disliked would be removed. Kofman agreed to these terms, a very unusual move for a documentary filmmaker. (As it turned out, Derrida asked that some of the footage of his wife Marguerite in their kitchen be removed and that he himself not be shown choking on yogurt at breakfast.) Kofman enlisted as codirector a much more experienced filmmaker, Kirby Dick.

Derrida shows Derrida in the midst of daily life: buttering toast, listening to the radio, walking down New York streets trailed by the movie's leather-jacketed directors, and sitting at home with his wife. After a lecture at Northwestern University, eager students surround him and ask him about the connections between his work and the kabbalah. One hapless young woman says to Derrida, "I read one of your novels over the summer." We then see Derrida giving a lecture in Paris, with Marguerite and Hélène Cixous sitting side by side in the audience, while he explains with some fumbling the presence of the film crew next to him.

In front of Kirby Dick's handheld camera, Derrida improvises monologues, usually rambling reflections on subjects like eyes, hands, and the other. While Derrida sits at dinner, a voice-over delivers a statement about "the economy of a much more welcoming and hospitable narcissism, one that is much more open to the experience of the other as other." A reporter asks him about *Seinfeld* as an example of deconstruction, much to his bewilderment.

The movie ends with Derrida's stunned reticence when Kofman asks him, first, if he would consider being psychoanalyzed ("No, I absolutely exclude this") and then if there have been any "traumatic breaks" in his life. Derrida answers, "There have been, yes," and then—in response to Kofman's unspoken invitation to discuss these traumas—"Again, no I won't be able to, uh, no, no. No." The voice-over repeats a Derrida passage on "the unconditional right to secrecy."

At another point in the movie, Kofman asks Derrida to talk about love. Derrida's response is "love or death?" to which she sensibly answers, "Love, not death. We've heard enough about death."

Derrida premiered at the Film Forum in New York on October 23, 2002. After the screening, Derrida and the two filmmakers participated in a question and answer session with the audience. Derrida was relaxed and funny. Asked about his interest in music, he recounted to the audience his experience of appearing onstage in July 1997 at the La Villette jazz festival with Ornette Coleman, at Coleman's request. While Coleman played the saxophone, Derrida read one of his own texts. He admitted with a smile that Coleman's fans, no adepts of deconstruction, booed and heckled him.

In Kofman and Dick's film, after a tantalizing, quickly dropped reference to his courtship of Marguerite, Derrida remarks, "I can't tell a story . . . I just don't know how to tell them." This is a real moment of insight into Derrida's philosophy, which is supremely nonnarrative (or even antinarrative). Throughout his work, Derrida remains relatively uninterested in the stories people tell to explain themselves. He lacks Nietzsche's fine hand for the summary psychological portrait; as I have argued, he would like to reject psychology altogether. Instead, he thinks of his own history, and anyone's, in terms of little details, mostly linguistic. Such details are for him ways of hiding personal identity rather than revealing it (as in the trivia of *The Post Card*). These seeming ephemera— little turns of phrase, a favorite term—provide for Derrida the equivalent of a Proustian concreteness. His discussions of Paul Celan prize exactly such secretive, yet strangely intimate, opacity.

The identification with a writer like Celan (another exile like him, a displaced Jew) might well stand at the heart of Derrida's identity. Derrida's true inwardness, one is tempted to think, remains distinct from both his early skepticism and his later, heavy-handed generalizations about justice and ethics.

In the last interview he gave before his death, Derrida said, "I am never more haunted by the necessity of dying than in moments of happiness and joy. To feel joy and to weep over the death that awaits are for me the same thing. When I recall my life, I tend to think that I have had the good fortune to love even the unhappy moments of my life, and to bless them. Almost all of them, with just one exception."[14] The poignance of this confession is remarkable—as is its claim to secrecy. Derrida will not tell us what the "unhappy moment" was, the one that he could not bless. Unlike his rival Lacan, but like Nietzsche, Derrida had a high, sentimental attachment to the inner self, whose desires and memories remain inviolable.

We can end here, with Derrida's moving testimony to his own life, and with the oddly telling reticence shown in Kofman and Dick's *Derrida*. The philosopher and his disciples had conquered the intellectual world—at least part of it, at least for a time. But, as his evasive comments to the filmmakers and interviewers indicate, Jacques Derrida retained his hiddenness to the end. His readers were left to wonder, at the last, who he was.

Coda

Two days after Jacques Derrida died of pancreatic cancer, on October 10, 2004, the readers of the *New York Times* saw a front-page obituary titled "Jacques Derrida, Abstruse Theorist, Dies at 74." The *Times* obituary called Derrida's works "turgid and baffling" and noted that he seemed to aim for an effect of maximum incomprehensibility. When asked to define his trademark term, deconstruction, Derrida would say only: "It is impossible to respond" (so the *Times* reported). The *Times*'s farewell to Derrida was, to say the least, not respectful: rarely has an obituary been so openly scornful of its subject. Why such resentment, on the part of America's newspaper of record, for a renowned French thinker?

Jacques Derrida, along with a few other French theorists, had spurred a great upheaval in the academic humanities, especially in literature departments: a revolution that decisively moved university-level literary study beyond the reach of the common reader. The average consumer of the *New York Times,* the audience for its book reviews and discussions of the arts, no longer understood what the professors were saying.[1] The frustration that attended this revolution, on the part of those unsympathetic to it, is understandable. Yet the rancor of the

Times, and of Jacques Derrida's many other opponents both inside and outside the academy, serves only to distort an accurate assessment of his work, of the kind that I have attempted in this book. Derrida was neither so brilliantly right nor so badly wrong as his enthusiasts and critics respectively claimed.

My central point remains Derrida's own sense of bafflement, his wish to find an escape from the battle between metaphysical assertion and deconstructive doubt that he had designed. Fairly early in Derrida's career, the conflict between metaphysics and skepticism, between logocentrism and the thought of différance, began to take on the look of an airless, unproductive paradox. He sought a way out by means of the prophetic style that he borrowed, at different moments, from Nietzsche in his high, rhapsodic pitch, and from the more sober Lévinas.

In the de Man affair of the late 1980s, Derrida's two paths leading away from the metaphysics-skepticism question, the Nietzschean and the Lévinasian, collided. Derrida suggested that, since the logos floats free of any controlling human agency, there is a basic irresponsibility encoded in all our words and actions: we cannot judge de Man because we remain incapable of defining and rendering accountable the biographical entity "de Man." This was the Nietzschean element, Derrida's assumption of a free play of meaning. (Nietzsche himself, of course, was more interested in psychological insight. Derrida takes as his guide not the proto-psychoanalytic Nietzsche but the deconstructionist Nietzsche of the late *Will to Power* fragments, who was busy dissolving the categories of personal intention and consciousness.)

After concluding that the de Man case was insoluble, Derrida then took a further, contradictory step. He decided that we are obligated to confront and forgive de Man, who was in this case the Lévinasian other suffering posthumously at the hands of his journalistic persecutors. We are bound to acknowledge the inscrutability of the person Paul de Man, and to respect this hiddenness. Since we will never know enough about him to judge him, we can truly confront and acknowledge him only by forgiving him.

At least in the instance of Paul de Man, Derrida proves unable after all to refrain from the psychological perspective he warns against: he envisions de Man's inner torment during the war. Such excursions into psychological drama are rare in Derrida's work. De Man elicits dramatization because of his cherished closeness to Derrida as friend and influence. More often, Derrida insists that we revere the cryptic character of the individual life by resisting the temptation to tell a story about others or about ourselves. The hiddenness of the self is a crucial theme in Derrida's essays on Paul Celan, and it motivates his resistance to psychological interpretation in Plato and Freud. Derrida explains his resistance to the theme of consciousness by his reverence for the integrity of the self, an integrity that renders it opaque to analysis. We should try not to imagine the consciousness of other people (or, by extension, of ourselves). Derrida therefore forfeits, or pretends to forfeit, any serious interest in explaining our words and deeds.

According to Derrida, my unconscious is more telling than my consciousness. The limitations of such an approach should be obvious. As in Derrida's account of de Man, what remains is an empty field for projections on the part of the interpreter. To be honest about this process means admitting, as Derrida did not, that we must continue inventing inwardness, that we cannot adopt an attitude of religious caution before the other's secret.

The lesson, then, is that psychology remains a necessary perspective: that we cannot live in Derrida's clean, imagined conflict between metaphysics and skepticism. Derrida himself broke with this pure opposition in his bouts of prophetic insistence; he was unable to decide whether the prophecy was of a new freedom (Nietzsche) or a new obligation (Lévinas). But he continued to avoid psychology.

My reason for writing this book is my belief that Derrida's confusion is instructive, because it tells us something about our current desire to evoke, in one gesture, imaginative diversity together with ethical responsibility. Derrida appealed to so many for a reason: he embodied a contradiction that is still ours, between the liberation that we sense in an expanded field of meaning and our ethical obligation to others. It is impossible to make one goal serve the other, despite our current inclination to see in the freedom from rigidly defined, artificially imposed notions of identity a demonstration of the dignity, and therefore the worth, of humans. On the level of aspiration—when we search for a commanding, motivating insight, a tablet of the law—Nietzsche and Lévinas remain incompatible.

But both are aspects of us already. Returning to psychology—to a necessary, rather than freely invented, myth of the self—is a way of reminding ourselves of how obligation interweaves with fascination. Derrida gave little attention to what interests us in people; he was too intent on safeguarding otherness. It is time to overcome his purity.

Notes

Introduction

1. The writings of Stanley Cavell are an essential guide to skepticism in this sense: see, in particular, *The Claim of Reason: Wittgenstein, Skepticism, Morality, and Tragedy* (New York: Oxford University Press, 1979). Cavell discusses Derrida in his *Philosophical Passages* (*Philosophical*).

2. On this point, see Stanley Rosen, *Hermeneutics as Politics* (New Haven, CT: Yale University Press, 2003). As Rosen states regarding the *Phaedrus* (and in objection to Derrida's reading of it), "There is no other 'relation with oneself' but the mythical" (85).

3. See Koethe, *Poetry*, 48–49.

4. Among the studies of deconstruction that I have found useful, in addition to those cited later in the main text, are Jonathan Culler, *On Deconstruction* (Ithaca, NY: Cornell University Press, 1982); John Ellis, *Against Deconstruction* (Princeton, NJ: Princeton University Press, 1989); Michael Fischer, *Stanley Cavell and Literary Skepticism* (Chicago: University of Chicago Press, 1989); Eugene Goodheart, *The Reign of Ideology* (New York: Columbia University Press, 1997); Barbara Johnson, *The Critical Difference* (Baltimore: Johns Hopkins University Press, 1981); Christopher Norris, *Derrida* (Cambridge, MA: Harvard University Press, 1988); and Raymond Tallis, *Not Saussure*, 2nd ed. (London: Macmillan, 1995). Also significant is the study by Michèle Lamont, "How to Become a Dominant French Philosopher: The Case of Jacques Derrida," *American Journal of Sociology* 93:3 (Nov. 1987): 584–622. More generally, several works on recent criticism have been

helpful: see David Bromwich, *Politics by Other Means* (New Haven, CT: Yale University Press, 1992); Morris Dickstein, *Double Agent* (New York: Oxford University Press, 1996); Denis Donoghue, *The Practice of Reading* (New Haven, CT: Yale University Press, 1998); Mark Edmundson, *Literature Against Philosophy, Plato to Derrida* (New York: Cambridge University Press, 1995); and Geoffrey Harpham, *Getting It Right* (Chicago: University of Chicago Press, 1992).

Chapter 1
From Algeria to the École Normale

1. See Albert Memmi, *Juifs et arabes* (Paris: Gallimard, 1974), 51.

2. For an influential and persuasive treatment of the Algerian conflict, see Alistair Horne, *A Savage War of Peace: Algeria 1954–1962* (New York: Viking/Random House, 1978).

3. See Benjamin Stora, *Algeria, 1830–2000: A Short History* (Ithaca, NY: Cornell University Press, 2004), 39.

4. See Jim House and Neil MacMaster, *Paris 1961: Algerians, State Terror, and Memory* (New York: Oxford University Press, 2006).

5. "Amoureuse beauté de la terre, l'effloraison de ta surface est merveilleuse. O paysage où mon désir s'est enfoncé! Pays ouvert où ma recherche se promène; allée de papyrus qui se referme sur de l'eau; roseaux courbés sur la riviere . . . J'ai vu se dérouler des printemps" (André Gide, *Les nourritures terrestres*, book 1, section 3 [Paris: Bordas, 1971], 87).

6. Jacques Derrida with Jean Birnbaum, *Learning to Live Finally: The Last Interview* (London: Palgrave Macmillan, 2007), 43–44.

7. Much to his credit, the young Derrida refused to emulate Sartre's politics. He also, in later years, resisted the Sartre-like engagement of Noam Chomsky and Edward Said, two idols of American leftist academics. Said and Chomsky sometimes applauded tyrannies just as long as they were anti-American, anti-imperialist, or anti-Israeli. Said, a longtime member of the political branch of Yasir Arafat's Palestine Liberation Organization, heartily approved of the repressive "Marxist" state of South Yemen, which was at least a step above Chomsky's well-known support for Pol Pot's Cambodia. Both were enthusiastic about Hezbollah.

8. Quoted in Harold Bloom, ed., *Jean-Paul Sartre: Modern Critical Views* (Philadelphia: Chelsea House, 2001), 2. Murdoch's book on Sartre, first published in 1953 and entitled *Sartre: Romantic Rationalist* (New York: Viking/Random House, 1987), remains one of the best treatments of his thought.

9. Bernard Henri Lévy, in his account of Sartre, expands on the notion of the desire for self-coincidence, and outlines its necessary collapse: "Ce sujet, d'abord, n'a plus d'interiorité. Il est cette chose qu'il vise. Celle-là. Il est la visée meme de la chose, le fait de se jeter ou projeter vers elle. Mais qu'il essaie de se reprendre, dit Sartre, qu'il essaie d'oublier un instant ces choses pour coincider avec soi-meme, se mettre 'au chaud, volets clos,' dans l'intimité d'une conscience qui ne serait plus que le lieu moite a partir duquel se prepareraient les incursions prochaines, et alors il s'efface, se dissout—Sartre dit 's'anéantit'" (Levy, *Le siècle de Sartre* [Paris: Grasset, 2000], 249–50).

10. For example, in Sartre's well-known vignette of the voyeur caught in the act, in *Being and Nothingness* (1943).

11. Dermot Moran, *Introduction to Phenomenology* (London: Routledge, 2000), 436–51.

12. Quoted in Herbert Spiegelberg, *The Phenomenological Movement: A Historical Introduction* (The Hague: Martinus Nijhoff, 1981), vol. 1, 81–82.

13. Natalie Alexander, "The Hollow Deconstruction of Time," in William R. McKenna and J. Claude Evans, eds., *Derrida and Phenomenology* (Dordrecht, Netherlands: Kluwer, 1995), 129.

14. David Wood, ed., *Derrida: A Critical Reader* (London: Wiley-Blackwell, 1989), 111.

Chapter 2
Writing and Difference and *Of Grammatology*

1. Claude Lévi-Strauss, *Tristes Tropiques,* tr. John and Doreen Weightman (New York: Washington Square Press, 1977 [1st French ed. 1955]), 51–52.

2. Lévi-Strauss, *Tristes Tropiques,* 136.

3. In *Of Grammatology,* Derrida produces something of a cartoon Rousseau. He transforms a sophisticated thinker into a nostalgist yearning for a world replete with innocent, fulfilling comforts, a place of perfect nurture. As his friend de Man suggested in *Blindness and Insight,* Derrida caricatures Rousseau's argument in order to get the better of him. As the Rousseau scholar Jean Starobinski notes, for Rousseau language "evolves into an antinature": "It is man's dangerous privilege to possess in his own nature the powers by which he combats that nature and nature itself. . . . Reasoned argument becomes necessary if man is to recover the voice of nature by means of a kind of interpretive archaeology. Man must devise

artificial substitutes for the 'immediate impulses' that ensured respect for others and preservation of his own life" (*Jean-Jacques Rousseau: Transparency and Obstruction*, tr. Arthur Goldhammer [Chicago: University of Chicago Press, 1988 (1st French ed. 1971)], 305–7). As Starobinski makes clear, Rousseau is in fact the master of the paradoxical knowledge that Derrida denies him (in order to attribute it to himself, Rousseau's reader).

4. Interview with the author (Houston, 2006).

5. The remark is quoted from Todorov, *Literature and its Theorists: A Personal View of Twentieth-Century Criticism*, tr. Catherine Porter (Ithaca, NY: Cornell University Press, 1989), 190.

6. My sense of Nietzsche has been informed by Stanley Rosen, *The Mask of Enlightenment: Nietzsche's Zarathustra* (New Haven, CT: Yale University Press, 2004 [1st edition 1995]); and Laurence Lampert, *Nietzsche's Teaching: An Interpretation of* Thus Spoke Zarathustra (New Haven, CT: Yale University Press, 1986).

7. Richard H. Armstrong, *A Compulsion for Antiquity: Freud and the Ancient World* (Ithaca, NY: Cornell University Press, 2005), 230.

8. Freud is presented as a Jewish thinker by Harold Bloom in *Ruin the Sacred Truths: Poetry and Belief from the Bible to the Present* (Cambridge, MA: Harvard University Press, 1989), 143–70. Bloom argues that Freud's notions of anxiety and repression are fundamentally indebted to the incommensurability of man and God as presented in episodes of the Torah (for example, Abraham's argument with God over the destruction of Sodom and Gomorrah, and Abraham's near sacrifice of Isaac).

Chapter 3
Plato, Austin, Nietzsche, Freud

1. For the English version of the *Phaedrus* I rely, with a few modifications, on C. J. Rowe's translation (Warminster, England: Aris & Phillips, 1998); I have also consulted the version by Alexander Nehamas and Paul Woodruff (Indianapolis: Hackett Publishing, 1995). I have cited the text by Stephanus numbers. Harvey Yunis in "Eros in Plato's *Phaedrus* and the Shape of Greek Rhetoric" (*Arion* 13:1 [Spring/Summer 2005]: 101–25) argues forcefully that Plato in the charioteer speech of the *Phaedrus* remakes rhetoric so that it is no longer oriented toward plausibility and the appeal to the audience's reasonable judgment, but rather toward their "capacity to imagine transcendence and human perfection" (116). See also 119–20, where Yunis credits Plato with moving rhetoric away from "mundane criteria of expedi-

ency and fairness," which are linked to the adversarial situations characteristic of law and politics. There is a later, somewhat parallel development of inspirational rhetoric when the Christian "need to convert souls" arrives (120).

2. Penelope Deutscher, *How to Read Derrida* (London: Granta Books, 2005), 12.

3. Charles Griswold, *Self-Knowledge in Plato's Phaedrus* (New Haven, CT: Yale University Press, 1986); and Giovanni R. F. Ferrari, *Listening to the Cicadas: A Study of Plato's Phaedrus* (New York: Cambridge University Press, 1987).

4. One of Austin's spectacular examples, in his essay "A Plea for Excuses" (in *Philosophical Papers*) details the difference between shooting a donkey accidentally and doing so by mistake: "You have a donkey, so have I, and they graze in the same field. The day comes when I conceive a dislike for mine. I go to shoot it, draw a bead on it, fire: the brute falls in its tracks. I inspect the victim, and find to my horror that it is your donkey. I appear on your doorstep with the remains and say—what? 'I say, old sport, I'm awfully sorry, &c, I've shot your donkey by *accident*'? Or 'by mistake'? Then again, I go to shoot my donkey as before, draw a bead on it, fire—but as I do so, the beasts move, and to my horror yours falls. Again the scene on the doorstep—what do I say? 'By mistake'? Or 'by accident'?" (185n).

5. Wittgenstein also questions this idea in the opening sequence of the *Philosophical Investigations,* the famous "Bring me a slab" discussion. But Wittgenstein writes with the aim of returning us to ordinary life rather than, like Derrida, removing us from this life. In this way Wittgenstein, and Austin too, differs decisively from Derrida.

6. Stanley Cavell, "What Did Derrida Want of Austin?" in Cavell, *Philosophical Passages* (*Philosophical*).

7. Austin believed in an essentially moral role for the philosopher. He noted that both Plato and Aristotle confused the difference between succumbing to temptation and losing control, a confusion "as bad in its day and its way as the later, grotesque, confusion of moral weakness with weakness of will" (*Papers* 198). (Often we succumb to temptation in high style, knowing perfectly well what we're doing; making this point, Austin sounds for a moment like Oscar Wilde.) And rather than being concerned in merely pragmatic fashion with whether actions or statements come off or misfire, Austin raises in a telltale footnote the question of whether they are *sound:* that is, fair or accurate (*Papers* 250).

8. On the early reception of Nietzsche, see Steven Ascheim, *The Nietzsche Legacy in Germany, 1890–1990* (Berkeley: University of California Press, 1992); on developments in feminist readings of Nietzsche after Der-

rida, see Peter Burgard, ed., *Nietzsche and the Feminine* (Charlottesville: University of Virginia Press, 1994).

9. Richard Rorty, *Contingency, Irony and Solidarity* (New York: Cambridge University Press, 1989), 129.

10. See Mark Edmundson, *Towards Reading Freud: Self-Creation in Milton, Wordsworth, Emerson, and Sigmund Freud* (Princeton, NJ: Princeton University Press, 1990).

Chapter 4
Gadamer, Celan, de Man, Heidegger

1. Maurizio Ferraris in *Jackie Derrida, Ritratto a memoria* (Turin: Bollati Boringhieri, 2006), 16, notes that Derrida, an anxious traveler, habitually arrived at airports hours before his plane was due to depart. For a few years, 1969 to 1973, his anxiety about flying led him to avoid air travel altogether. Another major event of these years was Derrida's affair with Sylviane Agaçinski, who worked with him in the organization of philosophers, GREPH, that he had helped found. When she was 39, in 1984, Agaçinski bore a son by Derrida.

2. As Fred Dallmayr puts it in his commentary on the Gadamer-Derrida debate, "Derrida's key notion of 'difference' shades over into a celebration of indifference, non-engagement, and indecision. . . . By stressing rupture and radical otherness Derrida seeks to uproot and dislodge the inquirer's comfortable self-identity; yet, his insistence on incommensurability and non-understanding tends to encourage reciprocal cultural disengagement and hence non-learning" (*Dialogue* 90, 92).

3. When the Paris exchange was published in a German edition, Gadamer supplied a response to Derrida in which he heatedly protested Derrida's wish to align him with Kantian ideas of morality. There is absolutely nothing moral, Gadamer claims, and also nothing "metaphysical" or "logocentric," about the desire to understand. Instead, understanding is what allows one to make a good argument. "That is to say, one does not go about identifying the weaknesses of what another person says in order to prove that one is always right" (*Dialogue* 55). In Gadamer's account, a real conversation (with a person or with a book) means trying to grasp another point of view, and even to strengthen that point of view, so as to have something real to struggle over. We need to lean toward someone else's way of seeing things: this is the only way we can really have something to say.

4. Paul Celan, "Meridian" lecture, tr. Jerry Glenn, printed as an ap-

pendix to Derrida, *Sovereignties in Question: The Poetics of Paul Celan* (New York: Fordham University Press, 2005), 181.

5. Bloom, interview with the author (New Haven, 2006).

6. Cited in Paul de Man, *Critical Writings: 1953–1978,* ed. Lindsay Waters (Minneapolis: University of Minnesota Press, 1989), xiv.

7. See J. Hillis Miller, *The Ethics of Reading: Kant, de Man, Eliot, Trollope, James, and Benjamin* (New York: Columbia University Press, 1987).

8. See Emmanuel Faye, *Heidegger: L'introduction du nazisme dans la philosophie* (Paris: Albin Michel, 2005). A summary of the book is contained in Faye, "Nazi Foundations in Heidegger's Work," *South Central Review* 23:1 (Spring 2006): 55–66. Especially striking are the pro-Nazi passages that Heidegger suppressed in 1961 from the published versions of his wartime lectures on Nietzsche (discussed in Faye, *Heidegger*, 410–59). Heidegger's complaint about the "*Verjudung*" of German intellectual life (*Geistesleben*) occurs in his letter to Victor Schwoerer of October 2, 1929 (see Faye, *Heidegger*, 59–60).

9. In a postwar exchange of letters with his Jewish student Herbert Marcuse, who tried in vain to elicit a measure of sympathy from him concerning the Shoah, Heidegger openly compared the sufferings of eastern Germans, many of whom had been displaced from their homes during the war, to the attempt to exterminate world Jewry. For him, Germany's actions had been no worse than those of its enemies.

10. Francois Cusset's *French Theory* (Minneapolis: University of Minnesota Press, 2008) accuses French intellectuals of abandoning the avant-garde in order to embrace a fashionable neoliberalism. For Cusset, Derrida is a shining counterexample to this trend. Francois Dosse's *Empire of Meaning* (Minneapolis: University of Minnesota Press, 1998), by contrast, welcomes the new interest in the individual shown by French theorists like Luc Boltanski, who abandoned the emphasis on the authority of systems so prominent in Foucault and other radical thinkers.

Chapter 5
Politics, Marx, Judaism

1. See Emmanuel Lévinas, *Nine Talmudic Readings,* tr. Annette Aronowicz (Bloomington: Indiana University Press, 1990), 98.

2. Susan Handelman, "The 'Torah' of Criticism and the Criticism of Torah," in Steven Kepnes, ed., *Interpreting Judaism in a Postmodern Age* (New York: New York University Press, 1996), 226.

3. Interview with the author, 2006.

4. Richard Rorty, *Philosophy and Social Hope* (New York: Penguin, 2000), 213.

5. Marshall Berman's stimulating *All That Is Solid Melts into Air: The Experience of Modernity* (New York: Simon and Schuster, 1982) notes that Marx, even in his vigorous protest against capitalism, also endorses its energy and its capacity to dissolve and remake social bonds in a radical way. Marx does not, as Derrida seems to imply, seek a remedy for capitalism's ills by repealing the phenomena characteristic of modernity.

6. Derrida in his lectures on hospitality is also intent on forging connections between Judaism and Islam. He points out that the tradition of Islamic hospitality often cites the example of Abraham. Islam is "the most faithful heir, the exemplary heir of the Abraham tradition," he comments. He goes on to cite a passage in Lévinas's book of Talmudic lectures, *Difficult Freedom,* which refers to the action of Mohammed V, the prince of Morocco, who shielded French Jews from the Vichy government (*Acts* 368).

7. The question of sexual harassment was to play a major role in Derrida's posthumous legacy. In 1990, Derrida willed his archives to UC–Irvine. Some material, including letters and manuscripts, is actually housed at Irvine. But in his will Derrida withheld any further documents unless the university dropped sexual harassment charges against Russian studies professor Dragan Kujundzic, who taught a popular course on vampires. Evidently, UC's Vampire Sex Scandal, as newspapers quickly christened it, was deeply disturbing to Derrida; the evidence against Kujundzic did in fact seem quite ambiguous. For several years after Derrida's death Irvine attempted to negotiate with Derrida's widow Marguerite, who continued to refuse to hand over Derrida's archives. The university sued Derrida's heirs in 2006, then finally dropped the lawsuit in February 2007, without regaining control of the archives.

8. For Roudinesco, by contrast, Chomsky was "perverse" in defending Faurisson (*For What* 132). She added, "I wonder what unconscious reason there could be for a Jewish intellectual like Chomsky . . . to adopt such a position" (133).

9. Said, after long membership in the PLO's political branch, had finally split with Arafat over the latter's signing of a peace agreement with Israel at Oslo in 1993. In an interview given shortly before his death with the Israeli journalist Ari Shavit (printed in *Haaretz,* August 8, 2000; and then as "The Palestinian Right of Return" in *Raritan* 20:3 [2001]: 34–52), he defined Israel as "a set of evil practices" (42) and strangely announced, "I'm the last Jewish intellectual" (52)—after insisting that Israel must be transformed into a non-Jewish state with a Muslim majority (46, 48). Said's belief that the

Jews, unlike the Palestinians, have no right to a nation of their own, and that the existence of the Jewish state is an obstacle to world peace, was shared (and continues to be shared) by large numbers of European and American leftists, including many academics (see *Rising* 167n).

10. According to a 2002 Anti-Defamation League poll, 29 percent of French citizens favored the Palestinians whereas 10 percent favored the Israelis, with the rest showing no preference. Yet the French Muslim population is more moderate, and more favorable toward Jews, than Muslims in the rest of Europe. While solid majorities of Muslims in other European countries, and even in America, refused to admit that Arabs carried out the terror attacks of September 11, 48 percent of French Muslims stated that Arabs were involved in the attacks (Pew poll released June 22, 2006: www.pewglobal .org/reports).

11. Edward Rothstein, "The Man Who Showed Us How to Take the World Apart," *New York Times,* October 11, 2004.

12. In her commentary in the 9/11 book, Borradori seconds another of Derrida's contentions: that there was no significant connection between Osama bin Laden and the Taliban regime in Afghanistan. Borradori argues that the "thesis that there are nations 'harboring' terrorist activity is hard to prove" (169). History has provided a sufficient answer to Derrida's and Borradori's opinion. Moreover, the facts demonstrating the relationship between Al Qaeda and the Taliban were already available before 9/11.

13. An earlier film about Derrida, *Derrida's Elsewhere,* directed by Safaa Fathy, appeared in 2000.

14. Interview with Jean Birnbaum published as *To Live Finally: The Last Interview,* tr. Pascale-Anne Braule and Michael Naas (London: Palgrave Macmillan, 2007), 52.

Coda

1. In its December 26, 2004, issue commemorating the most memorable people who had died during the year, the *Times Magazine* pointedly chose to memorialize the down-to-earth philosophy professor Sidney Morgenbesser, Columbia University's "sidewalk Socrates," rather than Derrida.

Index